'Frank C
He p
prevai
exami
closely
his worl ... ie
classro ... I
highly r ... or

Lynne Sedgmore CBE, Executive Director of the 157 Group of FE Colleges

'*Beyond Bulimic Learning* goes beyond identifying a medical metaphor for a sick sector, it prescribes the educational remedies that could lead to its cure. Essential reading.'

Joel Petrie, Advanced Lecturer, Dyslexia Support & Teacher Education, The City of Liverpool College

Beyond Bulimic Learning

This book is dedicated to some of the most underrated, underpaid, and constantly undermined of public servants – committed classroom teachers and workshop tutors.

Beyond Bulimic Learning

Improving teaching in further education

Frank Coffield with Cristina Costa, Walter Müller, and John Webber

Institute of Education Press

First published in 2014 by the Institute of Education, University of London,
20 Bedford Way, London WC1H 0AL
ioepress.co.uk

British Library Cataloguing in Publication Data:
A catalogue record for this publication is available from the British Library

ISBNs
978-1-78277-073-2 (paperback)
978-1-78277-078-7 (PDF eBook)
978-1-78277-079-4 (ePub eBook)
978-1-78277-080-0 (Kindle eBook)

Typeset by Quadrant Infotech (India) Pvt Ltd
Printed by CPI Group (UK) Ltd, Croydon, CR0 4YY
Cover image: Inspired by a flyer created by East Berkshire College

Contents

List of abbreviations

AfL	Assessment for Learning
AKC	Anderson, Krathwohl, and colleagues
AKF	Anderson and Krathwohl's framework
CAVTL	Commission on Adult Vocational Teaching and Learning
CPD	Continuing professional development
DBIS	Department for Business, Innovation and Skills
JPD	Joint practice development
FE	Further education
HMCI	Her Majesty's Chief Inspector
LS	Lesson Study
LSIS	Learning and Skills Improvement Service
Ofsted	Office for Standards in Education, Children's Services and Skills
PISA	Programme for International Student Assessment
PLC	Professional learning community
RDF	Research development fellow
RL	Research Lesson
SMT	Senior management team
TLA	Teaching, learning, and assessment

Acknowledgements

I have continued to use my 'community of discovery' to comment on my writing. This time they were faced with six substantial chapters, which have all been improved immeasurably by their close attention. So my sincere thanks go to Clare, Emma, and Tom Coffield; Charlotte Dixon; Tony Edwards; John Lowe; Ruth O'Rourke; Iain Rodger; Lynne Sedgmore; Amanda Spielman; and Paul Wakeling.

My thanks also go to Jim Gallacher, who generously provided me with materials to update my knowledge about Scotland's colleges; and to Jim Collins, Nicole Edmondson, Ali Moore, Sally Sigmund, and the rest of the publishing team at IOE Press, who have been a pleasure to work with.

I am also very grateful to my three co-authors – Cristina Costa, Walter Müller, and John Webber – who have each written a chapter on topics that extend the breadth and depth of this book, thus making it far more practically useful to tutors.

One person, however, discussed, enhanced, and typed every page from the earliest stage of submitting a book proposal to the final one of inserting the final changes. The help I have received from my wife, Mary, has been, as always, invaluable and unstinting, and I want to thank her publicly for it.

About the authors

Frank Coffield retired in 2007 after 42 years in education as a teacher in a comprehensive and then in a boys' approved school in Scotland, as a lecturer in education at Jordanhill College of Education in Glasgow, and at Keele University in Staffordshire, and as Professor of Education at the universities of Durham, Newcastle-upon-Tyne, and the Institute of Education, University of London. He was Director of the ESRC's Learning Society Programme from 1994 to 2000. He has written books on juvenile gangs, the so-called 'cycle of deprivation', drugs and young people, vandalism and graffiti, the impact of policy on the Learning and Skills sector, learning styles, and public-sector reform. Since his retirement he has written: *Just Suppose Teaching and Learning Became the First Priority…* (LSN, 2008); *All You Ever Wanted to Know about Teaching and Learning but Were Too Cool to Ask* (LSN, 2009); *Yes, but What Has Semmelweis Got to Do with My Professional Development as a Tutor?* (LSN, 2010); and (with Bill Williamson) *From Exam Factories to Communities of Discovery: The democratic route* (IOE, 2012).

Dr Cristina Costa is a Lecturer in Lifelong Learning (Technology Enhanced Learning) at the University of Strathclyde, Scotland, where she teaches and supervises students in the fields of Education and Technology Enhanced Learning. Her research focuses on the use of social and participatory media (also known as Social Media, Web 2.0) in a changing environment. She is particularly interested in analysing the advantages and implications of using the social web for learning and teaching, research and internationalization, engagement, and social enterprise. She has recently completed her PhD research on 'The Participatory Web in the Context of Academic Research: Landscapes of changes and conflicts'. Before joining the University of Strathclyde, Cristina worked at the University of Salford as the Learning and Research Technologies Manager. In 2010, she was named Learning Technologist of the Year by the Association for Learning Technology (ALT). (Web presence: www.knowmansland.com/)

Walter Müller is an Emeritus Professor of School Pedagogy at the University of Würzburg, Bavaria, Germany. He studied at the University of Erlangen-Nürnberg. In 1971, he took the state examinations to become a teacher, and in 1975 attained his doctorate in philosophy of education and school pedagogy, as well as political sciences, at the Universität-Gesamthochschule Duisburg. He was also an assistant to the chair of educational philosophy and the chair of school pedagogics. In addition, he managed the research site for classroom pictures and posters. In 1991, Walter Müller gained his postdoctoral qualification in the philosophy of education at the University of Duisburg. He worked as a professor of school pedagogy at the Julius-Maximilians-Universität Würzburg from 1997 until his retirement in 2013. His main publications are: *Zauberberg Erneut Bestiegen* (with Herwig Blankertz, Wetzlar, 1981 and 1984); *Skeptische Sexualpädagogik* (Weinheim, 1992); and (2009) 'Schnee von Gestern. Was ist das Neue an der Neuen Unterrichtskultur?' *Vierteljahrsschrift für Wissenschaftliche Pädagogik*, 1, 26–38.

John Webber (BSc, PGCE, PG Dip Couns) is the Professional Learning and Development Manager at Sussex Downs College, Lewes and Eastbourne. He moved from scientific research into teaching 27 years ago, training in middle school (upper primary/lower secondary) and specializing in maths and science. In 1990 he made the move into post-16 education to join the recently opened Tertiary College in Lewes. Since that time he has taught at every level, from entry level to postgraduate, across a range of subjects. He became increasingly interested in the processes of teaching and learning and has contributed, over the past 16 years, to teacher training and CPD both within his college and at the University of Brighton. His current role includes responsibility for promoting and developing effective, evidence-based practice among the 700+ teaching staff at the college. His research areas include an exploration of students' ideas and expectations about teaching and learning, and of themselves as learners, and how these develop during their time at college. In practical terms he is interested in how these ideas and expectations affect their engagement with learning and their subsequent achievement. He is working with teachers across the college to explore how they can best enable students to develop a more mature and effective orientation where this is needed. Recent publications include: H. McQueen and J. Webber (2009) 'What is Very Important to Learning? A student perspective on a teaching and learning model', *Journal of Further and Higher Education*, 33 (3), 241–53; H. McQueen and J. Webber (2013) 'What is an Effective Learner? A comparison of further education students' views with a theoretical construction of effective learners', *Journal of Further and Higher Education*, 37 (5), 715–35.

Chapter 1

Beyond bulimic learning

Frank Coffield

> *I dreamt of one day founding a school in which young people could learn without boredom, and would be stimulated to pose problems and discuss them; a school in which no unwanted answers to unasked questions would have to be listened to; in which one did not study for the sake of passing examinations.*
>
> Karl Popper[1] (1976: 40)

1) Introduction

The Romanian writer Panait Istrati was expressing his disenchantment with the brutalities of the communist regime in the Soviet Union when he was reminded of Lenin's dictum: 'In order to make an omelette, you need to break eggs'. 'Well,' he replied, 'I can see the broken eggs, but where's the omelette?' His riposte neatly sums up the contemporary scene in England and many other Western democracies with regard to the public services and especially to the health and education systems: we are now knee-deep in broken eggs, but there is still no sign of anything remotely resembling an omelette.

Last summer I read Vasily Grossman's novel *Life and Fate*, which at one level is about how one Russian family suffered during the Battle of Stalingrad in 1942. At another level, it raises the questions, posed by Stefan Zweig, that is not so much, 'How do I survive' such disasters, as 'How do I remain fully human?' (quoted by Sarah Bakewell, 2011: 219). In other words, how do I retain my integrity under either a Stalinist or a Fascist dictatorship, when I see decent colleagues, whom I have known well for years, being arrested, charged, and found guilty of being ideological enemies of the state? Some people, writes Grossman, will comfort themselves with the rationalization that 'innocent people don't get arrested'. A few will act out their courageous belief that 'it's never impossible ... to act morally and humanely even in a Soviet or Nazi labour camp' (Grossman, 2006: xxii). But not many of us are cut out to be heroes or martyrs.

Clearly there is a massive difference in scale between trying to behave decently in a police state and in a democracy, but I want to argue that there is a disturbing parallel that deserves attention. How, for instance, do professionals remain true to their basic values, of, say, their commitment to the public services as a vital public good, when they see those services being dismantled by a coalition government that has no democratic mandate for such fundamental reform? How are they to respond to root and branch changes that close down whole organizations doing valuable work, tipping hundreds of committed colleagues onto the scrap-heap of unemployment or underemployment?

In the meantime, the teaching profession in England is routinely derided by government ministers and politicians, no matter what their party persuasion. But they all have this in common: they are unable to manage the economy and so they compensate for their economic impotence by pushing around public-sector workers, especially teachers. Let me make my position clear. I am all in favour of democracy; it is just most politicians that I cannot stand. I will justify that harsh judgement in the final chapter.

Teachers also have to find a way of working with Her Majesty's Chief Inspector (HMCI), who boasted: 'If anyone says to you that staff morale is at an all-time low, you know you are doing something right' (Wilshaw, 2011). Either the man knows little about the psychology of his fellow human beings or, more likely, he is being deliberately provocative. He appears to be following in the footsteps of previous HMCIs such as Chris Woodhead, whose remit from government seemed to be: 'give the teaching profession a periodic public kicking'. Any Secretary of State, however, who had the welfare of the teaching profession at heart, would have found that remark of Wilshaw's unacceptable and would have made it the grounds for dismissal or at least a public rebuke. No action was taken. Ofsted will have to work hard to show it has not become a tool of government.

2) Responses to radical policies

The question that I want to discuss is therefore: how can educators best respond to policies that I describe as radical in the pejorative sense of being destructive, extreme or deliberately confrontational? (I prefer to use the word 'educators' to include all types of teachers, tutors, lecturers, mentors, coaches, outreach workers, assessors, and trainers in our schools, colleges, universities, communities, and workplaces, but will employ other terms from time to time for the sake of variety.) Educators are currently employing a wide range of adaptations, picking and choosing from the following list of six strategies and combining them in different ways as circumstances allow.

2.1) 'Compliance'

First, educators use a number of methods that I will lump together under the general title of '*compliance*'. For instance, new teachers and new managers quickly become 'data gatherers' and 'target followers' for they know little else, and, being the least powerful people in their organization, they cannot question established practices. Some heads of department are now employed not because they are outstanding teachers or curriculum innovators, but because they are good data managers. They try to make the new policies work, but at the same time many seethe internally, letting off steam in private to their colleagues or partner – or they kick the dog rather than the Secretary of State. By so acting, however, they are directing their anger inwards at considerable personal cost.

In classrooms the danger is that, in the interests of self-preservation, compliant tutors retreat to safe methods of teaching, transmitting via handouts and PowerPoint presentations all the information and skills that students need to pass exams. They take no risks in their teaching, nor do they innovate, because they have to be perpetually prepared for the 'no-notice' visits of their senior managers who will grade their lessons, in the same way that Ofsted inspectors grade individuals, departments, and institutions.

At the same time, their students are under pressure to obtain the best possible grades in order to get into the most prestigious jobs, apprenticeships, or universities by employing *bulimic learning*: they binge on large amounts of information and then, in government-induced bouts of vomiting, otherwise known as national tests, they spew it out. Let me say straight away that I am not using this term lightly or jocularly; that would be an insult to all those suffering from bulimia. Instead, I consider *bulimic learning* to be every bit as serious as its medical counterpart. Far from feeling better afterwards, they feel empty and educationally malnourished by resorting to what I call *bulimia academica*, which I define as repeated bouts of bingeing on information and regurgitating it in exams. They come to associate learning not with growing self-confidence, a sense of achievement, and a change in identity as competent students, but with stress, nausea, and self-disgust. Learning for them is reduced to the skill of passing exams rather than the means of understanding and coming to love the subjects they are studying. The testing regime in England is neither robust nor rigorous; it is purgative and emetic, and as such is both inefficient and ineffective.

Even our most successful students, those who obtain the highest grade of A* in five or six subjects, give up German or Shakespeare or statistics as soon as they can, because they do not want to be reminded of the tactics they are privately ashamed of, which they had to adopt to shine in the exams. According to employers and university tutors, even our brightest students understand less and less about a very narrow range of subjects, but they have become sophisticated test takers and officially recognized success stories.

It often takes years for students to recover from this government-induced disease of *bulimia academica*, as they slowly reconnect with the enchantment of poetry and the beauty of mathematics; but some never do.

The learning disorder of bulimia is compounded by its equally distressing twin, *anorexia academica*, which affects both individuals and the system as a whole.[2] Some students become anxious about being seen by their classmates to be clever and severely restrict their intake to bite-size chunks of information that makes them easier to swallow – the educational equivalent of chicken nuggets. In their teenage years, they seem to lose their previously keen appetite for learning, give lame excuses for repeated failures to learn, and pretend to have studied when they have not. They spend time reading self-help books about study skills without ever acquiring any. They miss classes, avoid working with fellow students, and withdraw from relationships with staff; they appear to disdain learning and actually take pride in being ignorant. This response may, however, be the self-harming outcome of having been tested every year since they were 5 years of age, a regime that has turned their stomachs against learning.

The education system itself also shows symptoms of the same malaise, with some curricula driven entirely by qualifications that have had much of the educational nourishment stripped out of them. So, groups of students can be found in schools and colleges earnestly discussing topics about which they do not have sufficient background information to form any opinions, and thus their learning remains shallow and fragmented. With the best of intentions, we have in this country offered our young people so-called 'transferable' skills such as critical thinking and then discovered that students need to be in command of a body of knowledge before they can be either critical or creative.

The contrasting approach adopted by the highly prestigious German system of vocational education is to provide all apprentices with a significant component of general education, to help them become not just skilled workers but also active citizens, wise parents, and discriminating consumers. Indeed, there is strong resistance in both academic and vocational education in Germany to modular courses, which are thought to encourage bitty, incoherent, superficial, and anorexic learning.

2.2) 'Strategic' and 'cynical compliance'

The second strategy can be seen when *compliance* becomes *strategic* or *cynical*; educators appear to implement the new policies, but subtly bend the rules to shield their institutions, students, and colleagues from the worst aspects of the changes; in short, they engage in damage limitation. Different responses fall within one term, 'gaming' – for example, developing the art of presenting potentially damaging data in the best possible light; creative accountancy to optimize outcomes; choosing courses that are thought to be the easiest to pass; early, double, or multiple entering of students for exams in the same subject with different awarding bodies; the inflation of one's achievements; creative non-implementation, when all the appearance of change is displayed without any of the substance; and currying favour with the powerful.

2.3) 'Survivalism'

A third approach has been called '*survivalism*', whereby colleges maximize their income by all legitimate means, even to the extent of employing teams of accountants to show them how to squeeze most money out of the tortuous and ever-changing government funding regulations; they pull out all the stops to ensure that they achieve all the targets they are set; and they compete effectively by, for instance, closely studying all 166 pages of Ofsted's new framework of inspection in order to become 'outstanding' (see Coffield, 2012 for a critique).

2.4) 'Resistance' or 'subversion'

Fourth, some staff *resist* or *subvert* those aspects of current policy that so offend their basic values that they retreat into whatever spaces they can find, from where they can reassert and celebrate their autonomy. After all, Messrs Gove and Wilshaw and their agents are not so numerous or ubiquitous that they can be inspecting in every classroom every day, so when the door is shut, educators seek to offer their students more than the 'trainability' offered by successive governments since 1988.

Stephen Ball's recent research, however, suggests that resistance is muted and marginalized; instead, he and his colleagues 'found evidence of discontents, murmurings, indifference and disengagements' (Ball *et al.*, 2012: 150). Performance management, Ball argued in an earlier publication, 'incites us to make ourselves more effective, to work on ourselves to improve ourselves and to feel guilty or inadequate if we do not. [It] works most powerfully when it is inside our heads and our souls. That is, when we do it to ourselves, when we take responsibility for working hard, faster and better as part of our sense of personal worth and the worth of others ... indeed it works best when we come to want for ourselves what is wanted from us.' (2008a: 51–2). Michel Foucault, the French philosopher, is frequently cited as the source of this insight, but I prefer to believe it was the graffiti I once saw on a toilet wall: 'Help your local police. Beat yourself up.'

A good example of educators 'internalizing the inspector' and offering more than is required of them is when senior managers offer the inspectorate data on the grades given as a result of observing the lessons of all members of the teaching staff. It is important to stress that Ofsted does *not* require lessons to be graded in this manner, nor does it insist on a standardized lesson. These are instances where managers, often at the insistence of governors, 'over-interpret' official policy, but in doing so they divert scarce resources from teaching, learning, and assessment (henceforth TLA); they increase the pressures on their own staff, and they restrict their professional autonomy – all unnecessarily. Colleges could reflect on whether they have more staff and resources engaged in measuring lessons than in helping tutors to improve them. The relentless pressures and the bureaucratic processes of statutory performance management and inspection are internalized by senior management and then they come to pervade the life of colleges. For instance, colleges and schools are marked down if their own self-assessment differs markedly from Ofsted's; so Ofsted's criteria are routinely applied to avoid that outcome.

Damien Page places the resistance of first-tier managers (for example, curriculum leaders and programme area managers) within further education (FE) 'on a continuum from overt acts such as principled dissent to covert acts such as ... cognitive escape', by which term he means activities such as searching for other jobs or making retirement plans. He goes further in claiming that their resistance 'may be the primary strategy to "shield" their teams ... from the excesses of managerialism and performativity. Managerial resistance from this perspective, rather than being detrimental to colleges, may be seen as an act of academic citizenship ... that attempts to fortify the borders around the professional autonomy of lecturers' (Page, 2011: 9).

2.5) 'Exit'

A fifth type of adaptation is simply to leave the profession, what I shall call 'exit' for short. When stress levels begin to destroy the intrinsic pleasures of working with young people or adults, then it is time to consider resigning, changing career, or early retirement. Over the past few years, surveys have reported significant increases among educators of stress-related absences and higher levels of requests for early retirement (Ratcliffe, 2012), which push up financial costs and staff turnover. More specifically, within the FE and Skills sector in England, no fewer than 51,000 staff are 'made up of fixed-term, casual, agency-employed or self-employed lecturers: just under 40 per cent' (Lingfield final report, DBIS, 2012: 33). This increasing casualization of the FE workforce is likely to have a deleterious effect upon the quality of TLA

– except, of course, where staff have deliberately chosen to work part-time for personal reasons and are determined that their students are not short-changed as a result.

I also include two other tactics under the general heading of 'exit' – securing promotion and 'internal exile'. The first of these approaches is adopted by able and ambitious classroom teachers for whom the standard career path is a post in middle management. In most large FE colleges and to a lesser extent in secondary schools, however, joining management nowadays means giving up teaching for good, and, as a result, a harmful gulf has opened up between those who do and those who do not teach. Now that Ofsted has changed the framework of inspection so that colleges can be judged to be 'outstanding' only if TLA are 'outstanding', the range of responsibilities placed on senior managers has been broadened still further. After FE colleges were removed from local authority control in the early 1990s, senior leadership teams had to learn quickly the skills needed to run their colleges as independent and successful businesses. Then they were urged to ensure that their FE college became 'the central player in a network of partnerships ... a dynamic nucleus at the heart of their communities' (Sharp, 2012: 5). These partnerships are charged with responding to the social, educational, and business needs of those communities, a demanding undertaking that requires a second set of entrepreneurial skills, including the building of local, co-operative partnerships in a highly competitive market.

Now senior managers are faced with a third major role: namely, providing leadership on TLA, a task for which many are ill-prepared. For the past 20 years, the job of improving the quality of TLA was often delegated to a director, but that strategy will no longer work because the whole culture of these institutions needs to change, a task I will discuss in Chapter 9. Headteachers and principals will now be called upon to demonstrate, as the leading TLA experts in their institutions, some *educational* leadership. They could, for instance, begin to demonstrate the overriding importance of TLA by returning to the classroom and teaching a variety of classes, including the most challenging ones. No easy task, I admit, if you have been out of the classroom for 10, 15, or 20 years. On the other hand, if the most powerful and best-paid people in an institution actually *do* the job they constantly claim is the most important, it has huge symbolic significance for students and staff alike.

Leadership in TLA requires more than being able to show colleagues, students, and governors that you can still manage a class of 25 or so 16–19 year olds; it also means having an extensive, and regularly updated, evidence base from which to select the most effective interventions, and to reject the least effective – the topic of the chapters that follow. A solid and constantly revised body of knowledge on TLA is now a prerequisite for leadership in education and should be considered to be as important (if not more important) as business acumen and the social skills needed to form local partnerships. Without that solid knowledge base in TLA, how would a principal, whose academic background is in, say, Business Studies, decide what advice to accept (and refuse) from a director of learning with a particular bee in his or her bonnet? How would principals understand the demands being made of 'front-line' teaching staff, if they have no recent and relevant experience of teaching themselves? Besides, one of the ways to deal with an overweening inspectorate is to know much more about TLA than the Ofsted inspectors; and, given that some of these are not even trained teachers or have no background in either the subject or sector they are judging, the task is less daunting than it appears on first hearing.

When one examines the advertisements for new principals and headteachers, however, the three key roles of educational leadership, financial acumen, and entrepreneurial collaborative skills are often reduced to, for example, 'assessment processes (which) will ensure that the College meets its annual performance targets and excels at inspection'.[3] Knowledge about, and continuing involvement in, TLA should, I think, be written into all job descriptions.[4]

By 'internal exile', I mean that small group of teachers who consciously decide to 'go through the motions' of teaching, which has become for them a job like any other job because of the relentless pressures to enrol more students, to retain as high a percentage as possible, and to improve test scores every year: it is the 'ratchet model' of schooling. They pour their creativity into other parts of their lives, such as gardening, amateur dramatics, or watching Newcastle United football club – an activity that can, however, seriously increase rather than decrease stress levels.[5]

2.6) Powerful, democratic professionals

I have deliberately kept to the end the *sixth and most positive response* – to become *powerful, democratic professionals.* I shall explore separately the significance of all three words in that latter phrase, although they are better seen as one united concept, made up of three interwoven elements. We can respond to the latest, ill-considered government initiative by deciding to deepen our professionalism; we can study the research on TLA with the aim of becoming not merely experienced, but expert or excellent teachers. The latter, according to John Hattie (2012: 24), have a secure and growing knowledge of their subject, can guide learning to desirable outcomes, provide feedback that helps students to progress, are alive to the emotional aspects of learning, and can offer convincing evidence that their students have learned from them. In Box 1.1, I offer a very brief summary of what I consider to be the key points from John Hattie's most recent book on how tutors can maximize their impact on their students' learning.

Box 1.1: Key points from John Hattie's research

1.	'The greatest effects on student learning occur when teachers become learners of their own teaching and when students become their own teachers ... Teachers need to use evidence to answer the question: what effect am I having on my students' learning? It is the teacher's role to evaluate the effect they are having on their students' learning.' (pp. 14–15)
2.	'The more the student becomes the teacher and the more the teacher becomes the learner, the more successful the outcomes.' (p. 17)
3.	'Teachers need to be in a safe environment to learn about the strengths and weaknesses of their teaching from colleagues.' (p. 16) (So there should be no grading of lesson observations.)
4.	'Teachers should seek negative evidence about their impact, for example, who has not learned?' (p. 25) (How many have failed to learn? What is the stumbling block? Does your teaching need to change? Assume that some students are not going to understand your lessons first time.)
5.	'Teachers see feedback as making statements about students and not about their teaching.' (p. 126) (We all need feedback to improve.)
6.	'Is the climate of this college conducive to the learning of teachers?' (p. 165) (Are the responses of tutors and managers to this question the same?)

Source: Hattie (2012)

Being responsible for the education of a group of students is the heart of the job of a powerful, democratic professional, but I join forces with Judyth Sachs in arguing that this central role needs to be expanded to include 'contributing to the school, the system, other students, the wider community, and collective responsibilities of teachers themselves as a group and the broader profession' (2001: 153). These additional roles for teachers are not being imposed from on high, but are emerging from the profession itself as educators realize they need to build alliances with students, parents, members of the community, employers, and other educational professionals, if they are to respond effectively and collectively to the torrents of new policy raining down on them from government. For Sachs, to define teachers' professionalism in this way calls for the identity of a politically engaged individual who is 'deeply rooted in the principles of equity and social justice' (ibid.: 157). It would also mean changing the present ethos and organization of our schools, colleges, and universities to enable students of all ages to experience democratic ways of living, learning, and working together, which so few do today.

Educators can no longer confine their role to improving TLA in classrooms, but also need to embrace the larger responsibilities implied by the two adjectives in the phrase 'powerful, democratic professionals'. This means, in the first instance, open discussions of how power is exercised in education nationally and within our educational institutions, for 'to ignore issues of power is to ensure our own powerlessness' (Taylor *et al.*, quoted by Ball *et al.*, 2012: 9). Power is here understood as the pattern of relationships within a group 'rather than taking power as a top-down and linear phenomenon' (Ball *et al.*, 2012: 9); and as such, it is subject to constant flux, internal divisions, and contradictory pressures. We need to understand more about how teachers' working and personal lives are being transformed through performance management, privatization, competition, and the pressures to become academies in an unregulated market; how, for instance, power at a national level is mediated at an institutional level so that educators, against their own best interests and almost without noticing it themselves, end up internalizing the language, values, and practices of the market and, by so doing, begin to inspect, limit, and regulate themselves more strictly than the inspectors. For example, those who 30 years ago were collegial heads of departments have become 'line managers', where the term itself denotes a shift in power, as well as a totally inappropriate industrial model because there is no production line in education, only in bulimic schooling.

To counteract these baleful influences, we need a stronger sense of ourselves as political agents, as agents of change rather than the passive recipients or 'implementers' of policy, devised by a self-serving elite. That means returning to the original Greek meaning of the word 'politics', where citizens (free-born men of property, admittedly) played an active part in the life of the polis – not slang for the Glasgow police, but the city state or local community. Nor should our political activities be confined to defending those values and practices we hold dear, but we should also be making demands on the 'system' by, for example, insisting on our professional and union representatives being routinely consulted in the formation of new policy as well as parents, students, and other concerned members of the community.

I also wish to defend the use of the adjective 'democratic' when attached to the noun 'professional'. The professions do not stand alone but are intimately connected to society, culture, and politics. The position adopted by any particular profession can range anywhere within the two extremes of a continuum. At one end, professions can (and do) behave at times like 'conspiracies against the laity', to use George Bernard Shaw's famous phrase (1907: 52). Somewhere in the middle of the continuum, professionals can also meekly acquiesce with the ideologically driven plans of the party in power, as the German medical and social work professions did during the Second World War in, for example, carrying out the extermination of mentally and physically disabled people, which was called 'the Liquidation of Valueless Life' (Klee *et al.*, 1991: xviii). At the other end of the continuum, professionals dedicate their working lives to the service of others, particularly those whom they consider to have suffered serious disadvantages and unjustifiable inequalities. I have repeatedly found that such a motivation – public service – is particularly strong among staff in the lifelong learning sector, although like most motives it is allied with other incentives such as the need to earn a living. So I am not suggesting that such altruism is universal or unalloyed within the sector, but rather that this ethical stance has a strong, political component in that it contains a vision of what kind of society and what kind of young people tutors wish to see.

Bill Williamson and I touched on these themes in our book *From Exam Factories to Communities of Discovery: The democratic route* (2012), and, on reflection, perhaps a better title would have been *Just Suppose We Lived in a Democracy, What Would Our Schools, Colleges, and Universities Look Like?* They would look very different from the present English 'system', which is the most centrally controlled in the world, where the Secretary of State for Education has taken direct and personal control over all academies and so-called 'free' schools, which should, as Sir Peter Newsam has argued, be more accurately called 'government' schools. The intention of the Tory-led coalition is that all schools should become academies so that all 21,000 in England may well end up being managed by Whitehall, a centralization of power that is inherently undemocratic, administratively unmanageable, and politically pernicious.

Over the past 25 years or so – ever since the 1988 Education Reform Act first introduced the National Curriculum and its drill sergeant, national assessment – democracy in education has become so attenuated that our claim to be a democracy can now be seriously questioned, as Michael Bassey has argued (in a letter to *The Guardian*, 19 September 2012). Democracy is not a given, a possession for all time; it can be quickly removed, as happened in Germany in 1933 for lack of defenders (Kershaw, 1998). It is a way of working together that has to be fought for in each generation by people from across the political spectrum. A Secretary of State for Education who ignores all those who must implement his or her reforms is in danger of losing the claim to democratic legitimacy. As Jules Petrie (2013) succinctly puts it, educators move within months from being *invisible* when policy is being developed to being *indispensable* when it has to be enacted.

To understand how extreme educational policy has become in England, we need a comparative dimension and, for once, why should England not try to learn some lessons from Scotland and Wales, as well as from Germany and Scandinavia? For a start, there are no longer any FE colleges north of the border, as they are now called *Scotland's Colleges*, to reflect the significant amount of higher education-level teaching they do that is independent of the universities. A major programme of regionalization has reduced their number from 43 to 31, thus creating large new regional colleges, which have been given three main tasks: lifelong learning, the utilization rather than just the supply of skills, and greater collaboration with schools and universities to ensure wider participation. The 'strong emphasis on collaboration' is structurally endorsed by a joint funding council for further and higher education, which was established in 2005 (Gallacher, 2009: 386). Moreover, regulation is carried out by by Her Majesty's Inspectorate of Education, who, like their former colleagues in England, conduct themselves as fellow professionals, and who have a developmental, rather than a punitive, role in helping to improve policy and practice. So, as Jim Gallacher concludes, in terms of policy, national frameworks, and funding, Scotland's Colleges have been slowly diverging from their counterparts in England over the past 20 years. There *are*, in other words, other options and we need to travel no further than Scotland or Wales to see them.

To sum up, it may seem strange to be discussing the prospect of powerful, democratic professionals in education when, for example, in the FE and Skills sector, because of government cut-backs, colleagues are being made redundant, contact time for teachers is being increased, class sizes are rising steadily, and pressure to 'ratchet up' test results is becoming even more intense. The state in England now has the legal authority to decide what is taught, to whom, and how; and it controls how learning is managed, funded, tested, and regulated. Above all, control is exercised by government by means of 'the performance tables which rank schools [and colleges] with implications for resources and student intakes, and which shape all school decisions' (Michael Young, 2013: 2). Besides, the performance measures that are used to draw up the tables are constantly changed; from now on, all 5 year olds in England are to be tested and 11 year olds will be ranked nationally. These are the very tight and tightening parameters within which English educators currently work. They will become only as powerful and democratic as the culture within which they work allows them to be; or, to put the point more positively, they will become as powerful and democratic as those educators can achieve through constant, collective struggle.

3) The outline of the rest of the book

No one, I think, can fairly accuse me of ignoring the political and managerial contexts within which educators currently operate. One of the problems for the lifelong learning sector, however, is that there is far more writing on those constraints than on what could be improved in classrooms. For example, I would have expected the first Ofsted Annual lecture on 'Learning and Skills' to contain some detailed discussion of TLA. But no; the topic is mentioned only in passing on the penultimate page (see Coffey, 2012). So in this book I want to offer some practical help to classroom teachers, particularly those in the FE and Skills sector. In particular, I want finally to respond to the oft-repeated and challenging question asked of me at in-service training days, namely, 'Yes, but what could I do more effectively in class next Monday?'. However, if you are looking for ways of magically boosting your own or your students' test scores, then please look elsewhere, for that is not my aim. Nor is it my intention to show schools and colleges how they can best manipulate the 159 criteria in the new Common Inspection Framework (see Coffield, 2012) in order to be judged 'outstanding'. Yet Ofsted's major, belated, but still welcome emphasis on TLA will slowly push educational institutions to change their culture by making it the first priority – and the following chapters are devoted to helping them do so.

I have searched the literatures in education, psychology, and technology for the most effective means of improving the quality of thinking and learning in ourselves and in our students, and I wish to convey them to a broad audience in clear English without recourse to jargon. In particular, I want to speak directly to one of the most constantly denigrated and poorly appreciated group of public-service workers, namely 'front-line' teachers, who do not have the time to read research reports for themselves. I hope the following chapters will also prove useful to teacher trainers (or 'educators', as I prefer to call them), to those with a management responsibility for improving the teaching of their colleagues and the learning of their students, and to parents and all those who aspire to be far more than academic bulimics with no respect for knowledge nor any love of learning.

The Education sections of bookshops are now bulging with explicit guides about how to get an A* at GCSE or A level, and they offer tips about how to refine one's exam technique or how to interpret a marking scheme. Instead, I want to offer help to those students (and their teachers) who arrive at FE colleges, sixth-form colleges, and universities, having sailed through their GCSEs or A levels, and who have, understandably, come to think of learning as memorizing facts to pass exams – because that has been their route to success up to this point. Yet within two or three years, their tutors hope to make them think, speak, and perform like builders, beauticians, or biologists, who have not only a deep understanding but a love of their subject. If the following chapters make a modest contribution to bringing that transformation about, I shall be pleased.

Most people would, I think, accept that a profession worthy of the name needs to possess a specialized body of knowledge. Some commentators, such as Gary Wilkinson, have claimed, however, as recently as 2005, that 'members of the education community have not united around any common body of knowledge which they collectively perceive to be essential for teaching' (2005: 428). While I accept that, in essence, education is a controversial subject that will always contain many competing theories and voices, I would contend that recently there has begun to emerge a growing consensus, based on reasonably hard evidence, among the relevant research community around the essential ingredients that make for effective TLA, and these will be presented in the following chapters (see, for example, Wiliam, 2009, 2011; Hattie, 2009, 2012; Higgins *et al.*, 2012; and Hargreaves, 2012). That having been said, my forays into the research literature soon revealed a plethora of competing approaches, all claiming to develop the minds of students and teachers alike. What I present in my six chapters is obviously a brief, personal selection from the very extensive literature, but a selection made as a result of applying the following four criteria:

- Approaches with compelling (or at least, strong) evidence of effectiveness. I have included in this book only those interventions with high-quality, consistent, and substantial evidence that they improve students' learning or educators' teaching.
- Those with explicit or emerging theories that have been tested in practice. As Vasily Grossman put it, 'today's theory is tomorrow's practice' (2006: 672).

- In addition to high impact, I also considered the cost and general applicability of interventions; for example, would it be necessary to employ additional members of staff or buy expensive hardware? And does the intervention work with all ages, students, and subject areas?
- Those interventions that can be easily accessed by students and overworked tutors. I rejected models where you need to learn a new technical vocabulary to understand them, or those that require a set of diagrams of increasing length and complexity to explain the central ideas. My rule of thumb became: if the diagram contained almost as many arrows as were fired in the battle of Agincourt, I needed to find something simpler. I have also included what I hope are interesting and entertaining examples and activities, because there is good evidence that they help us to understand new ideas, practices, or theories, as well as engaging us directly in the arguments (Tennyson, 1995).

Chapter 2 criticizes as ill-conceived and ineffectual one of the major strategies for reform, which has been used in this country for over 20 years: namely, that teaching will be improved by identifying and disseminating 'best practice'. I have come to the conclusion that there is no such thing as 'best practice', that the term and the strategy should be abandoned, and in its place we should be exploring a new model of professional learning, based on Joint Practice Development (JPD). This approach removes teachers from the isolation of their classrooms and involves them in jointly improving their own practice and that of their colleagues. The secret of JPD's success, I suggest, lies in its emphasis on mutual trust and respect between equal partners, rather than on one teacher trying to impart his or her 'best practice' to colleagues, who are implicitly being told that their practice is inferior.

John Webber, who is the Development Manager for TLA in a large general FE college, then describes in Chapter 3 an immensely practical approach to developing students' learning and thinking skills. He begins by discussing the challenge educators face when students, who have in the main relied heavily on their memory to regurgitate information to pass GCSE exams at 16, are suddenly required to formulate their own ideas, solve problems, and tackle intellectual challenges with increasing independence. He introduces the useful notion of 'studentship', which incorporates in one diagram the behaviours, skills, qualities, and beliefs called for in a successful student at this level. Then, drawing heavily on his own teaching experience and that of his colleagues, he shows how tutors can use Socratic questioning and other approaches to encourage thinking and to deepen understanding. Students can become owners of, and active participants in, their own learning.

He also evaluates a new approach called 'flipped learning', where students study the required knowledge, concepts, and techniques before coming to class, where time is then devoted to discussing, exploring, and extending their grasp of the material. As John argues, this approach restores the 'teacher–student relationship to the heart of learning'; it is heartening to read of such excellent work in the sector.

In Chapter 4, I discuss a well-known framework of different types of knowledge and thinking skills, which is a much-revised version of Benjamin Bloom's classic taxonomy or classification. The value of this framework (by Lorin Anderson, David Krathwohl, and colleagues) is that it gives students a useful overview of the main types of knowledge and thinking skills they are being asked to acquire. The value for educators is that the framework enables them to check quickly whether their lesson plans cover all the different types of knowledge and thinking skills or only a few, and perhaps the least challenging. I need time and space to discuss four different types of knowledge and six types of thinking skills, together with their interactions, and, as a result, Chapter 4 is one of the longest in the book. For those who may be coming new to these ideas, I have included a vignette or illustration, based on the teaching of Shakespeare's *Macbeth*; and I also evaluate the strengths and weaknesses of the framework.

Walter Müller is Emeritus Professor of School Pedagogy at the University of Würzburg in Bavaria and we have been friends since 1982, when we jointly set up an Erasmus exchange programme for educational students from the universities of Durham and Duisburg. His healthy scepticism, translated expertly in Chapter 5 by Joachim Schaudt, demonstrates that bulimic learning is by no means confined to these shores, but has become an international disease. He pinpoints three current tendencies in German schools that run directly counter to the liberal, humanist tradition of Wilhelm von Humboldt, who reformed the Prussian education system in the time of Napoleon: self-regulation and individualized learning; a concentration on results and outputs, standardized tests, and key competencies; and a focus on time management and the acceleration of learning. Helping students to become independent learners who can 'self-regulate' sounds progressive and modern, but it becomes a form of social control when students blame only themselves for failures to learn or are left to educate themselves. In short, the German education system is infected with the same dispiriting language, values, and ideas of neo-liberalism, where, schools, teachers, and students are assessed by economic rather than educational criteria. These tendencies, Walter argues, are changing the role of the teacher from a practitioner of the subtle art of teaching to a technician, competent in classroom management and the preparation of students for exams. In the process, education is eviscerated.

Chapter 6 does not offer a comprehensive tour of all the theories of motivation, but rather a highly selective exploration of those I have found most helpful in my professional and private life. So I examine the work of Jerome Bruner, Carol Dweck, Dylan Wiliam, and Jean Lave and Etienne Wenger. The last two, anthropologists Lave and Wenger, argue convincingly (to me at least) that the main problems of schooling are not about TLA, but about unequal access, selection, and control. That insight convinced me that I should include some economic approaches to motivation; for example, what are the incentives for students to learn? This led me to question some of the basic assumptions behind government policy in education and training, because it introduces into the debate some of the structural features of the British labour market (such as zero-hour contracts) that so dominate the working and personal lives of students.

No book on improving teaching in FE or education more generally would be complete nowadays without some discussion of the role of social media that have become such powerful catalysts in changing TLA. Cristina Costa, a lecturer in Technology at Strathclyde University, describes in Chapter 7 how she has learned the hard way through the experience of teaching a variety of different groups (such as Portuguese naval officers and university students on their placement abroad) that 'curious as it may sound, technology should be the last element to consider when it comes to the design of learning'. First, educators need to know their students well, and then decide precisely what they want them to learn and how they should learn it. Then and only then should a choice be made as to what technology to use. As she argues, one of the many virtues of using the new technologies is that it releases the creativity of students who can then 'become the driving force for change rather than being the passive recipients of it' (Hargreaves, 2012: 27). The social and participatory web is also changing the role of teachers, who need 'to know how to select, design, develop, share and review different types of digital teaching and learning activities' (CAVTL, 2013: 18). I would only add that tutors also need to impart to these students the skills of discriminating between the wheat and the more prolific chaff on the internet.

Tutors whom I have met at conferences or at staff-development days in college often ask what advice I have to offer them about where they should start to improve their practice. My answer is always the same – look at the evidence (which I discuss in Chapter 8) on what constitutes effective and ineffective feedback. I have been pleasantly surprised by the sheer quantity of that evidence, by its improving quality, and by the size of the impact it has on students. I stress, however, that the power of feedback is only potential, because feedback can have a negative effect on the recipients. But if educators want to have some quick successes, then internalizing what the research literature has to say on this topic is, in my judgement and experience, *the* place to start.

Finally, in Chapter 9, I return to the main themes that I outlined in this introduction. What is the likely future for FE and for education more generally? Are the pressures that governments currently apply to the system sustainable? What improvements can we make to the quality of TLA in classrooms and to the culture of our schools and colleges, irrespective of government policy? I attempt to provide practical, research-based answers to those questions, wherever possible. I write as a critical friend of the sector, with the emphasis firmly on the noun 'friend', because I want to defend and celebrate the uniqueness of FE in the educational world, as potentially *the* great transformer of the lives of people, most of whom have not had my advantages. I conclude, however, that what we need more than anything else is a major change of direction in policy and practice, a transformation that I think will be brought about by 'a new birth of democracy' in this country, just as President Lincoln, in the middle of the Civil War in the United States, called for 'a new birth of freedom' (Goodwin, 2013: 586).

Notes

[1] I once heard Karl Popper give a lecture at the Royal Society in the mid 1970s. His talk was entitled 'Evolution is false. Darwin Disproved' and I can remember every word of it. He shuffled forward on two sticks and in a thick Viennese accent he began, 'I used my theory of falsification to try to disprove Darwin's theory. I failed. End of Lecture. Any questions?' One questioner expressed his surprise that the lecturer had tried to disprove a theory that was backed by so much evidence. Popper broke in to say: 'You were surprised, Professor? Just think of the veritable shock I had when I first thought of the idea.'

[2] I am grateful to Amanda Spielman for suggesting this extension to the notion of 'bulimia academica'. The Italian writer Massimo Recalcati argues that 'Bulimics manifest the pure myth of consumption – they swallow, chew and grind up everything. But binging proves the impossibility of filling up the hole that lies at the core of their being and reveals the deception that ... everything can be purchased, except love. Anorexics, on the other hand, reject the logic of consumption ... They devote themselves to the narcissistic cult of the lean body. It is a private, autistic and anti-social cult ... What we are made to forget is that in human beings lack is not a deficit, but the condition of all creation' (quoted in Bauman, 2012: 114–15).

[3] Another example from a recent advert in the *Times Educational Supplement* for a principal and chief executive: 'You will be a results oriented, experienced leader with a proven track record in delivering change and a strategic awareness of the FE sector and the vision to ensure the College plays a full role in economic and skills development ...'. It continues for three paragraphs in this vein about 'revenue streams', 'productive relationships', and being 'commercially aware', without a mention of education or TLA.

[4] The job of changing the culture of FE colleges to make TLA the number one priority in reality as well as in rhetoric has still, in my experience, some way to go. The standard behaviour of SMT when I visit a college to deliver a day's input on TLA is for one of their number to introduce me warmly, to emphasize how TLA is their 'passion' and then to absent himself or herself for the rest of the day. The principals and senior staff who stay for the full day and engage fully in the discussions and activities are the exception; the others apparently have not heard of Viviane Robinson and her colleagues' research, which I discuss in section 3 of Chapter 9.

[5] Geoff Troman and Peter Woods (2000) offer a different set of adaptations that teachers make to the occupational stress caused by the intensification of their workloads. They suggest three main adaptations – *retreatism*, *downshifting*, and *self-actualization* (with some internal diversification within the second and third approaches) – that are interestingly similar and different from my six strategies. By their first category, 'retreatism', they mean that teachers submit to the imposed changes, but increased levels of surveillance mean that they can no longer withdraw into the private world of their classroom – an approach that I have called 'compliance'.

The second adaptation they label 'downshifting', whereby teachers seek to reduce their workload and responsibilities. This can take three forms: 'planned demotion' where, for example, a headteacher voluntarily accepts the post of a deputy head in another school; 'role-reduction', where teachers progressively disengage and, for example, sit it out for retirement; and 'role-redefinition', where teachers move from permanent jobs to supply or temporary teaching posts. In my classification, these tactics were subsumed within the heading of 'exit', which also helps to explain the increasing difficulty that schools and colleges have in getting skilled practitioners to put themselves forward for promotion.

Finally by means of 'self-actualizing', teachers seek new identities either through 're-routing' or through 're-locating'. The first adaptation describes teachers who find new opportunities to pursue their careers by becoming, say, an educational consultant, or a researcher, or a writer of textbooks. 'Re-locating' refers to those teachers who find posts in schools more in keeping with their values or those who devote themselves to voluntary activities outside school. The final adaptation of Troman and Woods is virtually the same strategy as what I have called 'internal exile'.

Whatever the labels being used, the main point we are making is the same: namely, that replacing 'older teachers with younger, cheaper, more instrumentally committed, compliant, and malleable ones' comes at 'a huge personal cost to some teachers and to the education system in general' because 'the profession may be losing some of its best teachers' (Troman and Woods, 2000: 269).

References

Bakewell, S. (2011) *How to Live: A life of Montaigne in one question and twenty attempts at an answer.* London: Vintage.

Ball, S.J. (2008a) 'Performativity, privatization, professionals and the state'. In Cunningham, B. (ed.), *Exploring Professionalism.* London: Institute of Education, University of London (Bedford Way Papers).

Ball, S.J., Maguire, M., and Braun, A. (2012) *How Schools Do Policy: Policy enactments in secondary schools.* London: Routledge.

Bauman, Z. (2012) *On Education.* Cambridge: Polity Press.

Coffey, M. (2012) 'Promoting social mobility and securing economic growth – how the further education and skills sector can help bridge the gap and lead the way'. The first Ofsted Annual Lecture in Learning and Skills, 12 July, City and Islington College, Ofsted.

Coffield, F. (2012) 'Ofsted Re-Inspected'. *Adults Learning*, 24 (2), 20–1.

Coffield, F. and Williamson, B. (2012) *From Exam Factories to Communities of Discovery: The democratic route*. London: Institute of Education, University of London.

Commission on Adult Vocational Teaching and Learning (CAVTL) (2013) *It's About Work … Excellent adult vocational teaching and learning*. Coventry: LSIS.

Department for Business, Innovation and Skills (DBIS) (2012) *Professionalism in Further Education*. Lingfield Final Report. Online. www.bis.gov.uk (accessed November 2012).

Gallacher, J. (2009) 'Higher education in Scotland's colleges: A distinctive tradition?' *Higher Education Quarterly*, 63 (4), 384–401.

Goodwin, D.K. (2013) *Team of Rivals: The political genius of Abraham Lincoln*. London: Penguin.

Grossman, V. (2006) *Life and Fate*. London: Vintage.

Hargreaves, D. (2012) *A Self-improving School System: Towards maturity.* National College for School Leadership.

Hattie, J. (2009) *Visible Learning: A synthesis of over 800 meta-analyses relating to achievement*. London: Routledge.

— (2012) *Visible Learning for Teachers: Maximising impact on learning*. London: Routledge.

Higgins, S., Kokotsaki, D., and Coe, R. (2012) *The Teaching and Learning Toolkit*. Education Endowment Foundation/The Sutton Trust.

Kershaw, I. (1998) *Hitler 1889–1936: Hubris*. London: Allen Lane, The Penguin Press.

Klee, E., Dressen, W., and Riess, V. (1991) *Those Were the Days: The Holocaust through the eyes of the perpetrators and bystanders*. London: Hamish Hamilton.

Page, D. (2011) 'From principled dissent to cognitive escape: Managerial resistance in the English further education sector'. *Journal of Vocational Education and Training*, 63 (1), 1–13.

Petrie, J. (2013) Personal communication.

Popper, K. (1976) *Unended Quest*. London: Fontana.

Ratcliffe, R. (2012) 'Rise in teachers off work with stress – and union warns of worse to come'. *The Guardian*, 27 December, 2.

Sachs, J. (2001) 'Teacher professional identity: Competing discourses, competing outcomes'. *Journal of Educational Policy*, 16, 149–61.

Sharp, M. (2012) *Colleges in their Communities: A dynamic nucleus*. Leicester: NIACE.

Shaw, G.B. (1907) *Dramatic Opinions and Essays*, vol. 1. New York: Bretano's.

Tennyson, R.D. (1995) 'Concept Learning: Teaching and assessing'. In L.W. Anderson (ed.), *International Encyclopaedia of Teaching and Teacher Education*, 2nd edn. Oxford: Pergamon Press, 457–63.

Troman, G. and Woods, P. (2000) 'Careers under stress: Teacher adaptations at a time of intensive reform'. *Journal of Educational Change*, 1, 253–75.

Wiliam, D. (2009) *Assessment for Learning: Why, what and how?* London: Institute of Education, University of London (Inaugural Professorial Lecture).

— (2011) *Embedded Formative Assessment*. Bloomington, IN: Solution Tree.

Wilkinson, G. (2005) 'Workforce remodelling and formal knowledge: The erosion of teachers' professional jurisdiction in English schools'. *School Leadership and Management*, 25 (5), 421–39.

Wilshaw, M. (2011) quoted in *Times Educational Supplement*, 13 December.

Young, M. (2013) 'The global search for education: UK on testing'. Online. www.huffingtonpost.com/c-m-rubin (accessed 8 January 2013).

Chapter 2

If there is no such thing as 'best practice', how can we improve teaching?

Frank Coffield

> *I hope I die during an in-service session because the transition between life and death would be so subtle.*
>
> Teacher quoted by Helen Timperley (2011: 1)

1) Introduction

It is a standard finding of educational research amounting almost to a cliché that it is extremely difficult to change the classroom practice of teachers. It is not, however, a problem confined to the teaching profession; indeed, the inability or unwillingness to change affects us all and no group more than those who are always badgering the rest of us to change: I refer in particular to senior politicians. Take, for example, Tony Blair's recent vision for the future: he would have us believe that 'the case for fundamental reform of the post-war state is clear ... how do we take the health and education reforms of the last Labour government to a new level ...?' (2013: 27). There is not a scintilla of doubt anywhere in his article: all of his policies, in his view, ushered in huge improvements. So no change there, nor any prospect of change.

I want to begin this chapter with a pertinent example of reluctance to change from the world of FE and Skills that will serve as an introduction to the main themes of this chapter. In 2009, Sheila Edward and I wrote a long, highly critical article on one of the strategies being used by government and Ofsted to effect radical reform of the education 'system'. In more detail, we found serious fault with the simplistic notion that post-compulsory education and training would be transformed 'by establishing a Standards Unit to identify and disseminate best practice' (DfES, 2002: 5). The Standards Unit, like so many other government agencies, has come and gone (with all its costly CDs, videos, and curricular materials), but the policy of identifying and transferring 'best practice' continues to be pursued by the Conservative-led coalition, government departments, and government agencies. So our strictures about, for instance, the terms 'good', 'best', and 'excellent' practice being used interchangeably, about the absence of any publicly agreed criteria for judging practice, and about the need to take into consideration the 'immense diversity and complexity of local contexts' (Coffield and Edward, 2009: 371) went unheeded. So far, so predictable.

I was therefore dismayed, but not surprised, to read in the consultation document to establish a Guild for the Learning and Skills sector (Guild Project Team, 2013a) that the phrase 'best practice' is used six times, 'good practice' twice, 'effective practice' once, 'the gold standard' once, and 'excellent practice' once. This does a disservice to the English language in that it suggests that the words 'best', 'good', 'effective', 'golden', and 'excellent' are all synonyms. The English language deserves to be used accurately and 'best' still means superior to 'excellent'; plus, there is often a chasm between 'good' and 'excellent'. As I shall continue to insist throughout this book, all of the football teams in the Premier League are excellent, but only one is the best – Newcastle United.

I took the trouble to attend one of the consultation meetings on the establishment of the FE Guild, which has since been renamed the Education and Training Foundation. I raised these objections and left the chair with a copy of our research article, then followed up the discussions by sending him a summary of the main arguments against their espoused model of change. I emphasized the danger of issuing a statement on teaching, learning, and assessment (TLA), which was unconnected to any underlying theory or research, and asked what the Guild's response would be if the 'best practice' they advocated turned out to be ineffective when tried by tutors. The FE Guild intends to set itself up as 'the expert voice' in TLA (Guild Project Team, 2013a: 11), so it cannot continue to avoid the issue of what theory (or theories) of learning underpins its recommendations; nor can it continue to ignore research that it finds inconvenient or challenging.

Four months later, in April 2013, the FE Guild Project Team issued its Implementation Plan and, yes, you have guessed correctly, 'developing provider good practice' is one of the Guild's five main themes. This document uses 'good practice' nine times, 'best practice' twice, and 'excellent practice' four times, sometimes on the same page without any awareness that the writing gives the impression of muddled thinking. It even includes the admission that many items in the Learning and Skills Improvement Service's self-styled *Excellence Gateway* 'are very rarely used and therefore of questionable value'[1] (Guild Project Team, 2013b: 21). So the members of the Guild Project Team themselves find evidence that tutors do not use the large, expensive repositories of 'good practice' in the *Excellence Gateway*; but that does not lead them to question the validity of these materials. Instead, their thinking appears to be: we must intensify our efforts to identify and disseminate what tutors neither use nor value, namely, our notions of what constitutes 'good practice' for others to use.

The need to change one's mind when confronted with disconfirming evidence appears to be pretty well entrenched at the highest echelons of the FE and Skills sector, so it is by no means confined to classroom teachers.[2] But the problem is universal. The attraction of familiar old ideas, even when they have been repeatedly discredited by research, acts as a sharp brake on progress – partly because we all tend to fight vigorously to continue thinking and behaving in the way we have always thought and behaved, and partly because when we get into positions of power, we may react relatively conservatively to new ideas, by behaving as if we were being threatened by a socially embarrassing disease.

When the economist John Maynard Keynes remarked: 'When the facts change, I change my mind. What do you do?', he was challenging the typical stance of so many senior politicians and civil servants who, if they were to respond honestly, would reply to his question as follows: 'We are only interested in evidence that supports what we already think or the policies we are determined to push through, irrespective of the research record.'[3] I have used this episode to make the general point that fundamental change is so easy to recommend for others, but unpleasantly challenging when we are the ones being called upon to drop ideas or practices that have long been part of our intellectual furniture or repertoire. We all need to be more tolerant of what is involved when we invite others to enact deep and lasting reform or even what appear to us to be rather obvious, effective, and practical innovations.

The rest of this chapter will present a fuller critique of 'best practice', suggest the alternative of Joint Practice Development (JPD), propose a shift from Continuing Professional Development (CPD) to professional learning, and end by discussing trust and how to regenerate it when it has broken down.

2) Why is 'best practice' such a bad idea?

For me, the central weakness in the strategy of identifying and disseminating 'best practice' is the psychological resistance it builds up within those at the receiving end, because they are being told implicitly, if not explicitly, that their current practice is, in comparison, poor or inadequate. If their practice is satisfactory, good, or outstanding, why are they expected to adopt someone else's 'best practice'? And the recipients of 'best practice' almost certainly think that their own practice is pretty effective, otherwise why would they be using it?

I first began to doubt the efficiency of the strategy when, along with student teachers, I watched a video of an 'outstanding' teacher working with a small group of highly motivated, well-dressed, and impeccably behaved pupils in a sunlit classroom, equipped with every modern resource and technological aid. The implicit message being transmitted to my students was: you can easily replicate the success of Miss Newly Qualified Teacher (NQT) of the Year in your run-down school serving a slum estate with 30 teenagers, few of whom have English as their mother tongue, some of whom are war refugees and all of whom would rather be in paid employment. In such circumstances, 'best practice' begins to sound like a con-trick played by the unimaginative on the unsuspecting, particularly if the students are left to work out for themselves how to transfer the 'best practice' of the video to their own classrooms. The 'best' can quickly become the enemy of the 'perfectly good enough' in challenging circumstances. The video, which was presented as an example of 'best practice', did not discuss *why* the NQT's practice was considered to be exemplary, and it served only to scare the average student teacher into self-doubt, inscecurity, and inaction.

My opposition to 'best practice' deepened as I reflected on a number of questions that are never posed, never mind answered, by the advocates of the strategy. Who, for instance, says that X is 'best practice'? On what grounds? Based on what criteria? Have the criteria been publicly debated and agreed before anyone's practice is examined? Have all the most important criteria been included; for example, effectiveness, value for money, other possible options, varieties of context, consistency, and quality? Would another observer looking at the same class choose this teaching episode or strategy as 'best practice'? And if not, neither evaluation can claim to be valid. Does the 'best practice' that has been selected capture the full 'complexity, ambiguity and problematic nature of teaching' (Anderson and Krathwohl, 2001: 110)? What warrant comes with 'best practice' and is it qualified in any way? How applicable is the 'best practice' in terms of impact? Is it equally effective, say, with all age groups and all subject areas? What I am objecting to is the consistent and causal connection being made between 'best practice' and better outcomes – in all classrooms, in all weathers.

Finally, what is the quality of the evidence advanced to support it? Is it backed, for instance, by a number of meta-analyses of methodologically sound primary studies, reporting consistently high, positive effects in standardized tests? Or, which is far more common, is the 'best practice' being advocated nationally nothing more than the views of one ex-principal who has been impressed by some teaching seen in a short visit to one class? This battery of questions deserves to be answered fully, before any teacher is put under pressure to adopt what some manager has labelled 'best practice'.

I have saved for last what some commentators[4] regard as the most devastating critique of all: namely, the notion that one 'best practice' can be applied in all contexts is an impossibility, and that it is naive in the extreme to expect any such panacea. Those familiar with the theory of situated learning[5] will be aware that the idea of a simple, optimum solution, regardless of context, to intractable problems of the kind teachers have to face every day, is a dangerous delusion. Teachers quickly see through all-purpose, easy-to-implement, sure-fire, student-proof recipes. In classrooms they constantly have to make quick professional judgements, which have immediate effects on diverse groups of individual learners with highly specific needs, interests, and attitudes, who come from different backgrounds with widely varying respect for education and the full range of opportunities and obstacles in their local labour markets. The strategy of transferring 'best practice' fails because it treats very differing contexts as if they were all identical. If there are still any proponents of 'best practice' out there, perhaps they could tell us what theoretical justification it has?

3) There *is* an alternative: Joint Practice Development (JPD)

To expose the weaknesses in a major government strategy for reform is, I think, a useful, if not always a welcomed, public service, but to be in a position to recommend a replacement is far more constructive. It is possible to avoid the difficulties involved in using the adjectives 'good', 'effective', and 'best' by talking instead of devising mechanisms for professionals to jointly (J) share their practice (P) in order to develop (D) it. Tutors, for example, whether in construction, child care, or chemistry, come together in their teaching teams to discuss their experiences of teaching their subject to a particular standard and for a particular board (Edexcel or Assessment and Qualifications Alliance, AQA). In an atmosphere of mutual trust and joint exploration far removed from the isolation of their classrooms, they explain their successes and their struggles in teaching their subject in order to learn from each other; and they then move on to observing and evaluating each other's classroom practice, in an atmosphere that encourages the creativity of both partners. This approach completely avoids the psychological disadvantages built into the 'best practice' model, where one teacher (with implicitly poor practice) is put into the embarrassing position of having to accept instruction from another with apparently superior practice, who may well be equally embarrassed at having been identified as the carrier of 'best practice' – crucially, their joint embarrassment is likely to inhibit, rather than encourage, learning.

I first came across the term 'JPD' in a research report written for the then Department for Education and Skills in 2005 by Michael Fielding and his colleagues (Fielding *et al.*, 2005). Theirs was an in-depth, qualitative research project involving classroom observations and interviews with over 120 practitioners who had been trying to transfer 'good practice' across a variety of secondary schools. Their main findings can by summarized as follows: first, they prefer the term 'JPD' to 'transfer of good practice', because the latter 'marginalizes the importance of developing a new way of working that fits the different context of the partner teacher' (2005: 1). Second, trusting relationships are fundamental to JPD, which also requires the significant investment of time, resources, and commitment from teachers, principals, and government.

Third, both partners in the exchange need to play the role of observer and observed, of being the originator and receiver of practical advice, and both roles are accorded equal status. This equality in the relationships between teachers in the JPD model compares very favourably with the superior–inferior status of the two tutors in the 'best practice' approach, which goes a long way towards explaining why the former is proving to be far more effective. Fourth, we need to 'build on systems which put teachers in touch with each other and leave space for professionals' skilled judgements rather than imposing orthodoxies' (ibid.: 5).

One question leaped to my mind when I first read this report in 2007. Policymakers are rightly on the look-out for means of 'scaling up' successful approaches from pilot projects to national systems. Why then, if this strategy had proved to be so successful, had it not been 'rolled out' across the system? Two ideas occurred to me. First, JPD is expensive – it takes considerable time to develop relationships so trusting that the partners begin to discuss their weaknesses as well as their strengths. JPD also involves 'observation and evaluation of teachers' practice in classrooms, which is far more challenging to participants' than just exchanging information, which for most teachers is the standard form of Continuing Professional Development (CPD) they receive (Sebba *et al.*, 2012: 5). Moreover, if teachers are put in touch with colleagues from neighbouring colleges to extend JPD, then there are obvious costs in terms of transport and covering for teacher absences to attend JPD sessions. Whether such collaboration should then develop into partnerships, alliances, or chains is a proposal that needs evidence rather than the automatic assumption that such partnerships create a self-improving system, as David Hargreaves appears to do (2012).

My second idea is admittedly more cynical, but perhaps also more accurate, because governments can always find sufficient money to do whatever they are determined to do. JPD also involves a loss of control from the centre; no matter the political complexion of the administration in power, education ministers have used their power to tell teachers what to teach and how to teach it. JPD, in contrast, restores trust in the professional judgement of teachers; it encourages collaboration rather than competition, and it respects the professionalism of all those involved, rather than believing that there is a large, hard core of inefficient teachers who must be got rid of.

4) From JPD to professional learning

What has happened to JPD in the 9 years since Fielding and his colleagues published their research in 2005? Whenever it has been used in the post-compulsory sector, tutors have responded very positively to it. Andy Boon and Toni Fazaeli, reviewing the evidence collected by the Institute for Learning over a four-year period, conclude that 'nearly all teachers carry out about double the number of hours of Continuing Professional Development required each year' (2014: 39). Now, just because teachers have spent a large number of hours studying a topic does not necessarily indicate that they have learned anything new, nor that they have changed their practice as a consequence of the hours invested. On the other hand, Fazaeli and Boon report that 'teachers value sharing critical reflection, testing practice and learning from each other, both within and outside of their place of employment' (ibid.). Before reading any further, I invite the reader to try the activity in Box 2.1.

Box 2.1: The give and take of Joint Practice Development (JPD)

Suppose you are in charge of introducing JPD into your college or organization or you are a tutor interested in taking part. What questions would you set the participants, to ensure that everyone came to the discussion with something to teach and left with something they had learned?

Question 1:

Question 2:

(See Hargreaves, 2012, for more information.)

For David Hargreaves, JPD is the first and central building block in his model of a mature, self-improving school system. In setting up groups of teachers for JPD, he suggests that they be invited to answer two questions, which I have adapted here: 'What could I offer a colleague who teaches the same subject as I do?' and 'What would I like to gain from that colleague?'. What we are witnessing here is nothing less than the emergence of a new model of professional development, which is:

> ... less about attending conferences and courses and more about school-based, peer-to-peer activities in which development is fused with routine practice. Professional development becomes a continuous, pervasive process that builds craft knowledge, rather than an occasional activity that is sharply distinguished in time and space from routine classroom work.
>
> Hargreaves (2012: 8)

I would also like to follow Helen Timperley's lead (2011) in suggesting that we make a shift in our thinking from professional *development* to professional *learning*, because the former phrase has become devalued by its association with mere participation in CPD courses. My own definition of professional learning is an amalgam of a number of wordings that have been suggested and reads as follows: *it is a collaborative process of improving practice in the light of experience, research, and reflection in order to become more effective and efficient at enhancing outcomes for students.* Such professional learning is not a task for classroom teachers alone, but should be in evidence at all levels in the education 'system'. Fat chance.

Helen Timperley's work is important because she shows in detail how teachers create new professional knowledge through interaction with their colleagues; also, when tutors access expert knowledge, the sequence is not one of theory being turned into practice, but theory and practice being built together. In her words: 'Professional learning is not a process of learning new things and then learning how to implement them. Implementation is part of how something is learned and more deeply understood' (2011: 60). The opposite approach is exemplified by those coaches who say: 'I told you how to do it. Why didn't you just do it?'

I have seen JPD used most effectively in a course run jointly by the Learning and Skills Improvement Service and Sunderland University for research development fellows (RDFs). Participants, who are drawn from all sections within the learning and skills sector, complete a small-scale piece of research of practical relevance to their job. For four years I have watched these RDFs learn from each others' practice in an atmosphere of mutual respect and trust; they also collaborate closely to improve the quality of each others' projects. In the most successful cases, the JPD approach has been picked up by colleagues who are not attending the RDF course, and so it begins to permeate the college, adult learning centre, or private training provider to which the RDF returns with the aim of slowly changing the learning culture of the parent organization as a result. (See Gregson *et al.*, 2013, who argue that one of the great strengths of JPD is that it does not dismiss the merits of the RDFs' current practice, but seeks to enhance it by having it discussed openly with supportive colleagues.)

One interesting variant of JPD goes by the name of Lesson Study (LS), which has been practised across Japan since the 1870s, but has only recently been introduced into this country. Briefly, LS brings together a group of teachers who want to work collaboratively at improving a lesson on a particular aspect of the curriculum – say, a topic that the teachers find difficult to teach or that students find difficult to understand. The teachers together plan a Research Lesson (RL), one of them teaches it while the others observe, then they all discuss the strengths and weaknesses of the RL, while making sure to involve the pupils as learning partners in improving it. A second RL is then jointly planned and three or so 'case pupils', who represent, say, high-, middle-, or low-attainment groups, are chosen for the teachers to observe. The second RL is then taught and discussed, again involving the views of the pupils, and the whole sequence is repeated a third (or even a fourth) time, until all of the participants (tutors and students) are satisfied with the lesson.

The claims being made for LS are that its focus on learning rather than on teaching provides a safe environment for teachers to learn from each other and from their pupils, to experiment with different approaches, and to suggest hypotheses about why their pupils learn (or do not learn), which are then tested. The different perspectives that the teachers bring to LS '*slow down* swiftly flowing, complex classroom activity in RLs, allowing teachers *to see more* of what happens in greater detail than they can alone and from several viewpoints' (Dudley, 2013: 118, original emphasis). I am fond of Michael Eraut's description of good teaching as being like riding a bike skilfully through heavy traffic without wearing a safety helmet, but LS moves the discussion away from lone practice to a collaborative focus on the specifics of how students learn – or not – in crowded classrooms.

The advocates of LS, and there are now over 2,000 teachers in England who have been trained to use it, also claim that the planning, the rehearsal, and the discussion of RLs help teachers to internalize new practices. In addition, explaining LS to others helps teachers to incorporate those new practices into their standard repertoire in ways that are likely to be lasting. Those who remain to be convinced point to the disruption caused by the staff cover and to the extra resources needed to release a group of teachers repeatedly to plan and improve RLs. Despite these disadvantages, LS is being seriously studied and developed as a technique in primary and secondary schools, and the time has surely come for it to be tried out in the post-compulsory sector.

Sometimes a concept can be more fully grasped if its opposite is described and, for me, the antithesis of the JPD model is *The Apprentice* programme on BBC television, which each year assembles, in my opinion, a group of arrogant, self-promoting, and untrustworthy young executives who stab each other in the back in the ruthless pursuit of winning at all costs. The potential danger of such a programme is that it implicitly suggests that you have to be an aggressively unpleasant self-seeker in order to succeed in British industry. This brings me to the final topic to be discussed in this chapter – the necessity of trust between colleagues and between staff and students.

5) Trust

Effective JPD depends crucially on developing trust, and the educational literature is replete with reference to its importance. For Helen Timperley, trust is forged through daily social interactions and she defines it as:

> ... a genuine sense of listening to others, personal regard shown by a willingness of people to extend themselves beyond what is formally required, and beliefs that colleagues have the knowledge, skills and/or technical capacity to deliver on intentions and promises.
>
> (2011: 108)

Trust also emerges as a key element in research into good leadership in universities, where it 'gives people the security to be open, honest and critical in discussing strategy development, and creative, experimental and risk-taking in their interpretation and implementation' (McNay, 2012: 8). Trust can also be very quickly destroyed as, for example, when a football manager publicly berates his players for making mistakes.

For David Hargreaves, school leaders have the potentially discomfiting task of not only modelling trust in their relationships within their institution, but also of monitoring the levels of trust the staff have in the senior leadership team and in one another, as well as the amount of trust students have in the staff. He encloses in an annex forms for auditing different dimensions of trust that could easily be adapted for the FE and Skills sector (Hargreaves, 2012). See Box 2.2 for an activity about the dimensions of trust and how it could be audited.

Box 2.2: Developing and auditing trust

What do you think are the main dimensions of trust? Can you list the ones you think are the most important?

1.
2.
3.
4.
5.

(See Box 2.3 at the end of the chapter to see a list of possible dimensions.)

Suppose now that you wanted to audit how much trust, say, the staff have in the senior management team (SMT). Can you think of a number of statements to exemplify the dimensions you have listed above and then produce a proforma where staff could agree or disagree with the item? For example:

1. Communications in this college are good because the SMT actively listens to complaints from staff and responds appropriately.

Agree strongly ☐ Agree ☐ Disagree ☐ Disagree strongly ☐

See Hargreaves (2012) for audits of trust in SMT by staff, by staff in one another, and by students in staff

How does the concept of trust play out in the FE and Skills sector? I agree with Denis Gleeson's assessment that over the years successive governments have created a culture of mistrust, where fear (rather than trust) has become the predominant driving force for change: 'Though FE colleges are officially independent of central government's control, the sector operates within a context of licensed autonomy, with professionals treated as trusted servants rather than as empowered professionals' (2014: 23). Increasingly, they are now treated as mistrusted servants. Similarly, Ofsted has evolved into a punitive arm of government and has lost the trust of the teaching profession.

It was only, however, when I was reading Richard Sennett's book on the rituals, pleasures, and politics of co-operation that I began to understand more fully why it has become so difficult for so many staff in the sector to make the leap of faith in their leaders that trust requires. He describes how, before the 2008 crisis in banks and investment houses, trust by the front-line financial specialists in their superiors was eroded by invidious comparison, because the latter were considered to be technically incompetent by the former: 'the top don't know what's going on every day in the firm; they lack hands-on knowledge' (2012: 171).

What I think has happened in a goodly number of FE colleges is this: as the SMT has steadily withdrawn from teaching since incorporation in the early 1990s, while at the same time proclaiming it to be the core business of the organization, classroom teachers have steadily lost respect for their leaders as educators, as opposed to financial managers, who in some cases become objects of ridicule from whom it then becomes impossible to learn. The result, according to Sennett, is a growing belief in 'an inverse relationship between competence and hierarchy, a bitter reversal which dissolves trust in those above' (ibid.: 172). Good teachers who see teaching as a craft, and who wish to continue improving just for the sake of it, tend not to be pleased but become embittered by such an outcome.

The culture of mistrust in colleges is a replication of the relationship between government and the institutional leaders in the sector, with the latter treated as assets to be controlled, 'sweated', and micro-managed by ministers in the interests of greater economic efficiency. A current example is the aggressive and inappropriate language of the Skills Minister, Matthew Hancock, who has, I understand, never been in charge of anything in his short life, but who writes of holding 'principals' feet to the fire on behalf of students' (2013: 4). The end apparently justifies the means. What also complicates the picture in education is the co-existence of two models that are in direct conflict – a professional model where all staff, teachers, and managers wish to be treated as members of the one profession; and a management model where SMTs run the organization and unions protect the interests of their members.

Mike Bottery, in addition to describing no fewer than seven different forms of trust, makes some useful suggestions about how trust between policymakers and professionals could be regenerated through a benign spiral (2003). A number of his suggestions could equally well be used by SMTs to remedy any breakdown in trust within an FE college; and with these proposals I shall end this chapter.

Governments and SMTs could, for instance, publicly and repeatedly acknowledge what a difficult job teaching is; they could reduce workloads that have become too heavy and stressful; they could lighten the administrative demands on teachers by cutting their incessant requests for data and so increase the time teachers could devote to TLA; they could trust the integrity of educators by allowing them greater freedom over pedagogy and curriculum; they could stop grading lesson observations and institute instead a policy of JPD; and they could introduce intelligent rather than punitive accountability, which replaces one-off, unrepresentative visits with more longitudinal evaluation of teachers' work. Above all, SMTs could return to teaching and discussing TLA with their colleagues from a basis of recent and relevant classroom experience.

Trust, however, is a two-way process and it may prove necessary for the teachers' unions and professional bodies to take the initiative in making proposals to management and government in order to get the benign spiral of trust started. Teaching staff could, for instance, demonstrate their commitment to raising the achievement of all students by offering 'wholehearted commitment to the provision of evidence of the monitoring of student progression, and of portfolio evidence of student improvement' (Bottery, 2003: 258). Tutors could also commit themselves to becoming a fully research-informed profession, and one aspect of that commitment would be a move to a new model of professional learning based on JPD, rather than wasting their time trying to identify and transfer 'best practice'. See Box 2.3 for a list of possible dimensions of trust.

Box 2.3: Dimensions of trust

1. Talking straight
2. Demonstrating concern
3. Creating transparency
4. Righting wrongs
5. Showing loyalty
6. Participating in professional learning with colleagues
7. Consulting before deciding
8. Confronting reality
9. Clarifying goals and expectations
10. Practising accountability
11. Active listening
12. Keeping commitments
13. Extending trust to all employees
14. Believing that colleagues can keep promises
15. Having a personal regard for all staff and students
16. Accepting and using principled dissent
17. Coping with risk and uncertainty
18. Relying on the integrity of professionals
19. Modelling trusting relationships with staff
20. Creating and enhancing a learning culture in the college

Source: adapted and extended from Hargreaves (2012: 14)

Notes

[1] I shall not pursue further the logical non sequitur of this statement, which suggests that ideas are of dubious worth if they are rarely used, because that would rule out philosophy, Christianity, and thinking itself.

[2] The strategy of first identifying and then disseminating 'best practice' is alive and well, despite all of its attendant problems, in all of the main texts being produced by and for the sector; to take just one more example, the report from the Commission on Adult Vocational Teaching and Learning (CAVTL, 2013) within 34 pages uses 'best practice' six times, 'good practice' twice, and 'effective', 'innovative', 'sophisticated', 'sustained', and 'leading edge' practice once each. I suspect that all of these terms are being used loosely to mean the same thing. If not, I think we should be told what the differences are.

[3] A good example is Michael Gove's determination to introduce free schools to England, all the while claiming that Swedish evidence supported his insistence. In fact, that evidence showed that free schools lowered standards.

[4] See, for example, James and Biesta (2007).

[5] Situated learning, as proposed by Jean Lave and Etienne Wenger, two American anthropologists, shifts 'the analytic focus from the individual as learner to learning as participation in the social world, and from the concept of cognitive process to the more-encompassing view of social practice' (1991: 43). In my words, their theory explains how newcomers slowly learn the knowledge, skills, and dispositions of experts by being drawn in from the periphery to the centre of their activities. Please do not be put off by the intimidating title of their book – *Situated Learning: Legitimate peripheral participation* – it is an insightful and novel demonstration of the quintessentially social character of learning. They studied the cognitive apprenticeships of novices who changed their identities as they slowly became midwives, tailors, quartermasters, butchers, and non-drinking alcoholics (that is, those who no longer drink but remain alcoholics). As Lave and Wenger argue, if you want to take a fresh look at authentic learning, the last place you would study is an educational institution, because so many of them have been turned into exam factories (see Coffield and Williamson, 2012).

References

Anderson, L.W. and Krathwohl, D.R. (eds) (2001) *A Taxonomy for Learning, Teaching and Assessing: A revision of Bloom's Taxonomy of Educational Objectives*. New York: Longman, abridged edition.

Blair, T. (2013) 'Labour must search for answers and not merely aspire to be a repository for people's anger'. *New Statesman*, 12–25 April.

Boon, A. and Fazaeli, T. (2014) 'Professional bodies and continuing professional development: A case study', 31–53. In S. Crowley (ed.), *Challenging Professional Learning*. London: Routledge.

Bottery, M. (2003) 'The management and the mismanagement of trust'. *Educational Management, Administration and Leadership*, 31 (3), 245–6.

Coffield, F. and Edward, S. (2009) 'Rolling out "good", "best" and "excellent" practice. What next? Perfect practice?'. *British Educational Research Journal*, 35 (3), 371–90.

Coffield, F. and Williamson, B. (2012) *From Exam Factories to Communities of Discovery: The democratic route*. London: Institute of Education, University of London.

Commission on Adult Vocational Teaching and Learning (CAVTL) (2013) *It's About Work ... Excellent adult vocational teaching and learning*. Coventry: LSIS.

Department for Education and Skills (DfES) (2002) *Success for All: Reforming further education and training: Our vision for the future*. London: DfES.

Dudley, P. (2013) 'Teacher learning in lesson study'. *Teaching and Teacher Education*, 34, 107–21.

Fielding, M., Bragg, S., Craig, J., Cunningham, I., Eraut, M., Gillinson, S., Horne, M., Robinson, C., and Thorp, J. (2005) *Factors Influencing the Transfer of Good Practice*. Research Brief RB615. London: DfES.

Gleeson, D. (2014) 'Professional identity, trading places: On becoming an FE professional', 20–30. In S. Crowley (ed.), *Challenging Professional Learning*. London: Routledge.

Gregson, M., Nixon, L., Spedding, T., and Kearney, S. (2013) *Unlocking Improvement in Teaching and Learning: A leader's guide to joint practice development in the FE system*. London: LSIS.

Guild Project Team (2013a) *Consultation to Establish a Guild for the Learning and Skills Sector*. London: AOC/NIACE/AELP.

— (2013b) *FE Guild Implementation Plan: Summary version*. London: AOC/NIACE/AELP.

Hancock, M. (2013) 'A sector in charge of its own destiny'. In I. Nash (ed.), *Twenty Years of College Independence*. Online. www.feweek.co.uk (accessed 24 April 2013).

Hargreaves, D. (2012) *A Self-improving School System: Towards maturity*. National College for School Leadership.

James, D. and Biesta, G. (2007) *Improving Learning Cultures in Further Education*. Abingdon, Oxon: Routledge.

Lave, J. and Wenger, E. (1991) *Situated Learning: Legitimate peripheral participation*. Cambridge: Cambridge University Press.

McNay, I. (2012) 'Leading strategic change in higher education – closing the implementation gap'. *Leadership and Governance in Higher Education*, 4, 46–69.

Sebba, J., Kent, P., and Tregenza, J. (2012) *Joint Practice Development: What does the evidence suggest are effective approaches?*. National College for School Leadership.

Sennett, R. (2012) *Together: The rituals, pleasures and politics of cooperation*. London: Allen Lane.

Timperley, H. (2011) *Realizing the Power of Professional Learning*. Maidenhead: Open University Press/McGraw-Hill Education.

Chapter 3

Stimulating thinking, creating challenge, extending learning

John Webber

> *Some recent philosophers have given their moral approval to the deplorable verdict that an individual's intelligence is a fixed quantity, one which cannot be augmented. We must protest and act against this brutal pessimism.*
>
> Alfred Binet (1909: 141), founder of the IQ test

1) The challenge

Listening to students discussing their beliefs about learning can be very illuminating. Listening to those who have rediscovered a love of learning and the knowledge that they are learning for themselves can be delightful. Listening to teachers, who help develop this love of learning in their students, can be really inspiring. This chapter arose from the habit of doing all of these as part of my role supporting the development of teaching and learning in a large FE college. It explores what underlies the difference between students who approach learning with dull reluctance – like Shakespeare's schoolboy[1] – and those who will climb walls and surmount any obstacles to get the learning they want. Drawing on published research, cross-referenced to the lived experience of students and teachers, it seeks answers to the many related questions that arise as students mature, or fail to mature, as learners in post-16 education.

When invited to talk about the differences they have found between learning at school, on the one hand, and FE or sixth-form college on the other, students almost always make two related statements: 'at school they spoon-feed you'; 'at college there is more independent learning, it's more up to you'. Interestingly, students pick up this idea very early. Prospective students when they attend 'introductory days' in early summer already talk about this contrast and express positive anticipation, speaking of being treated as adults, having choice, and learning for themselves.

So consistent are these responses that there is a danger of being lulled into thinking that this transition is problem-free. However, there is much more to changing one's fundamental orientation to learning and to developing the relevant behaviours, skills, and personal resources that will enable this transition, than simply thinking it is an attractive idea. Habits, beliefs, and expectations formed during secondary school often run strongly counter to this. Thus, a cohort of prospective students who talked enthusiastically about taking greater responsibility for their learning, when asked what questions they had come with to the introductory day, looked blank or puzzled, as if the idea that they would have any questions of their own about college was quite alien. When asked 'Why did you come in today?', the majority answered either 'Because I got a letter from the college that told me to do so' or 'Because my parents said I should'.

Perhaps this should not surprise us. Arguably, the historical premise on which our educational system is built assumes that teachers are the people with the knowledge and expertise, and the role of successful pupils/students is to follow instruction and absorb as much of this precious knowledge and expertise as their ability allows. The end-points – qualifications earned – have the dual function of rewarding these behaviours, and of providing future employers, or indeed future educators, with a classification of individuals into more or less able, and more or less diligent.

There are several questionable assumptions behind this premise. Three in particular are of immediate relevance to this chapter. The first assumption is that teaching is the process of pouring knowledge into the waiting minds of the students. The origin of the word 'lecture', meaning to read, is worth reflection. The medieval practice of reading aloud from a text, of which there was only one copy, so that students could reproduce this in their own notebooks, was clearly essential before the days of printing. Given how much knowledge and expertise we can now access both in print and via the internet, we have scope to rethink. Students think so too:

Box 3.1: Students in their first year of college talking about different approaches to teaching

Note: in this and all following transcripts in this chapter: 'S' = Student, 'I' = Interviewer, 'T' = Teacher

S1: 'I'd say teachers handle it in very different ways. Some teachers will write on the board and you will copy down everything. Other teachers will tell you what you need to do and then let you go and do it.'

I: 'Which do you find more useful?'

> S2: 'I think writing and copying are very old-fashioned and you need a different approach. But you also need direction. You need quite a lot of encouragement, so that you know exactly what you need to do and then you can do it.'
>
> S3: 'When people are just writing on the board and you are writing it and they are speaking at the same time you cannot really process it. [What helps you process it?] Like these guys were saying, when it's more interactive, with class discussions ... If they are just writing on the board they might as well not be there, you could just read it.'

The second assumption is that the knowledge of prior generations is sufficient to meet the needs of the current generation of students, whereas realistically, to thrive in their uncertain future, young people will need to question our assumptions and generate new knowledge and ideas. This is not to deny the importance of the knowledge and expertise of their teachers. Instead, it is about establishing ways of helping students achieve a higher order of engagement with this knowledge than simply reproducing it like human photocopiers.

The third assumption, that ability is a fixed quantity determined at birth or early in the development of the child, is arguably the most pernicious. This has not only been shown to be false but also, as Binet himself asserted (see the quote at the start of this chapter), profoundly damaging to the way people engage with the challenges of learning (see, for example, Dweck, 1999).

Although these assumptions have been the focus of much critical commentary, they have been the common school experience of both parents and teachers for generations. They are reproduced in much of current educational practice and embedded in the culture that surrounds it. It is not surprising that students reflect this back to us – and all the more reason for us to challenge them.

With notable and important exceptions, under pressure to meet league table targets, secondary teaching appears to have increasingly adopted a didactic and controlling approach. Commonly, pupils are supplied with a stream of printed handouts that stipulate not only exactly what they need to know, but also how they should go about demonstrating this knowledge when answering exam questions. However, this chapter will not be a smug critique of secondary education that seeks to eulogize the work of FE and sixth-form colleges in repairing the damage done. Ironically, while many college teachers identify this as a problem, they too are under pressure from the various ranking statistics based on graded assessments, 'success rates', 'benchmarks', and 'value added', and can easily find themselves rationalizing similar approaches.

This is reflected in a recent Cambridge Assessment Group publication (Mehta *et al.*, 2012). Their focus group research with university lecturers indicates that '... most of the new undergraduates, irrespective of previous grades, are not prepared for university study'.

New undergraduates were considered to be least prepared in:

1. critical/higher-order thinking skills
2. academic writing skills
3. independent inquiry/research skills.

As if rubbing salt into the wound, the report states that 'the participants perceived teaching at A level to involve a lot of spoon-feeding ... and to focus on teaching-to-the-test'.

It is easy in the light of such accounts to become pessimistic about the prospects of improving this situation without a radical, and currently unlikely, release from the intensive measuring of education through grades. However, the appearance of an irreducible dilemma is misleading. As reflected throughout this book, there is accumulating evidence that it is possible to create teaching and learning experiences that enable students to become more actively engaged learners while enhancing their chances of achieving higher grades.

This chapter will explore specific approaches that stimulate students to think, to formulate questions of their own, and to develop an appetite for the challenges of deeper learning. It aims to show that it is possible to help students to develop new habits of mind, new ways of responding when they hit difficulties, new beliefs and expectations about learning and themselves as learners. In the process, students can rediscover the love of learning that is so apparent in preschool children:

> The inclination to learn from life itself and to make the conditions of life such that all will learn in the process of living is the finest product of schooling.
>
> Dewey (1924: 60)

Box 3.2: An opportunity for reflection: think, puzzle, explore

Before reading any further, it would be valuable to pause and consider your own ideas about the above. I suggest the following questions, which incidentally can be adapted to use with students to stimulate their own thinking when approaching any new topic:

1. What ideas do you already have about stimulating students' thinking and their appetite for learning?
2. What puzzles you about this? What questions do you have about it?
3. What interests you about this? How might it relate to your work?

2) Modelling the change: The four dimensions of 'studentship'

I was led to explore this topic after repeatedly hearing experienced teachers claim that the problems associated with transition from school to college were deepening. They perceived students as being unwilling to recognize their part in the learning process. What was the relationship to learning that students had developed prior to college and how might this need to change for them to become mature learners, well prepared for their lives as adults?

Invited to complete the sentence 'I wish our/my students would ...', teachers commonly focus first on behaviours: arrive on time; bring a pen; do their homework; pay attention; answer questions; contribute to group work. When asked, 'What would you like them to develop apart from subject knowledge?', their answers commonly switch to skills such as the ability to produce well-structured written work. When encouraged to go further, some will talk about increasing self-confidence, being more ready to take risks, coping better with failure.

Researching the literature on learning to learn and what makes an effective learner complicates the picture still further. However, a pattern slowly emerges. My research led to the creation of our four-dimensional model of 'studentship' (see Box 3.3), the name being inspired by the analogy with craftsmanship[2] or musicianship.

This model attempts to condense into a simple tree-like structure many theories and ideas about learning. Thus, for example, the branch labelled 'Qualities' is inspired in part by the work of Bill Lucas and Guy Claxton (2010), which shares common ground with that of Art Costa and Ben Kallick (2000). Carol Dweck's research (1999) contributed key ideas to the root labelled 'Beliefs'.

Box 3.3: A model of 'studentship' in four dimensions

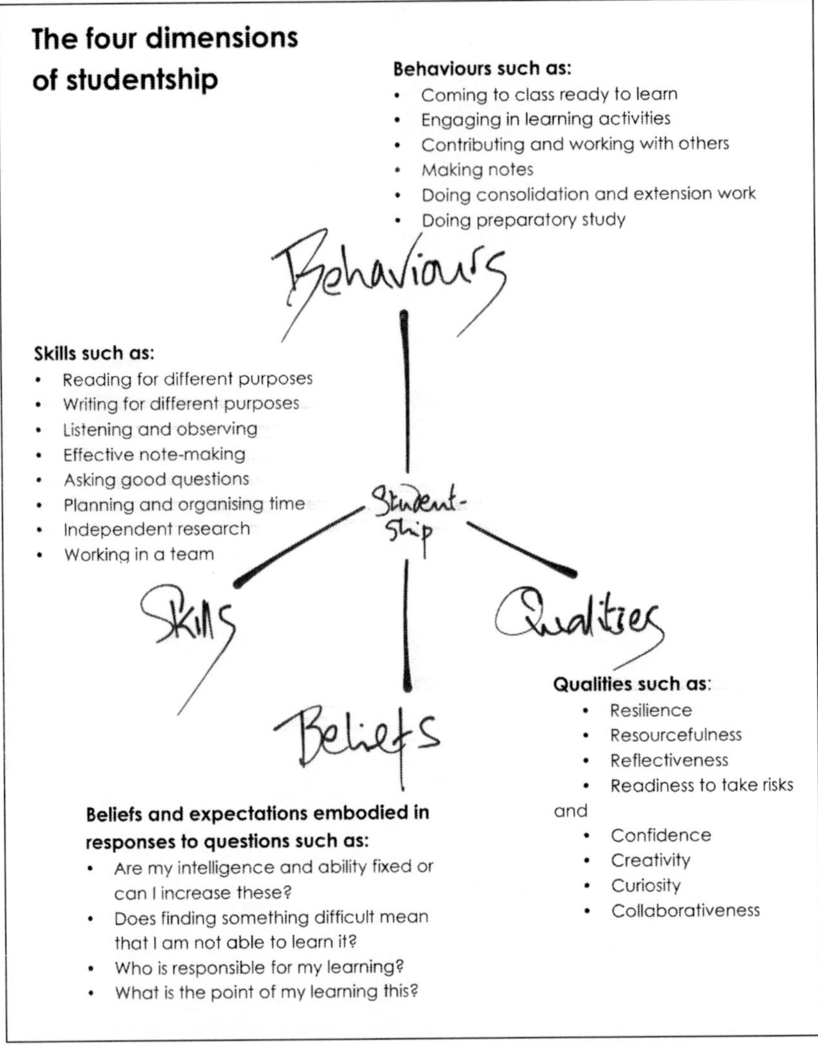

The value that I and others have found in working with this model comes from the recognition both of the distinctness of each of the four dimensions and of their interrelatedness. Thus, at the simplest level, students' note-making behaviours depend in part on their note-making skills and at a deeper level on what they believe is the purpose or value of taking notes. Equally, the most basic of learning behaviours – for example, attending classes – may be determined by their answer to the question 'What is the point of my learning this?' or more subtly by a combination of their skills, personal qualities, prior behaviours, and beliefs. Thus a student's lack of skills might lead to their failing an assignment. This dent in their self-confidence, coupled with a belief that ability is a fixed commodity and failure identifies its limits, may lead them to withdraw rather than risk further humiliation. A slightly more resourceful student with an equally impoverished model of learning might copy his or her next homework, to hide the difficulty. Later in this chapter we will explore possible interventions that can help students to develop more effective ways of navigating this complex territory.

3) Responding to the challenge

3.1) Developing students' learning and thinking skills

The recognition that there is more to learning than simple recall of knowledge is, in principle, embedded in current education. In particular, graded assessments commonly discriminate between lower-order and higher-order thinking skills. 'Bloom's taxonomy' of cognitive skills, originally one of three taxonomies produced, in 1956, by an educational committee chaired by Benjamin Bloom, still dominates the field. Its commonest representation, as a triangle with six boldly coloured portions, has 'knowledge' at its base and 'evaluation' at the summit. A recent review of the model (Anderson and Krathwohl, 2001) proposed significant changes, including the recognition that knowledge runs throughout learning and that the crucial differences lie in how the learner interacts with this (an idea explored further in Chapter 4). However, the original taxonomy underpins much current formal assessment. It is commonly transcribed with little modification into the grading criteria for A levels, vocational qualifications, and higher education assessments.

Nevertheless, while such assessments aim to differentiate the achievements of students using this model, approaches to teaching often fail to reflect this. A vivid example of this is provided by research into teachers' habitual use of questions, such as a 1993 study by Brown and Wragg. They found that over half of questions asked (57 per cent) were managerial: 'Who has finished all of the worksheet?'; another third required pupils simply to recall information provided previously by the teacher. Only 8 per cent called for any form of higher-order thinking.

Given how widely questioning is used to provide a teacher with an immediate assessment of learning, this habit of asking 'lower-order' questions merits attention. Take a moment to answer the following questions in Box 3.4 about the first verse of Lewis Carroll's famous poem 'Jabberwocky'.

Box 3.4: Questions for understanding?

'Twas brillig, and the slithy toves
Did gyre and gimble in the wabe;
All mimsy were the borogoves,
And the mome raths outgrabe.

1. Where did the slithy toves gyre?
2. How were the borogoves?
3. What did the mome raths do?
4. Why might the borogroves have been mimsy?

You were probably able to answer the first three of these questions correctly with minimal thought. Did your ability to do so provide any evidence that you understood the poem or indeed your own answers? The fourth question at least, while still not requiring you to understand the meaning of the nonsense words, is likely to have engaged you in thinking a little more creatively. When used with a group, this final question commonly stimulates a variety of answers, each with a different rationale to support it. This brief exercise, whether used with teachers or students, can stimulate some interesting reflection on questioning to check understanding and to stimulate thinking.

In fact, teacher questions can be a powerful tool not only to check a variety of different aspects of learning but also to stimulate students to think in a variety of ways.

Consider the questions in Box 3.5 below.

Box 3.5: Questions for thinking

1. When was ... invented?	2. What factors might have contributed to it being invented at this time?	3. Has the use of ... changed since it was invented? In what way?
4. How has the invention of ... affected ...?	5. If ... hadn't ever been invented, how do you think our lives today might be different?	6. Do you think the invention of ... has been a good thing? Why?

While the first question seeks simple recall, others potentially stimulate a variety of forms of thinking: analytical, evaluative, or creative.

A second example (see Box 3.6) illustrates the same process with a more practical, task-related focus.

Box 3.6: Questions for practical thinking

1. What is the first thing you need to do if you are trying to ...?	2. List the six steps you need to take to ...	3. Which of the steps could you skip if ...?
4. What would happen if you missed out step 3?	5. If ... happened, what could you do to get round the problem?	6. In a similar way, now decide the steps that you would need to take to ...

Such sets of questions can be used both progressively to probe students' understanding and to stimulate fresh thinking. They can also be used to provide different levels of challenge for different students, where this is appropriate.

We have adopted 'questioning for thinking' as a focus for various developmental activities throughout our college. A common obstacle to effective questioning reported by teachers is when students just answer 'I don't know' if asked a direct question. Unfortunately, teachers often – more often than they might believe or intend – respond to this by answering their own question. This can reinforce students' learned helplessness. It appears to confirm the idea of the teacher as the expert always on hand to compensate for the deficiencies of the students, rather than helping them develop their own thinking.

The alternative strategy of opening up the question to volunteers may appear slightly more successful, but such volunteers are often limited to a familiar minority of the most confident students. This can rapidly reinforce inequalities in a classroom, ensuring that some students not only engage in more thinking but also receive more confidence-building attention and affirmation, while others slip further into a resigned sense that they are 'not very good at this sort of thing'.[3]

3.2) Questions to scaffold[4] learning

To address this issue, Kevin, a teacher and member of my development team, has been working with a systematic framework for questioning, based on the work of Walsh and Sattes (2011: viii) and further developed in Fisher and Frey (2007: 37–41) and Frey and Fisher (2011). Rather than rescuing students who answer 'I don't know', the teacher responds with prompts or cues to assist them in thinking their way through to an answer (see Box 3.7). Kevin says, 'The point is, you are not going to give up on them now'.

Box 3.7: Not giving up on students when they say 'I don't know'

T: If I wasn't here, how could you find out?

S: I could Google it.

T: OK, so what might you Google?

S: 'Input buttons'.

T: OK, and what response do you think you might get?

S: I would see all the different types of input button.

T: Which ones have we covered so far?

S: Well we did ... and ... and ...

T: Yes, and which one do you think would be most suitable for this scenario?

S: Umm, maybe the one that ...

Kevin commented:

> It is crucial that they get to the right answer themselves. When I began to use this technique, I was amazed at the impact. Students were working a lot harder. It required practice. Initially, I sometimes found that I was just rewording the question. Now it just feels natural.

A student commented in the written end-of-year feedback:

> The thing I like about Kevin's teaching is that he never gives you the answer. He always makes you figure it out for yourself.

It is encouraging to note that the AS summer exam results for this cohort of students showed a marked improvement compared to the previous year: 54 per cent achieved an A or B grade compared to the national benchmark of 25 per cent, whereas the previous year only 20 per cent achieved these grades. It appears that stimulating thinking is not only good for learning, but it is also useful in exams!

In the words of another cohort of students:

> S1: 'I think the best teachers ask you questions rather than just tell you things' [S2 agrees verbally, S3 is nodding] 'because that encourages you to go away and do the work yourself. If you have

> to think out the answer or research it yourself, you are more likely to remember it.'

These students are taking increasing ownership of their learning, a theme we will return to below.

Josh, their Spanish teacher, commented:

> It is key that the students try to figure the answer out for themselves, even if in the end you have to give them help with this ... 'You said this and this. Well, notice that this and this go together but this and this don't work.' You use what they have already given you to come up with the rule, a theory, an explanation.

3.3) Socratic questioning to extend students' thinking

The technique of using questions to stimulate students to arrive at deeper or more articulated insights is sometimes called 'Socratic questioning', in acknowledgement of its famous ancient Greek exponent, Socrates. Some teachers have developed this to become a key teaching strategy. Box 3.8 illustrates the method, using an excerpt from a recorded lesson with AS English Literature students who are studying a play. The students initially worked in small groups to annotate a brief section of the text, identifying ways in which the dialogue brings out key themes in the plot. Then, in turn, they came to the front of the class to annotate a projected version of the text.

Box 3.8: Example of Socratic questioning

S: *[annotating a section of the text where one character, Beverly, is talking to Tony, a guest at her party, about her dream of drinking Bacardi on the beach]* 'Drinking on the beach is something you normally do as a couple but she doesn't mention Laurence.'

T: 'Very interesting.'

S: 'So she is either trying to create sexual tension or she actually is alone.'

T: 'Yes. So what are you saying there? Are you saying that this is about Beverly or is it about Laurence as well?'

S: 'Both of them, really. She doesn't get fulfilled by Laurence. So she needs to be somewhere else, to have someone with her, to see her in a sexual light.'

> T: 'Ah! [*To the group*] Write that down – the lack of sexual chemistry between Laurence and herself. [*Pause*] And a question for you there. How does Leigh portray this as it develops later in the play? Is there a difference in the relationship between Beverly and Tony in Act 1 and Act 2?'
>
> S: 'Well, they become more intimate as Beverly and Laurence start to argue more.'
>
> T: 'That's interesting. Write that down everyone. The intimacy between Beverly and Tony develops as the rows develop between Beverly and Laurence. Very good.'

In an interview following the lesson, Mark, the teacher in the quoted section above, talked about his use of questions to extend learning:

> I think it is really important that you are challenging comments that need to go further. So a student will say, 'I think Beverly is presented as a man-eating monster' and I will say, 'How? Why? Can you go further with that?'. It is really important that they go as far as possible with their evaluation and analysis.

Mark also talks of how the approach allows him to scaffold the thinking of students, who may be struggling, by directing their attention through prompts and leading questions. This can help them to achieve insights or a fuller understanding.

Again, recent exam results support these claims. A third of this cohort of students (and those in the parallel classes) achieved an A grade at the end of their first year and all 65 students passed. A2 students, including a cohort quoted later in this chapter (see Box 3.15), were even more successful. Over a third of them achieved an A* and 82 per cent either A*/A or B.

3.4) Stimulating students' questioning

One of the risks we face as teachers is deadening students' curiosity by always giving them the answers to questions that they have not yet asked. There are a number of ways to address this, some of which I will return to later (for example, in the section on 'flipped learning'). One powerful route into this area is the use of 'question stems'. Students are asked to generate a set of questions about a topic, an idea, a picture, or an object. They are given a variety of question stems that they might use, such as 'Why ...?', 'How would it be different if ...?', 'What if ...?', 'What might be the reason for ...?', 'What is the purpose of ...', 'Suppose that ...?', 'What if we knew ...?'. Working in teams to generate, say, a dozen useful questions can add the spice of competition. Sets of questions are then reviewed to select the most interesting. This can lead into discussions about how one might go about seeking answers to selected questions. It can also stimulate a valuable discussion about what makes a good question, and good questions are the starting point of much valuable learning.[5] As J.S. Bruner (1974: 127) observed:

> Good questions are ones that pose dilemmas, subvert obvious or canonical truths, force incongruities upon our attention.

3.5) Activities to promote thinking and develop understanding

While high-quality questioning can be a powerful stimulus for extending students' thinking, there are many other ways of achieving this. However, before exploring these, we need to address a common myth that has developed along with the recent focus on defining measurable learning objectives.

Teachers are commonly advised that learning objectives should use verbs that describe what the student will be able to do if they achieve the intended learning. The underlying precept is that learning needs to result in a measurable change in what the learner is able to do. This in turn leads to the advice that verbs such as 'understand' should be avoided, on the grounds that understanding cannot be directly observed. Reasonable as this is, it carries a significant risk that understanding is discounted or ignored when lessons are planned or assessment tasks are written. Knowledge and skills become the exclusive measures of learning and hence the exclusive goals.

Discounting understanding is nonsense. I hope you would be hard-pressed to find a teacher who would not want students to understand key ideas or principles in their subject appropriate to their level. However, you are likely to find teachers who teach with the implicit assumption that understanding is not essential as long as students are able to successfully complete the relevant assessments.

Unfortunately, a lack of understanding is likely to contribute to one of the most commonly bemoaned features of student learning – that is, they fail to transfer knowledge or skills from one context to another because of some superficial differences in the appearance of a task. Thus, a teacher spoke with acute frustration about a large cohort of students who did not attempt a high-mark exam question similar to another that they had answered successfully just two days before. 'I said to them, "but we covered a similar question on Tuesday and you all did very well". They said, "but the question included the name of a chemical that we didn't know, so how could we do it?"' Their understanding of the topic was insufficient for them to realize that they did not need to know anything more about this chemical than was presented as data within the question. (The problem of transfer is discussed further in Chapter 4.)

Understanding enables you to think about, adapt, and apply your knowledge and skills to new situations. It is crucial even in subjects where there is no need to articulate this understanding verbally.

'Teaching for understanding' was the focus of a six-year research project led by Martha Wiske, David Perkins, and Howard Gardner at the Harvard School of Education. This is reported in the eponymous book (Wiske, 1997) and it continues to inform developmental work with schools under the heading 'Visible thinking'.[6]

Their approach is based on the precept that learning is very often achieved through doing. You cannot learn maths just by watching someone else do sums nor to skate just by reading a manual. At some point you need to pick up a pencil or put on some skates. They argue that thinking and understanding are no different and that understanding 'is a matter of being able to perform in a variety of thought-demanding ways with the topic, for instance, to: explain, muster evidence, find examples, generalize, apply concepts, analogize, represent in a new way, and so on' (Perkins, 1993).

These observable behaviours involve higher-order skills that need to be developed through practice – not in the abstract, but in the context of the actual subjects being studied. Hence the Harvard team worked extensively with teachers to design and evaluate learning activities that develop students' thinking and understanding in a variety of subject domains. Many of these seek to make thinking more explicitly visible to both the teacher and the learner. This serves both to highlight the value of this often hidden process, and to make errors and misconceptions more readily visible and hence available for correction.

A simple example is the 'think, puzzle, explore' activity in Box 3.2. This can help reveal students' prior knowledge and preconceptions and engage them in thinking about a topic before you tell them anything. Another example is to say, 'What makes you say that?', which encourages students to provide evidence or an example to support their statements. This is similar to the questioning process exemplified above in Box 3.8. A variant of this, which I have found works well, is to show students a photograph or a short video clip that they have probably not seen before. The subject of the picture or video clip needs to be one that is slightly puzzling, ambiguous, or in some way requires interpretation. The students are asked to try to interpret or explain what they see, answering three questions:

- What is going on in this picture?

- What do you see that makes you say that?
- What more can you find?

This can work well in pairs, small groups, or as a plenary. As a teacher-led plenary it can provide ample opportunities to discuss the process of observation, speculation/interpretation, and justification from evidence. If the video clip or picture is relevant to the topic you are about to introduce, it can also serve as a useful way to stimulate interest and engagement.

There are many more examples of these 'thinking routines' available on the Visible Thinking website.[7] *The New York Times*'s blog 'The Learning Network'[8] also has a further discussion of the activity, 'What is going on in this picture?', along with some intriguing photographs (Schulten, 2013).

3.6) The power of meta-cognition

A recent review, carried out for the Sutton Trust (Higgins *et al.*, 2011), of educational research into which approaches to teaching and learning make most measurable impact on pupil progress, identified the following three as having potentially the greatest impact:

1. effective feedback
2. meta-cognition and self-regulation strategies
3. peer teaching/peer-assisted learning.

They define meta-cognitive strategies as 'teaching approaches which make learners' thinking about learning more explicit in the classroom'. Their review confirmed that strategies such as those discussed above 'have consistently high or very high levels of impact'. We will meet other examples in the remainder of this chapter (the topic of meta-cognition is also discussed further in Chapter 4).

3.7) Students as owners of their own learning

> The main difference is that you have got to want to do it. If you don't want to do it, there is no way you are going to make yourself do it. Whereas at school it is all more controlled and if you don't want to go to a class you go to it anyway because you are in school and you'll get in trouble if you don't go. Here it is a lot more relaxed. You have got to have a lot more self-drive.
>
> Student at the end of her first year at college

Like many concepts in education, the notion of students as owners of their own learning is open to use and misuse. (See also Walter Müller's discussion in Chapter 5.) However, it remains a fundamental issue, particularly during this phase in students' lives, as they mature into adulthood.

In the introduction to this chapter, I quoted students talking in focus groups during a recent college pre-enrolment introductory day. These quotes illustrated consistent, positive expectations of increasing independence, ownership of their learning, and being 'treated more like adults'. This is an encouraging starting point, matching the intended culture and expectations of the college, but it is only the idea that they are relating to. Many students find the reality more challenging (see Box 3.9).

Box 3.9: Students reflections on their changing experience of learning

Students looking back on their first year at college:

S1: '... at school you are aware that teachers are there to get you through the exams whereas here, teachers want to help you, but it is up to you.'

S2: 'I think the one thing I would change, looking back, is I would try to do more independent learning because I did copy homework when I was struggling. I think I would have done better if I hadn't done that.'

S3: 'You rely very much on yourself. The teachers aren't constantly after you for homework or any assignments that they have set. It is much more down to you whether you do it or not. If you want to pass you have to do it. They're not going to force you to.'

S4: 'It's much more equal. They talk to you as adults.'

A2 student looking back at the end of her two years at college:

S5: 'Before I came here I had no idea what I wanted to do ... The thing I have enjoyed most is learning about things I didn't know anything about before and finding a subject, Sociology, which I really enjoy studying for its own sake.'

Alongside the previous quotes, these capture a progression that successful students make during their time at college, not all at the same pace, nor all as fully as the final student in the sequence. Having interviewed a diversity of students at different phases in their maturation as learners, I would characterize four phases that they commonly go through (see below).

3.8) Learning to cope with freedom

During the first phase, students will talk positively about being less spoon-fed, being treated as adults, and doing more independent learning, with just a hint of anxiety about their ability to balance study with their burgeoning social lives.

In the second phase, often after a failure or disappointing grades, they will talk of this change with a hint of ambivalence. This is an uncomfortable stage. Often, beneath their words, for instance, S1 in Box 3.9, there is a hint of feeling slightly abandoned. Are the teachers leaving them more to their own resources to help them mature as learners or because they care less about them? This may well echo their experience at home as their parents or carers adapt to their growing independence.

It is a challenging phase for teachers to handle. Attempts to give more direction or support are commonly rejected or ignored, particularly by the students who need it most. And yet a timely intervention can sometimes have a dramatic benefit. The extended quote in Box 3.10 illustrates this.

Box 3.10: Student at the end of his first year at college reflecting on almost dropping out

'I thought the transition from school was very different from what I expected it to be. At school they are always beating down on you to do your homework or you get a detention. Whereas at college it's your own problem, not anyone else's, and if you don't do it, you are not wasting anyone else's time but your own. So it was quite difficult, but I would rather there being a lot of freedom than no freedom at all like at school. There's a lot more respect.

'At first, to be totally honest, I didn't really cope at all. I was just terrible at getting my work done on time. I had no sort of strategy. By December, I was really on the rocks. I contemplated dropping out of college because it wasn't for me. Eventually I spoke about this to my teacher and my tutor and they helped me write a strategy that still left some free time for me too ... I wasn't expecting it, but I really enjoy it.'

This student has successfully negotiated the third phase, a period during which students gain fresh insights into the process of learning and the choices they have. He needed to acknowledge he was in trouble and to seek help with this rather than hide it.

The second student quoted in Box 3.9 (S2) reveals two interesting underlying assumptions that are apparent in the thinking and behaviour of quite a large number of students at an early stage in their time at college. First, that the only reason to do homework is to stay out of trouble (why else would you bother to copy it?), and second that when you are struggling, you should try to hide it. Hiding a difficulty is an understandable impulse, especially if you suspect it is due to a limitation in your ability that cannot be changed. He too appears to have achieved crucial insight.

The transition being explored here is not a minor shift in perspective. It is a core aspect of emerging as an adult learner with all the complexities of any aspect of becoming an adult. This recognition is explicit in the reflections of students S3 and S4 in Box 3.9. While some students achieve this transition without much difficulty, for many it is a bumpy ride. As another AS science student said, 'The January exams came as quite a shock because we none of us did as well as we thought we would'. Students often refer to the January exams as 'a wake-up call'. As a Business Studies student remarked, 'Suddenly you realize that they weren't just saying that [you needed to do more independent study]. You really do need to'. Another added, 'You come to realize that you have to do the learning yourself'.

The fourth phase exemplified by student S5 in Box 3.9 and in the final two sentences in Box 3.10 is a period when students have integrated these insights sufficiently to take charge of their own learning and in the process rediscovered how enjoyable and rewarding this can be. In the remainder of this chapter we will explore further how teachers can contribute to this process of moving students through these four phases.

3.9) Stimulating students to become active participants in their learning

What conditions can most effectively scaffold this awakening to the importance of students' active participation in their own learning? We have been exploring this at my college, and I will summarize three of the approaches below:

1. students co-creating their understanding
2. flipped learning
3. peer mentoring, peer teaching, and peer assessment (see section 3.10).

3.9.1) Learning through discovery and co-creation

One valuable approach to engaging students in a more active ownership of their process of learning is to lead them to work out the knowledge they need to learn, rather than simply telling them. Graham, curriculum leader for English as a Foreign Language, strongly favours this approach.

Box 3.11: International students learning English as a Foreign Language, being helped to discover the reasons we use the passive voice

T: '... can you read sentence number three to us?'

S1: 'Basketball is played all over the world.'

T: 'Right. Why use the passive?'

S1: 'Because basketball is the main subject.' [This was the first rule.]

T: 'Okay, that's one reason. There is another reason.'

S1: [tentatively] 'The world can't play basketball.'

T: 'Okay, good ...' [To another student] 'Go on.'

S2: 'If you change it to active, it's already well known that it's humans who play, so you don't need to mention it.'

T: 'Aha, that's really interesting. So who plays basketball?'

Students: 'Humans, people.'

T: 'What sort of people?'

S3: 'Basketball players.'

T: 'Okay. So we have a nice sentence now: "Basketball players play basketball all over the world." Is that a good sentence?'

Students in chorus/laughing: 'No!'

T: 'Why not?'

S4: 'Because it's ... um ... redundant.'

T: 'Ah, I like that word!' [To another student] 'What does that mean, "it's redundant"?'

This can be a very effective technique. Using it, Graham enabled the students to identify six distinct reasons for using the passive voice in English. Unaided, I doubt that many native speakers could do this. As he commented in interview, 'If you can get the students to work something out for themselves, there will be a certain amount of cognitive processing that will make it more likely that they will retain it and be able to use it later'.

Throughout this session, students were alert and actively engaged. They were enjoying the challenge.

3.9.2) 'Flipped learning'

Flipped learning, where students are set activities or watch videos that introduce them to key factual knowledge, underpinning concepts or essential techniques before a lesson, is currently experiencing a stellar rise to fame. 'Google trends' reveals that searches for 'flipped learning' or 'flipped classroom' more than tripled in six months between November 2011 and April 2012 and continued to rise into 2013. Such a sudden emergence is more usually associated with new technologies such as YouTube or Twitter.

Why this sudden interest – is it not just 'prep'? Some of its kudos comes from its association with technology, for example at the Khan Academy. However, Salman Khan, the creator of over 3,000 mini online lessons distributed via YouTube, claims that this is not 'cyborg learning'. Instead, the approach can restore the teacher–student relationship to the heart of learning because it allows teachers to spend more time working with students individually. Although technically and pedagogically simple, these brief videos have stimulated an extraordinary response, including headlines such as 'One man, one computer, 10 million students: How Khan Academy is reinventing education' (Noer, 2012).

Is this just 'techno-hype' that promotes the penetration of smartphones and iPads into education, or is there something of value to learning here?[9] In my role, leading the development of teaching and learning practice in our college, I have been keen to support small action research projects that have explored this in more depth.

One example is a project led by Richard, a PE teacher. Richard had been researching how the team might address the poor performance of boys studying A level PE. He wondered if the approach promoted by Khan might help address the problem. This led to an action research project supported by funding from my department. He developed his own short videos ('screencasts') that students could watch before a lesson. During the lesson, time was spent discussing and putting this learning into practice. Anyone who didn't do this before the class was asked to sit at the back and watch it on an iPad before they joined in the class activity. In a focus group, the students spoke of this as the 'iPad of shame'!

Though initially suspicious, students rapidly embraced the approach (see Box 3.12).

Box 3.12: AS PE students talking about the use of 'flipped learning' videos

S1: 'At the start, we thought, "Here we go, homework". When we actually started watching it, I much preferred doing that.'

S2: 'Yeah, because at first I didn't do a couple, then when I got to lessons I realized it was quite helpful to have actually done it!'

S3: 'It made you feel better in class because you were prepared. You knew something about what you were going to be doing.'

S2: 'Yeah, it made you feel more confident because Rich would ask you a question and you'd think, "Oh yeah, we covered that in the screencast, I know that", and you would be able to discuss it more.'

The approach also had a notable impact on their exam success, particularly for the boys. (The girls' results also improved, but they had been quite strong already.) In the previous two years, a third of all boys had failed the science-based unit on Anatomy and Physiology, whereas in this year the pass rate was 100 per cent. Furthermore, while previously only 2 per cent had achieved A or B grades, in this year 25 per cent did.

Box 3.13: AS PE teacher talking about his use of short videos for 'flipped learning'

'I started by analysing my scheme of work and selecting concepts that students found hardest. I then created screencasts for these. I kept them very short, so that in the lesson there was still much more they had to learn, talk about, and apply.

'A key thing that I got them to do was bring a couple of questions about the content of the screencast to the lesson. One question was about something they did understand and another was about something they didn't. We then dealt with these questions in class. That's been really helpful. If a student hasn't understood something specific, I have time to talk to them individually.

'It enables me to very quickly assess where everybody is at. I could see when they are struggling with a concept and can sit with them and say "Have you tried this, have you thought about it this way?" Or, because everyone else has also seen the video, I can get quite a lot of peer teaching and group-work going. A student who has understood that concept can explain it to others. If I overhear something that is not quite correct, I can fine-tune it.'

How can watching a short video providing some basic knowledge have such a dramatic effect? Actually, what Richard and others have rapidly discovered is that it is not so much the screencasts but what can then happen in the lessons that has the real impact.

Steve, a Sociology teacher, also experimented with creating his own short videos, in this case to support a series of brief revision sessions for students retaking a module that they had previously failed. Previously, he had found students arrived at these sessions not having done any preparation, apparently thinking that he would just fill them up with his knowledge. He said:

> This didn't give me any time for the things they need the most help with. It isn't necessarily the knowledge, for those students it is often decoding the exam question, or putting their answer together into a coherent structure.

So he created brief videos to cover this basic knowledge. Students were required to watch and make notes before the session. They were also asked to bring at least one 'interesting question' about the topic that was not covered in the video. If they arrived at the session not having done this, they were sent to the library to do so. By the second session all but one had done so:

> I found that I got to know these students better because I didn't have to stand in front and lecture them. I could go round and help them individually with things they were still struggling with such as 'What does the examiner mean when the question is raised in this way?', 'What knowledge is relevant?', and 'How do I structure this?'

Did it work? Of the 12 students retaking the module, three chose not to participate in these sessions. These students, perhaps unsurprisingly, achieved virtually no improvement in their grades. In contrast, the nine who participated (who previously had achieved 3 Ds, 3 Es, and 3 Us) scored 5 As, 1 B, 2 Cs and a D. Though a small sample, it has been enough to encourage Steve to embed this approach into his teaching from the start of the coming year.

No single approach is a total answer. Students can start to turn off if this approach is used all the time. However, used selectively, for example with the topics that students commonly struggle with, it creates valuable space in class for higher-order engagement and more individualized support. In the process, students become more active participants in their own learning.

3.10) Working with students' beliefs and expectations

3.10.1) Fixed or growth 'mindsets'?

As mentioned in the earlier discussion of the model of studentship (section 2.1), the beliefs and expectations that students bring to learning can have a profound impact on how they respond to challenge and difficulty. The work of Carol Dweck and her co-researchers (which is explored further in Chapter 6), especially around 'fixed' and 'growth mindsets', provides valuable insight into this. Unaddressed, a fixed mindset – that is, the belief that intelligence and ability are determined early in life – can lead students to avoid challenge or give in when they meet difficulty or initial failure. Such students may choose to copy homework to hide difficulty, or drop out of college altogether, rather than ask for help.

In contrast, with skilled teachers, once students have learned that difficulties and errors are part of learning, they come alive in the lessons that challenge them.

3.10.2) Cultivating a growth mindset through peer teaching and peer assessment

It is therefore crucial to examine how teachers can help students develop a growth mindset. One valuable contribution can be made through positive recognition of effort and individual progress, celebrating students' readiness to try something new, even when they are not sure they will succeed:

> I think the key to encouraging a growth mindset is good-quality formative assessment and getting students to really focus on the diagnostic aspect of feedback that helps them improve. This is why I don't think we should always grade work. My feedback sheets include comments on the student's progress. I always encourage them to notice particular progress they've made since their previous piece of work.
>
> Steve, sociology teacher

> I think that it is really helpful when teachers give you feedback that identifies strengths in how you learn and things you are not so good at. Then they set you targets, or you can set them yourself. You sit with your teacher and they say you have done really well in this, but this is what you need to improve. How are we going to work on this? And you do it together. It is not like your teachers are just grading you [makes face].
>
> First-year student

Dweck has also shown that a growth mindset can be inspired by learning about – or from – others, who overcame initial failure. We have observed this, in our college, when students retaking a module voluntarily start peer teaching.

Box 3.14: Growth mindsets and the mutual benefits of peer teaching

'In my AS classes the last two years, I've had second-year students attending, who want to retake a unit after poor results. They have become examples of how, if you persevere despite initially failing, you can overcome barriers and make real progress. Some of them got a D grade and go on to get an A or a B when they retake. The AS students notice this and say, "Wow, it can be done!"

'I was worried that this might send the wrong message – "Don't worry, you can get a D the first time and come back again next year". But, strangely enough, it doesn't because the AS students think, "I'd rather get it right first time".

'The A2 students are really helpful because they explain what they are doing differently now. They say, "When I was in your shoes I wish I had done more preparation for lessons", or "I can see what mistake you are making, that's where I went wrong".'

(Sam, accountancy teacher)

Other research, for example Higgins *et al.* (2011), confirms how peer teaching, such as Sam describes in Box 3.14, can bring a wide range of benefits to students' relationship to learning. She has also noted how much both the AS and A2 students enjoy the process.

The same can be true of peer assessment, if it is introduced and pursued with care and conviction. We have found that it is critical that students are given a clear explanation of the potential benefits of the process and are periodically reminded of this. They also need careful step-by-step guidance on how to assess and give effective feedback, starting with jointly assessing model answers or anonymous examples of previous students' work. With regular practice, they can become both competent and highly positive about the process of peer assessment.

Box 3.15: Students praising peer assessment

S1: 'If you are peer assessing and you find something good, Mark says don't just say that it is good, you have to write what assessment objective it answers and exactly pinpoint what it is that makes it good. So you know in yourself how to get the good marks and you can see for yourself what you are doing or not doing.'

I: 'How do you feel about it?'

S2: 'I think it's great.'

S1: 'I love it.'

S3: 'I think everyone is a little apprehensive when you start. You don't want to offend anyone and write "It's terrible!" [laughter]. But you just get used to it and it is a really useful tool.'

S1: 'Yes, it is really refreshing to have feedback from someone who is working at a similar level to you, because they bring a completely new perspective.'

(AS students at the end of their first year)

Note how it builds confidence for both parties: the peer assessor and the student whose work is being assessed. It is also worth noting that this confidence was matched by a significantly high level of achievement in their subsequent exams for the whole cohort, with them scoring among the top 10 per cent for 'value-added' nationally in their first year and a third of them earning A* in their A2 exams.

This brings us back to my opening remarks. League tables may seem to demand chasing exam success at the expense of deeper learning. However, substantial gains are to be made when the focus is on engaging students in real thinking and empowering them to take a greater ownership of their learning.

4) Final comments

I believe that what we have been exploring here and what the staff and many of the students are working to develop is nothing short of changing the culture of learning and, in particular, the nature of the partnership between students and teachers. This is not a trivial task and it would be both rash and dishonest to pretend that we have completed it. Even in the most favourable of circumstances, such a process takes considerable time, and it can be argued that the current political climate surrounding education may work against this. However, the successes and enthusiasm of both students and staff who make progress along this road are surely motivation enough to persist despite the difficulties.

I believe that the culture/social environment and activities that support students developing as deep learners, and as owners of their own learning, apply equally to teachers as to the professionals developing their practice. Thus, in our college we are seeking to use coaching rather than telling to help staff explore areas that need to be developed. (We no longer grade lesson observations.) Our aim is to encourage and support reflective dialogue about teaching and learning among peers, to welcome innovative experiments, and the related risks of failure (so long as these are managed in such a way that they do not harm students), and to foster a collaborative approach to development through the use of Joint Practice Development.

What is heartening is that teachers who engage in this process find it highly motivating. It appears that even the most experienced teacher can, like our students, revitalize their love of learning and, through this, rediscover their enjoyment of teaching.

Notes

[1] 'Then, the whining schoolboy with his satchel / And shining morning face, creeping like snail / Unwillingly to school;' from Shakespeare's *As You Like It*.

[2] Richard Sennett (2008) defines craftsmanship as 'an enduring, basic human impulse, the desire to do a job well for its own sake'. He argues that this entails three dimensions: skill, commitment, and judgement. In this chapter we will see how these are all involved in students' maturing relationship to learning.

[3] See Wiliam (2011: 80–4), for further discussion.

[4] 'Scaffolding' is a metaphor, inspired by the work of Lev Vygotsky and Jerome Bruner, now widely used to describe processes by which the teacher or peers can support a learner to develop new understanding or insight.

[5] There are many other examples of activities of this kind in the 'Resource' section of Walsh and Sattes (2011).

[6] The web page www.pz.gse.harvard.edu/visible_thinking.php, on Harvard's 'Project Zero' website (accessed May 2013), introduces this work and has onward links to the Visible Thinking website, www.visiblethinkingpz.org/VisibleThinking_html_files/VisibleThinking1.html (accessed May 2013), which contains many relevant resources and suggested activities.

[7] There is a helpful index to these thinking routines at www.visiblethinkingpz.org/VisibleThinking_html_files/03_ThinkingRoutines/03b_Introduction.html (accessed May 2013), grouped under tabs in the left-hand margin.

[8] See http://learning.blogs.nytimes.com/ (accessed 3 February 2014).

[9] Cristina Costa will explore this and related questions more fully in Chapter 7.

References

Anderson, L.W. and Krathwohl, D.R. (eds) (2001) *A Taxonomy for Learning, Teaching and Assessing: A revision of Bloom's Taxonomy of Educational Objectives*. New York: Longman, abridged edition.

Binet, A. (1909) *Les Idées Modernes sur les Enfants*. Paris : Flammarion.

Brown, G. and Wragg, E.C. (1993) *Questioning*. London: Routledge.

Bruner, J.S. (1974) *Beyond the Information Given*. London: Allen and Unwin.

Costa, A.L. and Kallick, B.L. (2000) *Habits of Mind: A developmental series*. Alexandria, VA: Association for Supervision and Curriculum Developers.

Dewey, J. (1924) *Democracy and Education*. New York, NY: Macmillan Company.

Dweck, C.S. (1999) *Self-Theories: Their role in motivation, personality and development*. Philadelphia, PA: Psychology Press.

Fisher, D. and Frey, N. (2007) *Checking for Understanding*, 37. Alexandria, VA: ASCD.

Frey, N. and Fisher, D. (2011) 'Guiding learning: Questions, prompts and cues'. *Principal Leadership*, January 2011. Online. www.fisherandfrey.com/wp-content/uploads/2011/03/pl-guided-learning.pdf (accessed May 2013).

Higgins, S., Kokotsaki, D., and Coe, R. (2011) *Toolkit of Strategies to Improve Learning*. Durham: Durham University Press.

Lucas, B. and Claxton, G. (2010) *New Kinds of Smart: How the science of learnable intelligence is changing education*. Maidenhead: Open University Press.

Mehta, S., Suto, I., and Brown, S. (2012) *How Effective are Curricula for 16 to 19 Year Olds as Preparation for University? A qualitative investigation of lecturers' views*. Cambridge: Cambridge Assessment.

Noer, M. (2012) 'One man, one computer, 10 million students: How Khan Academy is reinventing education'. *Forbes*, 19 November 2012. Online. www.forbes.com/sites/michaelnoer/2012/11/02/one-man-one-computer-10-million-students-how-khan-academy-is-reinventing-education/ (accessed June 2013).

Perkins, D. (1993) 'Teaching for understanding'. *American Educator: The Professional Journal of the American Federation of Teachers*, 17 (3), 8, 28–35. Online. www.exploratorium.edu/ifi/resources/workshops/teachingforunderstanding.html (accessed May 2013).

Schulten, K. (2013) 'What did you think of "What's Going On in this Picture"?'. *New York Times*. Online. http://learning.blogs.nytimes.com/2013/06/03/what-did-you-think-of-whats-going-on-in-this-picture/ (accessed June 2013).

Sennett, R. (2008) *The Craftsman*. London: Allen Lane/Penguin.

Walsh, J.A. and Sattes, B.D. (2011) *Thinking through Quality Questioning: Deepening student engagement*. Thousand Oaks, CA: Corwin Press.

Wiliam, D. (2011) *Embedded Formative Assessment*. Bloomington, IN: Solution Tree.

Wiske, M.S. (ed.) (1997) *Teaching for Understanding: Linking research with practice*. San Francisco, CA: Josey Bass Education Series.

Chapter 4

'Facts alone are wanted in life.'

The unwelcome return of Mr Gradgrind

Frank Coffield

In the mid-1970s, a friend and colleague, Phil Robinson, and I won a research grant to study Sir Keith Joseph's notion of 'the cycle of deprivation'. After we had been working for over a year, Sir Keith convened a seminar to discuss emerging findings at the Civil Service College at Sunningdale, to which he invited all the relevant ministers and senior civil servants. I, as a very young researcher, was somewhat daunted to discover I was speaking immediately after Professor Basil Bernstein, who was at that time at the height of his fame for his theory of restricted and elaborated codes of language. Basil began speaking, mentioned the notion of a hierarchy of knowledge, and turned to the blackboard and wrote the word 'heirarchy' on it. Sir Keith intervened immediately: 'Professor', he hissed, 'you have spelled hierarchy wrongly'. Basil did not turn round to check. Instead he threw the chalk up in the air, caught it, and replied: 'Sir Keith, you pay me a lousy £100 for this talk and you expect spelling as well?'

1) Introduction

Charles Dickens made education one of the main themes of his novel *Hard Times*, which introduced us to the schoolmaster Thomas Gradgrind and his pupils, those 'little vessels ... ready to have imperial gallons of facts poured into them until they were full to the brim' (1955: 2). Dickens was ridiculing a form of schooling where pupils learned by heart to define a horse as a 'Quadruped. Graminivorous. Forty teeth ... sheds coat in the spring' (ibid.). For Dickens, 'imagination is as important as the multiplication table and more important than business or banking', as Claire Tomalin puts it in her biography of the novelist (2011: 251), and it was imagination, creativity, and innovation that he thought should be nurtured in children.

What, however, is the relevance of this Victorian, hard-grind model of education to our present concerns over TLA? In February 2013 the coalition government issued for consultation a framework of a new National Curriculum for England, which has since been modified, but not significantly. It would take too long to review the whole framework, so I am going to home in on a few aspects of the document for primary schools – which runs to 221 pages; within it, the section on English covers 36 pages, with separate Appendices on spelling, grammar, and punctuation, plus a Glossary of 69 terms such as 'active voice', 'past tense', and 'word family'. My immediate reaction on reading this official document was that there is something deeply absurd, undemocratic, and dangerous about any Secretary of State for Education (from whatever political party) prescribing this level of detail. My opposition was to harden as I read on.

The programmes of study, which are presented in full for each subject in the curriculum, consist of statutory requirements, together with notes and guidance that are non-statutory. So, for example, under Handwriting for Year 1 (5–6 year olds), the statutory requirement stipulates that: 'Pupils should be taught to sit correctly at a table, holding a pencil comfortably and correctly' (DfE, 2013: 20). The non-statutory notes and guidance for handwriting include the following: 'The size of the writing implement (pencil, pen) should not be too large for a young pupil's hand' (ibid.). I do not wish to be misunderstood here. I am aware that pencil-grip and handwriting are important skills for young children; it is the over-prescription by the Secretary of State for Education to which I am objecting.

Who are the insensitive, patronizing know-alls who write such prescriptive instructions? What image must the DfE have of teachers to issue them? What kind of teacher needs that level of direction? Teachers in this DfE document are treated as unprofessional, low-level technicians, whose job it is to carry out the statutory requirements in the order specified so that, if they perform all the necessary steps correctly, the result will be the outcome predetermined by the government. If you think the worst of teachers, they may very well be tempted to respond by serving up the worst, except that they are too committed to their students to behave so unprofessionally. Teachers, nowadays, are not even treated as well as apprentices, who are given increasing discretion in carrying out tasks: they are there to be told what to do. In all these DfE pages there is not the slightest suggestion that teachers could aspire to become something more than the curriculum *implementers* of the ideas of government ministers, namely, *curriculum makers*, capable of designing their own programmes of study.

Classroom teachers are essential to the task of curriculum development, because they know from experience how long it takes students to become fluent in a new skill. Teachers who are experts in particular subject areas also have to constantly put themselves into the shoes of beginners who find it difficult to understand what the experts have understood for so many years that they have forgotten that they too once found it difficult. The other danger that they must guard against is reducing what may be a broad and balanced curriculum to bite-size chunks of information that have been especially prepared to answer highly predictable exam questions. Examiners are familiar with those exam candidates who repeat a model answer, which has probably been dictated to them, to a question that does not appear on the exam paper: 'I know this and you are going to get it, whether it's in the exam or not'.

Of the 221 pages that set out the framework for the new National Curriculum for primary schools, only two, I repeat two (or 0.9 per cent), are devoted to citizenship. Space, however, is found within these two pages to mention volunteering and teaching pupils about 'a range of financial products and services', but there is no space for suggesting that pupils should experience democratic ways of living, learning, and working together *within their schools*. In my view, citizenship in schools and colleges should give students of all ages the opportunities to *practise* democracy so that they come to appreciate its strengths and weaknesses and become 'attached' to it as their best hope of effecting change (see Reiss and White, 2013: 30). Instead, this government treats it as yet another, rather unimportant subject worthy of only two pages, where students have to learn facts about Parliament, the constitution, and the monarchy.

My critique of these new proposals for the 'national' curriculum, which, incidentally, will apply neither to private schools, academies, and free schools in England, nor to any kind of school in Scotland or Wales, stems partly from a genuine fear that they will reintroduce some of the worst features of the schooling that I received in a grammar school in Glasgow in the 1950s.

For example, when I was 16 in 1958 and studying History for O Grade (the equivalent in England then of O level and now of GCSE), I copied into my jotter from the board the four causes and the three consequences of the French Revolution, without for a moment reflecting on the arrogance that suggested there were only four of the former and three of the latter. (I did not have the intellectual apparatus to make such a judgement, nor was I encouraged to acquire it.) I committed the seven 'facts' to memory and was subsequently delighted to find on the examination paper a question inviting me to: 'Give the four causes and the three consequences of the French Revolution'. This I did; I employed the same technique to answer similar questions and so passed easily. Teaching, learning, and assessment were all in perfect alignment.

Only one problem. I had totally failed to understand the significance of the revolution that transformed the history of Europe and turned subjects of the king into citizens of the world. Only when, many years later, I read Simon Schama's chronicle of the revolution did I begin to realize that it was 'a much more haphazard and chaotic event and much more the product of human agency' than of the inexorable forces of social change (1989: xv). History, as it was taught to me, had been reduced to what was easily assessed – lists of dates of kings and queens – and bloody, violent revolutions were watered down to a few easily memorized but anaemic causes and consequences. As Schama explained his intentions: 'to write history without the play of imagination is to dig in an intellectual graveyard, so that in *Citizens* I have tried to bring a world to life rather than entomb it in erudite discourse' (ibid.: xix). And that world does come to life in his writing.

For the very best of reasons – the desire to give all children (and especially those from disadvantaged backgrounds) an excellent grounding in the basics – a new curriculum has been produced that may unintentionally return education to the attempted transmission of disconnected facts without understanding of the kind that I and millions of others were subjected to in the 1940s and 50s. No one in his or her right mind wants to prevent children from learning the basics, but at the same time surely no one wants them to be taught in such a lifeless and uninspiring way that they are put off learning from then on?

I would now like to invite you, the reader, to try the activity in Box 4.1 before reading any further; its aim is for you to judge what prior knowledge you have of this topic before I discuss the literature on it.

Box 4.1: Types of knowledge and thinking skills

A. KNOWLEDGE

Please write down in the space provided below your ideas about different types of knowledge. I do not mean the different subject areas such as the physical sciences, the social sciences, and the humanities, but categories, such as factual knowledge.

1. Factual knowledge
2.
3.
4.

B. THINKING SKILLS OR COGNITIVE PROCESSES

Please write down in the space provided below your list of different types of thinking skills or, to use the technical term, 'cognitive processes'. To give you a hint about the types of skills I am thinking of, I have provided the first one:

1. Remembering
2.
3.
4.
5.
6.
7.
8.
9.
10.

Once you have completed this activity, you may wish to compare your suggestions with those provided in Boxes 4.4 and 4.5.

2) A framework for knowledge and thinking skills

There are powerful, educational reasons for objecting to any curriculum that depends for its success on a very heavy emphasis on memory work by students. One of these reasons will also act as a useful means of introducing the main topic of this chapter, namely the need for a framework to introduce different types of knowledge and thinking skills, or 'cognitive processes', to use the technical term. (I shall use both in this chapter for the sake of variety.) Lorin Anderson, David Krathwohl, and colleagues, in their well-known framework, henceforth AKF (2001), list no fewer than 19 thinking skills, only two of which are concerned with remembering: namely, identifying and retrieving knowledge from memory. So they have added a total of 17 processes that go beyond remembering, such as understanding, applying, analysing, evaluating, and creating, of which more shortly.

Their approach has profound implications for TLA, because, if our aim is for students to be able to transfer their knowledge from one situation to new, unfamiliar contexts, then they will need to be able to do much more than just remember that knowledge – they will have to become adept at understanding, applying, analysing, evaluating, and, yes, at times going beyond it, to create new knowledge.

Nor can we assume that tests which call for the recall of facts will at one and the same time measure more complex thinking skills such as applying or evaluating knowledge. On this point the research literature is clear: we cannot 'rely upon tests of information to provide a valid indication of a student's ability to apply, analyse or interpret' (Airasian, 1994: 83, quoted by Marzano and Kendall, 2007: 117). If we want students to be able to apply, analyse, or interpret knowledge, we will have to teach them explicitly how to do so and test them afterwards to see how effective our teaching has been, although they could have developed these abilities on their own.

So the educational argument is that we obviously want our students to remember what we have taught them; but that is only the first stage in a long process. We must also teach them to be aware of, and to know how to use, all 19 thinking skills, and our tests need to be so varied and sophisticated that they can assess whether they can use all 19, and not just the two processes concerned with memory. Richard Fox sums up the point well: 'To memorize without understanding is indeed mostly pointless ... But to understand without ever remembering is also equally useless, for it condemns us to repeat each episode of learning over and over again, ad infinitum' (2001: 32). My plea here is for a healthy balance to be struck between teaching low-level, but essential, knowledge and skills and higher-order knowledge and skills, and part of that balance consists in respecting the important role in education of rote learning, of learning facts such as spelling and arithmetical tables by heart.

I now need to justify my selection of AKF to study in some detail; after all, there is a kaleidoscopic array of frameworks to choose from, and David Moseley and his colleagues evaluated 35 of them in 2004. I have chosen AKF partly because it is a successful, practical, and easy-to-use revision of Benjamin Bloom's famous *Taxonomy of Educational Objectives* (1956), which in its day was more influential than any other, having been translated into more than 20 languages and having 'been used by educators in virtually every subject area at virtually every grade level' (Marzano and Kendall, 2007: 1). Anderson, Krathwohl, and colleagues (hereafter AKC) do, however, admit that Bloom's original handbook was 'one of the most widely cited yet least read books in American education' (2001: xxiii).

Their taxonomy – or classification system – provides an organizing framework that I think will help students and teachers to talk with more precision and understanding about TLA. It also provides 'a common way of thinking about and a common vocabulary for talking about teaching that enhances communications among teachers themselves' and among students and teachers (AKC, 2001: ii). It imposes a hierarchical order on different types of knowledge and thinking skills, from those at the lowest level (such as remembering) to those at the highest level (for instance, creativity). The advantages of this framework, however, go well beyond the desirable inclusion of more complex thinking skills in TLA: it encourages tutors to broaden their teaching repertoire; it enables them to develop and to evaluate curricula; it provides them with a checklist that they can use to see whether they are using the full range of types of knowledge and thinking skills in their lesson plans; it always connects thinking skills with some form of knowledge; and it constantly reminds teachers to ask 'that most fundamental of all curriculum questions: "what's worth learning?"' (AKC, 2001: 236).

The AKF also contains one crucial message that needs to be communicated to all students, no matter how successful (or not) they have been in their GCSE exams before they move on to a sixth-form or FE college or to an A level form in a comprehensive school: namely, it will no longer be sufficient to remember information and reproduce it to do well in most exams. From now on, they will be required to make sense of, to be able to apply, and sometimes to go beyond, a collection of facts. This will mean in many cases that students will have to change patterns of learning that have served them well in the past, but that are now very likely to prove counterproductive; for example, students will have to move away from any dependence on 'spoon-feeding'[1] to a more active engagement with the subjects they are studying. In this way, sixth-form and FE colleges act as 'halfway houses' between school and university, or between school and the world of work. This important shift in attitudes can be presented to students as a challenge to become better at learning and thinking, a challenge in which their tutors will encourage and support them to become more independent, critical thinkers by changing their implicit view of learning as simply memorization of facts and regurgitation – the *bulimia academica* I criticized in Chapter 1.

I do not present AKC's approach, however, as a finished or a flawless product. Since its publication in 2001 it has been widely used (for example, Pickard, 2007), just like its famous predecessor, but its weaknesses have also been pointed out by, for instance, Marzano and Kendall (2007), so I will include their critique in Section 7 of this chapter. Before that, I shall provide a quick overview of the AKF, and then explain it in more detail. First, it may be helpful to the reader to illustrate how the framework could be used in classrooms by means of a vignette (below).

3) Vignette

AKC use six vignettes from a variety of subject areas (history, maths, science, language, and health studies) to deepen the reader's understanding of the Taxonomy Table and how it can be used in classrooms. For reasons of space I have decided to discuss briefly the vignette from English literature – namely, a curriculum unit on Shakespeare's *Macbeth* – and I want to offer an alternative reading to the conventional one. But first, it is important to stress that the six vignettes are not presented as examples of 'best practice', a strategy that I consider to be deeply flawed and that I criticized heavily in Chapter 2. Instead, as is the case here, the intention is to show how teaching objectives, classroom activities, and assessment can all be aligned by means of the AKF in order to improve TLA.

The important distinction between subject knowledge (in, say, English literature) and the content of curricular materials (to teach, say, *Macbeth*) is explained by AKC, who use the convenient fiction of imagining four teachers, each of whom has a different objective in teaching the Scottish play. Mrs Patterson, for instance, wants her students to be able to recite by heart some of the famous lines from the play, such as Lady Macbeth's soliloquy:

> Glamis thou art, and Cawdor; and shalt be
> What thou art promised. Yet do I fear thy nature.
> It is too full o' th' milk of human kindness
> To catch the nearest way. Thou wouldst be great;
> Art not without ambition, but without the illness should attend it.
>
> (Act 1, Scene 5, lines 12–16)

The teacher's concern here appears to be increasing her students' factual knowledge and perhaps also their love of the language.

In contrast, Ms Chang thinks that the central ideas in the play should show her students how, for example, ambition proves the tragic flaw in Macbeth's character – so she is more concerned with teaching conceptual knowledge. Mr Jefferson takes a third approach and has his class discuss the development of the plot and how the play is constructed; he then challenges them to extrapolate from that knowledge to see what they could learn about plays in general. He could be said to have a predominant interest in getting his students to apply their newly acquired procedural knowledge to a new situation.

Finally, Mrs Weinberg gets her students to identify with the characters in the play in the hope that they will learn something about themselves, their own strengths and weaknesses and perhaps their own ambitions – in doing so, she is stressing the significance of meta-cognitive knowledge.

Box 4.2 reflects the differing interests and concerns of the four teachers and also shows how consulting the cells in the table encourages teachers to create classroom activities, assignments, and tests that cover the whole range of cognitive processes and types of knowledge. So instead of restricting the tests to the recall of factual information (for example, 'What country is the main setting for *Macbeth*?'), I have devised questions and activities that call for: analysis of conceptual knowledge (for example, 'What similarities and differences do you detect in the characters of Lady Macbeth and her husband?'); evaluation (invite able students to judge whether they prefer Shakespeare's or Verdi's treatment of the subject or to compare the film versions of Orson Welles, Roman Polanski, or Akira Kurosawa; and what criteria would they use to make such judgements); and creation (plan and stage a production of the play, which will require staff and students to employ all the types of knowledge and cognitive processes and more besides).

Box 4.2: Four teachers teach *Macbeth*

THE KNOWLEDGE DIMENSION	THE COGNITIVE PROCESS DIMENSION					
	1 REMEMBER	2 UNDERSTAND	3 APPLY	4 ANALYSE	5 EVALUATE	6 CREATE
A. FACTUAL KNOWLEDGE	Mrs Patterson					Devise a reliable and valid test of the factual details of the play
B. CONCEPTUAL KNOWLEDGE		Ms Chang		Can Macbeth be written off as just another callous sociopath and murderer?	Is ambition or success the main theme of the play?	Organize a debate between those who take different views of the play's main themes
C. PROCEDURAL KNOWLEDGE			Mr Jefferson	How have different theatre and film directors presented the drama?	Which version do you prefer: Shakespeare's or Verdi's, based on what criteria?	Stage a performance of the play
D. META-COGNITIVE KNOWLEDGE			Mrs Weinberg	Looking back, what knowledge and skills did you need to understand and appreciate *Macbeth*?	What have you learned about your own character, its strengths and weaknesses, from reading the play?	Can you think of a modern setting for the play, e.g. gangs in Glasgow or New York?

Source: adapted from Anderson and Krathwohl (2001: 144)

I want to use this vignette to emphasize one particular aspect: the overriding importance of the role of the teacher and his or her understanding of the play. AKC's four fictional teachers are clearly teaching devices to draw out the significance of four types of knowledge that each require different types of classroom activities and tests, but it is far more likely that all four sets of objectives, activities, and tests would be chosen by one English teacher who is planning to teach *Macbeth*. But if the central conceptual idea in the play is *not* about ambition being the tragic flaw in Macbeth's character, as AKC propose, then the students' understanding of the play is being restricted by only one interpretation of the play.

At one level, the play presents a devoted and loving couple (Lady Macbeth says of her husband: 'my dearest partner of greatness', while he calls her 'dearest chuck'), who become corrupted by ambition, who kill Duncan and then descend into the moral abyss by ordering the murders of MacDuff's wife and children. But Macbeth has become king before a third of the play has been heard and the rest is taken up with the question of who will reign after the childless Macbeths. Russ McDonald makes this point forcefully: 'too many teachers misunderstand ... Macbeth is not about ambition. The play examines not the drive to succeed but the result of having succeeded, it's about paying the price for having got what you wanted. Success is one of the play's essential nouns. In gaining success, Macbeth guarantees that he will have no successors' (2010: 95).

What I have offered here is an alternative reading of the play, but there are other interpretations. What we need to give students is access to a range of views and the skills to evaluate them against their own. There is no substitute for great teaching.

4) Overview and explanation of the framework

As can be seen in Box 4.3, the framework consists of two dimensions: a knowledge dimension and a cognitive process dimension; and their interrelationships are presented in what AKC call the 'Taxonomy Table'. The *knowledge dimension* (the rows in Box 4.3) consists of four categories: Factual, Conceptual, Procedural, and Meta-cognitive, which 'are assumed to lie along a continuum from concrete (*Factual*) to abstract (*Meta-cognitive*)' (AKC, 2001: 5). The cognitive process dimension (the columns in Box 4.3) has six categories: *Remember, Understand, Apply, Analyse, Evaluate*, and *Create*. These six processes are assumed to lie along a continuum of increasing cognitive complexity from the simplest (*Remember*) to the most complex (*Create*), a contentious issue to which I shall return later in section 7 of this chapter.

Box 4.3: The Taxonomy Table

THE KNOWLEDGE DIMENSION	THE COGNITIVE PROCESS DIMENSION					
	1 REMEMBER	2 UNDERSTAND	3 APPLY	4 ANALYSE	5 EVALUATE	6 CREATE
A. FACTUAL KNOWLEDGE	X					
B. CONCEPTUAL KNOWLEDGE		X				
C. PROCEDURAL KNOWLEDGE			X			
D. META-COGNITIVE KNOWLEDGE						

ANDERSON\KRATHWOHL\AIRASIAN\CRUIKSHANK\MAYER\PINTRICH\RATHS\WITTROCK, A TAXONOMY FOR LEARNING, TEACHING, AND ASSESSING: A REVISION OF BLOOM'S TAXONOMY OF EDUCATIONAL OBJECTIVES, ABRIDGED EDITION, 1st, ©2001. Printed and Electronically reproduced by permission of Pearson Education, Inc., Upper Saddle River, New Jersey.

The Taxonomy Table consists then of 24 cells (four types of knowledge x six cognitive processes) and it can be used to evaluate, say, the draft proposals for the National Curriculum. That exercise reveals that only three cells out of our 24 are heavily used: A1 (remembering factual information), B2 (understanding conceptual knowledge), and C3 (applying procedural knowledge), with most of the learning required of primary pupils being A1, and that required of secondary students being B2. The table demonstrates the need for TLA to be broadened beyond a narrow focus on a few, rather simple thinking skills to encompass the full range of skills and types of knowledge that students will need in order to become independent, critical, and innovative thinkers. With such a table at their disposal, teachers can quickly check which cells are covered by their lesson plans and which are left blank. Such an exercise will also lead them to consider whether, as the table implies, all of the cells are of equal size and whether their size varies considerably by subject.[2] Annual examinations that concentrate on testing only a few, low-level skills have convinced students that it is more important to learn what will be tested than what is worth knowing – and the table exposes the weaknesses in that approach in a vivid and memorable way.

Let me now try to flesh out the very basic outline of their approach, which is all that I have offered so far. I shall do so by offering a gloss first on each of the four types of knowledge, then on the six cognitive processes, and finally on their interactions.

5) Four types of knowledge

By *Factual Knowledge*, AKC mean 'the basic elements students must know to be acquainted with a discipline or solve problems in it' (2001: 46). They divide *Factual Knowledge* into two subtypes: *knowledge of terminology* (for example, scientific terms such as 'synapse' or 'ganglion'); and *knowledge of specific details and elements* (for example, the battle of Trafalgar took place on 21 October 1805).

The second category is *Conceptual Knowledge*, which I define as knowing how a particular subject matter such as chemistry is structured and how the different parts of it fit together. AKC divide this type of knowledge into three subtypes: *knowledge of classifications and categories* (for example, knowing how to parse a sentence into noun, verb, adjective, and adverb); *knowledge of principles and generalizations* (for example, Pythagoras's theorem or Gresham's law about bad coinage driving out good); and *knowledge of theories and structures* (for example, different models or metaphors of learning such as acquisition, participation, and becoming [see Coffield, 2008, for further information on these models]).

Procedural Knowledge means (pretty obviously) knowing what sequence of steps to follow in order to carry out a procedure. This category is broken down into three subtypes: *knowledge of subject-specific skills* (for example, methods for solving quadratic equations); *knowledge of subject-specific methods* (for example, research methods in education such as interviewing techniques); and *knowledge of criteria* for determining when to use appropriate procedures (for example, the criteria for deciding which statistical technique to use, such as chi squared).

The fourth and final type of knowledge is called *Meta-cognitive Knowledge*. 'Meta-cognition' is one of those highfaluting terms used so often in education that actually conveys two rather simple ideas: first, it refers to being aware of how one thinks and learns in order to plan, evaluate, and so improve one's thinking and learning; and second, it also means knowing about knowledge itself; for instance, that it is 'generated by human minds, that it is uncertain, but can be revised according to agreed/negotiated standards' (MacLellan and Soden, 2012: 34). In Jerome Bruner's words, it is knowing the distinction between 'personal knowledge' – for example, that Newcastle United is the greatest football team the world has ever known – and 'objective' knowledge, so called because 'it has stood up to sustained scrutiny and been tested by the best available evidence' (1996: 61) – for example, that I am right in thinking that Newcastle United is the greatest football team the world has ever known. I jest.

For AKC, *Meta-cognitive Knowledge* consists of three subcategories that they call *strategic knowledge*, *knowledge about cognitive tasks*, and *self-knowledge*. I shall devote more space to these ideas, as I think they are practical and useful to students and tutors alike.

Strategic knowledge refers to the large variety of learning strategies that can be summarized under the three headings of: *rehearsal* (for example, repeating to yourself over and over again whatever you want to remember); *elaboration* (for instance, fastening onto the key ideas in a text or using a mnemonic, such as the one for remembering the six wives of Henry VIII, Catherine of Aragon, Anne Boleyn, Jane Seymour, Anne of Cleves, Catherine Howard and Catherine Parr: 'Cate and Anne and Jane, And Anne and Cate again and again'; and *organizational* (say, transforming the material to be learned into a mind map or a tree diagram or a Venn diagram).[3] Strategic knowledge also includes the methods that students find themselves to solve problems and to spot errors in their own work.

Knowledge about cognitive tasks is knowing how, when, and why to use different learning strategies and being aware that there may be local or cultural norms for using them (for example, allowing students to play with new materials may be appropriate when introducing mathematical blocks but less so in chemistry if the novelty element is a Bunsen burner). See Box 4.4 for an example of learning strategies that I call 'Twenty Questions'.

Box 4.4: Twenty Questions

This is an activity that explores the strategies students use to solve problems. Twenty Questions is a game about how to handle knowledge that can bring some light relief into the classroom as well as providing teachers with an insight into how their students are thinking.

A simple version of the game runs as follows: 'I am thinking of a number between zero and 80 and you have to discover this number by asking me as few questions as possible. Each question can be answered only "yes" or "no".'

Research by the psychologist Ian Hunter (1974) showed that there are two patterns of questions used by students: half-split questioning (HSQ) and particular questioning (PQ). Bright students will immediately begin to use HSQ by asking, for instance, 'Is the number higher than 40?', 'No.', 'Higher than 20?', and so on until they get the right answer. Students can be asked how many questions they think they will need to identify the target number, and how many questions if the task was to identify a number between zero and a million. Can they also describe the principle they have adopted to solve the problem?

Some of the interesting issues that have emerged from this research are: how soon do students who at first use the PQ strategy (for example, 'Is it 69?', 'No.', 'Is it 28?', 'No.') realize how ineffective it is and start imitating their fellow students who are using HSQ? Do students learn the HSQ approach more quickly if the roles are reversed and the teacher asks the questions and one student who has used PQ gives the answers? Can students work out what are the advantages of using HSQ? There appear to be three. First, the answers are so packed with information that the possibilities are speedily narrowed down. Second, the load on working memory is minimal because you need only to keep in mind the answer to the question you have just asked. Third, there are fewer decisions to make because: 'HSQ provides, from the start of the game, a plan of action which eases the moment-by-moment decisions about what to do next' (Hunter, 1974: 811).

Finally, can students transfer their learning on this game to new and perhaps more difficult contexts, such as with all of the characters in Shakespeare's plays, or the kings and queens of England from 1066 to 2014, or the elements in the Periodic Table, or what is the title and author of the book I am currently reading?

Self-knowledge is, as you would guess, knowing one's own strengths and weaknesses as a learner (for example, being aware as a tutor that you are better at explaining in accessible ways the complex ideas of others than at creating original ideas of your own). Students may not realize that they have become over-reliant on a particular learning strategy, so it would be the tutor's job to remind them of the total range of strategies and the type of tasks for which they are most suitable. Similarly, if students are unaware that they have gaps in their factual or conceptual knowledge, they will not act to close them on their own, without prompting. AKC conclude that teachers need 'to help students make accurate assessments of their *self-knowledge* and not attempt to inflate students' academic self-esteem' (2001: 60, emphasis as in original).[4] To summarize, I have listed the major types and subtypes of knowledge in Box 4.5.

Box 4.5: Major types and subtypes of knowledge

A	FACTUAL KNOWLEDGE AA Knowledge of terminology AB Knowledge of specific details
B	CONCEPTUAL KNOWLEDGE BA Knowledge of classifications BB Knowledge of principles BC Knowledge of theories, models, and structures

C	**PROCEDURAL KNOWLEDGE** CA Knowledge of subject-specific skills CB Knowledge of subject-specific methods CC Knowledge of criteria for determining when to use appropriate procedures
D	**META-COGNITIVE KNOWLEDGE** DA Strategic knowledge DB Knowledge about cognitive tasks DC Self-knowledge

Source: adapted from AKC (2001: 46)

6) The six cognitive processes

The AKF is predicated on a particular view of students as 'active agents in their own learning; they select the information to which they will attend and construct their own meaning from this selected information. Learners are not passive recipients, nor are they simple recorders of information provided to them' by teachers or anyone else (AKC, 2001: 38). Students use their prior knowledge, their knowledge of themselves as learners, and the opportunities and constraints afforded them by the college to make sense of whatever tutors present them with; and in so doing they construct their own meaning, which may (and which often does not) accord with what they have been taught.

Some students, for instance, retain with great persistence some of the misconceptions about the world that they formed as young children. Howard Gardner has collected substantial evidence that: 'Nearly all students without formal science training and a disconcertingly high percentage of those with such training offer explanations that are at variance with simple and well-established laws' in physics, biology, maths, and economics (1993: 155). We do not, however, need to dwell on the misunderstandings of students; think instead of those well-educated friends who believe in astrology and try to convince you of the pervasive influence of your birth sign on your life; in this way the twelfth century lives on into the twenty-first. These arguments undercut any notion that TLA should focus on remembering or rote learning, as if learning was nothing more than the unproblematic acquisition of unconnected bits of information.

The first cognitive process dealt with in the AKF is *remembering*, which is subdivided into *recognizing* (for example, identifying that the Spanish word 'minusválido' means 'handicapped' or 'disabled'; literally translated as 'less fit or valid' – I know, it is incredible, but this is still the standard term); and *recalling* (for example, retrieving from long-term memory that during the

Second World War the Red Army in Russia suffered 'nearly 9 million dead and 18 million wounded' (Beevor, 2011: 428).

The next cognitive process – *understanding* – is perhaps the one most widely used in schools and colleges and is the ability to construct meaning from oral, written, and graphic communications. AKC subdivide this process into seven subtypes, which I simply list here and explain very briefly in Box 4.6, because most are self-explanatory: interpreting, exemplifying, classifying, summarizing, inferring, comparing, and explaining.

The third of the six cognitive processes is *applying* or using procedures to solve problems, which consists of both *executing* (when the task is familiar, as when students are faced with page upon page of mathematical problems to which they unthinkingly apply a standard formula); and of *implementing* (when the task is unfamiliar, where the students must choose an appropriate procedure to fit a problem that they have not met before).

The fourth process – *analysing* – is defined as 'breaking material into its constituent parts and understanding how the parts are related to one another' (AKC, 2001: 79), although analysis often needs to concern itself with what has been omitted or ignored. This is a vital skill for students of all subject areas and consists of three separate processes that AKC define as follows: *differentiating* = distinguishing relevant from irrelevant parts, determining how the parts fit into the overall structure; *organizing* = finding coherence within the elements of a structure; *attributing* = ascertaining the point of view, intention, or bias in the material presented.

Box 4.6: Six categories and 19 thinking skills or cognitive processes

1.	REMEMBERING 1.1 recognizing = matching new information with previously learned information 1.2 recalling = retrieving information from long-term memory
2.	UNDERSTANDING 2.1 interpreting = translating, students putting arguments in their own words 2.2 exemplifying = giving an example of a principle or concept 2.3 classifying = deciding that something belongs in a category 2.4 summarizing = abstracting the main points or themes 2.5 inferring = drawing a logical conclusion 2.6 comparing = detecting similarities and differences 2.7 explaining = constructing a cause-and-effect model of a system

3.	APPLYING 3.1 executing = using a procedure to perform a familiar task 3.2 implementing = using a procedure to solve an unfamiliar problem
4.	ANALYSING 4.1 differentiating = discriminating, distinguishing 4.2 organizing = finding coherence 4.3 attributing = ascertaining values or biases
5.	EVALUATING 5.1 checking = testing for fallacies or inconsistencies 5.2 critiquing = judging the merits of a solution
6.	CREATING 6.1 generating = suggesting possible solutions 6.2 planning = designing a workable plan 6.3 producing = carrying out the plan successfully, inventing a product

Source: Adapted from: AKC (2001: 67–8)

These three processes – differentiating, organizing, and attributing – are often combined in different ways when, for instance, students are asked to describe the motives of a character such as Iago in Shakespeare's *Othello*, and they may need to use the skills of differentiation, organization, and attribution, as well as adding some psychological insight, in order to provide a comprehensive analysis.

A number of my undergraduate students over the years have misunderstood the fifth main cognitive process – *evaluating* – treating it as an open invitation to criticize the work of, say, Jean Piaget or Lev Vygotsky. It is better understood as making judgements based on criteria or standards, the most frequently used of which are quantity/quality (is it enough/is it good enough?), effectiveness, efficiency, and consistency. The AKF divides evaluating into two subprocesses:

- *Checking* = making judgements about internal consistency: do the data support the hypothesis? Are there any internal inconsistencies or logical flaws? Have the procedures been carried out correctly?
- *Critiquing* = making judgements based on external criteria: what are the strengths and weaknesses of a product, procedure, or theory, based on predetermined criteria? How effective is this solution? How reasonable is this hypothesis? In mathematics, which method is more efficient, effective, or elegant? What, for instance, are the positive and negative consequences of performance-related pay for teachers? What is the quality of the evidence that has been advanced to support a case?

The sixth and final category is *creating*, which, as you would expect, involves putting elements together to form a coherent, functional, or original whole. AKC make the sensible point that 'many students will create in the sense of producing their own synthesis of information or materials to form a new whole, as in writing, painting, sculpting, building, and so on' (2001: 85). Often we require our students to draw on a large variety of sources, and to weave them into a new structure or pattern that moves their thinking beyond their prior knowledge. For example, education students are frequently invited to produce a review of the literature on a topic such as 'What are the main theories of learning?', and their submission must present a coherent and integrated argument, not just a discrete account of the work of theorist A, plus that of theorist B, C, etc. AKC break the creative process down into three distinct phases:

- *Generating* = coming up with alternative, divergent, and possibly original hypotheses or solutions; transcending the constraints of prior knowledge and existing theories; solutions are assessed according to explicit, publicly agreed criteria such as practicality, cost, and reasonableness.
- *Planning* = students examine the possibilities and design a workable plan.
- *Producing* = students carry out the plan successfully and produce a solution or a product, which, as argued earlier, does not have to be either unique or original, but may be useful, functional, and in accordance with the specifications laid down in advance.

I prefer Ken Robinson's treatment of these three phases, which he calls *imagination* (where we step out of the here and now), *creativity* (where we develop original ideas that have value), and *innovation* (where we put our creative ideas into practice). He has devoted his working life to providing evidence that everyone has creative potential and not just a select few, that we can all learn to be more creative, and that we now know how to nurture cultures of creativity in our schools and colleges. I shall draw on his ideas again in the final chapter, but for the present here is a flavour of his powerful argument: 'We all have creative capacities but very many people conclude that they are not creative, when in truth they have never learnt and practised what is involved' (Robinson, 2011: 165–6).

I am aware that providing even this brief account of the AKF may have tried the patience of the reader. In my defence, I would point out that the abridged version of the AKF runs to 302 pages, so I have been highly selective, but perhaps too concise or pedantic in places. I offer in Box 4.6 a summary chart of all 19 cognitive processes within the six categories of remembering, understanding, applying, analysing, evaluating, and creating. The value of this long list is that it makes it abundantly clear that to confine either teaching or assessment to the first two processes (recognizing and recalling) within the category of remembering is to do students a major disservice. If we want to help them develop higher-order thinking and learning skills, then we need to build the other 17 processes into our curricula and tests; and students are likely to use three or four of them together rather than in isolation, when, for instance, carrying out a personal project that calls for summarizing, organizing, planning, and producing.[5]

7) Evaluation

What I propose to do now is to use some of the ideas I have just presented to evaluate the AKF by using the two suggested subcategories of checking and critiquing. Under *checking* I will raise the question of whether it makes good educational sense to talk of decontextualized thinking skills or cognitive processes. Under *critiquing*, as promised earlier in this chapter, I will deal with a serious objection raised by Marzano and Kendall.

For the purposes of exposition, AKC deal separately with the two dimensions of knowledge and cognitive processes, but their Taxonomy Table constantly reminds us that it is the interactions between particular types of knowledge and specific cognitive processes that we deal with in TLA. Besides, they are aware of the importance of context in learning because they argue explicitly that experts in, say, history or biology will think, address problems, and use methods appropriate to their subject area, and that these will vary markedly from subject to subject. This stance resonates well with the long Germanic tradition, which insists that the internal logic, the specific nature of the subject, and its means of verification will require a pedagogical approach suited to that subject – so that engineering, for instance, cannot be taught in the same way as English.

Let me give an example of AKC's approach from modern languages, where we want to teach students the ability to grasp the spirit of the language in question. Recently, outside what we would call a licensed grocer in Orihuela in south-eastern Spain, I saw a sign that read 'Bocadillos elaborado al momento'. The translation, probably made by someone relying on a dictionary or a computer rather than on his or her brain, read 'sandwiches elaborated to the moment'. Every word is English but the phrase is nonsense; even the word order has to change to catch the meaning appropriately: 'Freshly made sandwiches'.

What I think needs to be added to AKC's account is a more dynamic and holistic understanding of *context*, as, for example, in the research of Ball *et al.*, where it is treated as 'an "active" force ... not just a backdrop against which schools have to operate' (2012: 24). For Ball and his colleagues, context consists of four overlapping features: the particular situation (locale, history of the college, and student intake); professional cultures (the values and experiences of the teachers and the management style of the Principal); resources (staffing, budget, and technology); and externalities (competition from local rivals, and pressures from other government policies, such as Ofsted rating, league table position, and exam requirements).

The work of Stephen Johnson, however, moves us on from checking to critiquing because he doubts whether there are entities called 'cognitive processes'; he also thinks that 'transfer of training' is a myth (the notion that thinking skills can be shown to be effective in different but similar circumstances from those in which they were first taught); and he also contends that cognitive processes encourage a checklist approach to thinking and to a disparagement of knowledge. I have to admit that I have sat at times in disbelief at education conferences listening, in the main, to IT specialists informing delegates that no one needs a strong knowledge base nowadays as long as he or she has access to the internet. And anyway, knowledge is changing so fast that it is impossible to tell what knowledge will be useful in ten or even five years' time. It was partly in opposition to such poppycock that Michael Young wrote his book *Bringing Knowledge Back In* (2008).

Johnson's criticisms deserve to be taken seriously and he is certainly right in arguing that the transfer of training from one context to another is a deeply complex and unresolved problem in education and psychology.[6] He is also right to complain about 'the checklist approach', which I have been guilty of in Boxes 4.2 and 4.3, but wrong to suggest, for example, that the AKF disparages knowledge as passive, inert, or theoretical. The Taxonomy Table has been specifically constructed to emphasize not just the interactions between, but the inseparability of, different types of knowledge and thinking skills when dealing with TLA.

One way of reconciling these conflicting viewpoints would be to *add* the valid points of Johnson's arguments to the AKF. I for one have no difficulty whatsoever in accepting that our thinking and learning are by no means captured by the 19 processes listed earlier in this chapter, because they are also frequently intuitive, emotional, embodied, and social. Besides, I support Johnson's contention that our notion of meta-cognition should be enlarged to include cultivating certain habits of mind and intellectual virtues such as:

> respect for truth; concern for accuracy; openness and charity towards different ideas, while maintaining a critical spirit;

> determination; willingness to conjecture; patience with the frustrations and *longueur* of learning and confidence to question authorities and tackle difficult questions.
>
> (Johnson, 2010: 45)

Indeed, I would like to go further by suggesting that we also adopt the formal properties of productive dialogue[7] suggested by the German philosopher Jürgen Habermas: namely, that it must be characterized by mutual respect and equality between the speakers, an open sharing of information and knowledge, and a willingness to accept the 'force of the better argument' (Habermas, 1988: xvi).

To continue with critiquing, a more specific weakness has been found in the AKF. Marzano and Kendall criticized the assumption that the six cognitive processes are ordered hierarchically according to difficulty from the simplest (remember) to the most complex (create). They reviewed the empirical research, which showed that even educators trained in the use of the AKF 'were consistently unable to recognize questions at higher levels as more difficult than questions at lower levels of the taxonomy' (2007: 8). They go further by pointing out that the complexity of a mental process is not just dependent on its inherent difficulty, but also on the level of familiarity you have with the process, a familiarity that will change with time and practice. So, for instance, an experienced taxi driver will be able to discuss with you whether the ban on the Liverpool footballer Luis Suarez for biting an opponent was too severe, while skilfully negotiating traffic in the London rush hour, but a learner driver will still be using the mnemonic MSM (for mirror, signal, manoeuvre) before changing lane. Students' performance may be limited neither by their lack of ability nor by the inherent difficulty of a particular concept or skill but by the amount of time it takes to integrate new knowledge with existing knowledge in order to produce a smooth performance at a higher level. This is a fair point, but so, I think, is my observation, which Marzano and Kendall themselves acknowledge, that there is a hierarchy of difficulty within their own taxonomy because recognition (where a student chooses a synonym from a list of words) is a simpler process than recall (where a student is asked to define a word, which involves him or her in recall plus an appropriate response).

The question is likely to be asked: why did I chose the AKF over Marzano and Kendall's new taxonomy, especially when the latter claim that it represents not just a framework but nothing less than a theory of human thought? My answer is that, despite the welcome inclusion of both psychomotor procedures as a form of knowledge and the meta-analysis[8] of teaching strategies that involved over 2,500 effect sizes,[9] their model is even more complex than the AKF and the practical returns from it are so thin. Let me give two examples to substantiate that second objection. First, although Marzano and Kendall claim that their theory deals with human emotions much more extensively than AKC, their treatment of this topic borders on the farcical:

> Although the nature and function of emotions is a complex topic, for instructional purposes students can be presented with the simple model that there are four basic emotions: glad, sad, mad and afraid.
>
> (2007: 164)

I cannot speak for Marzano and Kendall's students, but such a statement deserves the emotional response of being called insensitive, patronizing, and superficial. In making that criticism, we have rather quickly moved way beyond four simple emotions.

Second, their explanation of problem-solving cannot be taken seriously, at least by me. They claim that their eight-part strategy is 'more robust' than previous procedures suggested by rival psychologists and yet the first two steps run as follows:

> 1. Determine whether you really have a problem. Is the goal truly important to you, or is it something you can ignore?
> 2. If you determine that you really do have a problem, take a moment to affirm the following beliefs:
>   a. There are probably a number of ways to solve the problem, and I will surely find one of them.
>   b. Help is probably available if I look for it.
>   c. I am perfectly capable of solving this problem.
>
> (2007: 159)

There are six more procedures in a similar vein, but two are enough. Pity that Tony Blair did not know about this 'robust' strategy when he became Peace Envoy to the Middle East or all the problems of that war-torn region would have been settled long before now.

8) Final comments

This has been a long chapter, but I wanted to show in detail that teaching is very far from being a simple process of transmitting isolated bits of information from a knowledgeable tutor to a passive student. On the contrary, the previous pages have explored some of the ambiguities, complexities, unpredictabilities, confusions, and controversies that make up the sheer messiness which goes by the name of TLA. To help tutors cope with these difficulties, I have explained in detail AKC's taxonomy 'that captures the complexity and comprehensiveness of our knowledge base while being relatively simple, practical and easy to use' (AKC, 2001: 41). Many of their ideas have proved pedagogically powerful when I have tried them out, and I hope other teachers have the same experiences. Tutors and students have also responded very positively to this framework, which, they have informed me, has given them a memorable overview of knowledge and thinking skills.

When, however, should students be introduced to a framework like the AKF? Earlier I suggested that an appropriate time would be when students first arrive at FE or sixth-form college at the age of 16, by which time bulimic and anorexic learning will most likely have become a way of life for most students. On the other hand, Lauren Resnick has been arguing since 1987 that we should be teaching students how to think and learn from the moment they start in primary school, so that they do not develop the bad learning habits that they then have to spend so much time unlearning later on – on the balance of the evidence, I agree with her.

Let me end this chapter by quoting from the English philosopher A.N. Whitehead, who warned: 'above all things we must be aware of what I will call "inert ideas" – that is to say, ideas that are merely received into the mind without being utilized or tested or thrown into fresh combination' (1962: 1–2). The main argument of this chapter has been that it is not good enough for students of whatever age to acquire and regurgitate mountains of factual information; they must understand concepts and principles deeply; they must be able to apply, analyse, and evaluate subject knowledge; and they must be helped to discover their creative strengths so that they can produce new knowledge.

Notes

[1] At a staff development day in one FE college, a colleague remarked that to ensure an annual improvement in test scores, she and her closest colleagues had gone well beyond 'spoon-feeding'; they were now 'breast-feeding' their students.

[2] I am grateful to Amanda Spielman for making this useful point.

[3] Geoff Petty has a useful chapter on graphic organizers and other visual representations, though he cautions against 'leaping on the first representation that occurs to you', because ideas can be represented in a variety of forms and some are more powerful (they explain more) and more economic (in the simplest possible form) than others (2009: 116).

[4] The AKF at this point deals with motivation, but as I prefer an approach that combines the psychological notions of Jerome Bruner with the economic ideas of Ewart Keep, I postpone a discussion of this topic to Chapter 6.

[5] A commercial product – Thinking Dice, available at www.thinkingdice.com – has been introduced that consists of six differently coloured dice, each of which has a question on its side. The dice aim to promote questioning and higher-order thinking, using the six main categories of cognitive processes in the AKF. For example, the six questions on the blue evaluating dice are: 'What are the strengths and weaknesses of ...?'; 'Do you agree/disagree with ...?'; 'Why ...?'; 'If you could change one thing about ... what would it be?'; 'What is the most important ...?'; 'How would you select ...?'; 'What do you think about ...?'. I have seen 14–16-year-old students happily using the dice to ask more challenging questions of their learning partners, but I have two reservations: the questions on the dice could be more searching, and I object to any firm advertising their products as 'Higher Order Thinking made simple'. If only.

[6] The idea that subjects such as Latin would make students think more logically in the other subjects they undertook – the classical problem of transfer of training – has been studied since the 1920s, when Thorndike showed convincingly that classical scholars performed no better in other school subjects. Readers interested in this topic are referred to a key text by Tuomi-Gröhn and Engeström, who argue, for example, that 'what is transferred is not packages of knowledge and skills that remain intact; instead, the very process of such transfer involves active interpreting, modifying and reconstructing the skills and knowledge to be transferred' (2003: 4).

[7] Adopting Habermas's rules would help to improve the quality of the national debate in education, which has recently degenerated into a slanging match, with the current Secretary of State for Education, Michael Gove, accusing the 100 academics (of whom I am one) who publicly criticized his policies of being 'the modern Enemies of Promise ... more interested in valuing Marxism, revering jargon and fighting excellence' (Gove, 2013). Such extreme language from any politician would be serious, but it is particularly reprehensible in an Education Secretary. Instead of responding to the serious concerns raised by the academics, commentators such as Harry Mount, writing in *The Daily Telegraph*, construct a travesty of our argument that is then ridiculed: 'His [Gove's] opponents are of such a deep strain of perverse idiocy ... anti-knowledge ... brainiacs, warped by their doctorates and professorships ... obscure theories concocted by their knowledge-hating contemporaries' (Mount, 2013). Such immoderate language breaks all of Habermas's rules, obscures rather than illuminates the debate, and is bad for democracy.

[8] For explanations of this term, please see the first few pages of Chapter 8.

[9] As above.

References

Anderson, L.W. and Krathwohl, D.R. (AKC) (eds) (2001) *A Taxonomy for Learning, Teaching, and Assessing: A revision of Bloom's Taxonomy of Educational Objectives*. New York: Longman, abridged edition.

Ball, S.J., Maguire, M., and Braun, A. (2012) *How Schools Do Policy: Policy enactments in secondary schools*. London: Routledge.

Beevor, A. (2011) *Stalingrad*. London: Penguin Books.

Bloom, B., Engelhart, M.D., Furst, E.J., Hill, W.H., Krathwohl, D.R. (1956) *Taxonomy of Educational Objectives: Handbook 1: Cognitive domain*. New York: David McKay.

Bruner, J.S. (1996) *The Culture of Education*. London: Harvard University Press.

Coffield, F. (2008) *Just Suppose Teaching and Learning Became the First Priority...* London: Learning & Skills Network.

Department for Education (DfE) (2013) *The Proposed Programmes of Study and Attainment Targets for the National Curriculum Subjects*. London: DfE.

Dickens, C. (1955) *Hard Times*. Oxford: Oxford University Press.

Fox, R. (2001) 'Constructivism examined'. *Oxford Review of Education*, 27 (1), 23–35.

Gardner, H. (1993) *The Unschooled Mind: How children think and how schools should teach*. London: Fontana.

Gove, M. (2013) 'Why I refuse to surrender to militant Marxist teachers hell-bent on destroying our schools'. *The Mail on Sunday*, 24 March.

Habermas, J. (1988) *Legitimation Crisis*. Cambridge: Polity Press.

Hunter, I. (1974) 'How to play Twenty Questions'. *New Society*, 26 December, 810–11.

Johnson, S. (2010) 'Teaching thinking skills'. In C. Winch (ed.), *Teaching Thinking Skills*. London: Continuum.

MacLellan, E. and Soden, R. (2012) 'Successful learners, confident individuals, responsible citizens and effective contributors to society: Exploring the nature of learning and its implications in curriculum for excellence'. *Scottish Educational Review*, 1, 29–37.

Marzano, R. and Kendall, J. (2007) *The New Taxonomy of Educational Objectives*, 2nd edn. Thousand Oaks, CA: Corwin Press.

McDonald, R. (2010) 'Serving the poet'. In *Programme to Glyndebourne Opera Season*, 95–9.

Moseley, D., Baumfield, V., Higgins, S., Lin, M., Miller, J., Newton, D., Robson, S., Elliott, J., and Gregson, M. (2004) *Thinking Skill Frameworks for Post-16 Learners: An evaluation*. London: Learning and Skills Research Centre.

Mount, H. (2013) 'Children can't think if they don't learn facts.' *The Telegraph*, 20 March.

Petty, G. (2009) *Evidence-Based Teaching: A practical approach*. Cheltenham: Nelson Thornes.

Pickard, M. (2007) 'The new Bloom's Taxonomy: An overview for family and consumer sciences'. *Journal of Family and Consumer Sciences Education*, 25 (1), 45–55.

Reiss, M. and White, J. (2013) *An Aims-based Curriculum: The significance of human flourishing for schools*. London: Institute of Education Press.

Resnick, L. (1987) *Education and Learning to Think*. Washington, DC: National Academy Press.

Robinson, K. (2011) *Out of Our Minds: Learning to be creative*, 2nd edn. Chichester: Capstone.

Schama, S. (1989) *Citizens: A chronicle of the French Revolution*. London: Viking.

Tomalin, C. (2011) *Charles Dickens: A life*. London: Viking.

Tuomi-Gröhn, T. and Engeström, Y. (2003) *Between School and Work: New perspectives on transfer and boundary-crossing*. Oxford: Elsevier Science.

Whitehead, A.N. (1962) *The Aims of Education*. London: Ernest Benn.

Young, M.F.D. (2008) *Bringing Knowledge Back In*. Oxon: Routledge.

Chapter 5

'Everyone is his own boss.'

Current threats to educational attainment in German schools

Walter Müller

Reinhard Kahl's well-known film series, *Incubators of the Future: How schools in Germany succeed*, includes an episode about the Neue-Max-Brauer school in Hamburg.[1] This progressive school is considered a pioneer for schools of the future and has received multiple awards – for example, the German school award in 2006 and the Theodor-Heuss Medal. Furthermore, the school was admitted to the illustrious circle of 'Club of Rome Schools'.[2] The title of the episode is: 'Everyone is His Own Boss'. The viewer is shown how the 'boss-system' works in the classroom. Every child is responsible for a particular learning task, which means that he or she is the expert, go-to person, and coach for the other pupils, and also evaluates their work. Moreover, every child is the boss of his or her own learning, the success and failure of which is monitored via so-called competence grids. When asked whether this kind of learning tempts the children to do nothing and just 'stare into space', a girl replies: 'It would be our own fault, if we did not learn and thus did not know anything afterwards'. The commentator, Reinhard Kahl, emphasizes how positive it is that the school did especially well in the Programme for International Student Assessment (PISA) survey and that until around the age of 15, pupils are one year ahead of their peers in other schools.

This short film shows what the prevalent maxim of German school politics has been since the late 1990s and since PISA. It also provides examples of what has become popular in the performance management of primary and secondary schools:

First, effective time management and efficiency, and the acceleration of the learning process (students can be advanced by one whole school year).

Second, competence and output orientation, which means a departure from curriculum-bound, content-centred lessons in favour of transdisciplinary competencies, which are predetermined in the form of testable standards (in a compulsory competence grid).

Third, self-regulated and highly differentiated learning (everyone is his own boss).

In contrast to the mainstream, I do not see positive signs of the 'required change in mentality of the German educational system' (Annette Schavan)[3] in these three tendencies. Instead, I see evidence that schools increasingly (have to) submit to non-pedagogic, economically motivated concerns and objectives. They are well on the way to losing entirely their educational aspirations (which many people have called into question all along) and are increasingly degenerating into sites of non-education and dulling of the mind.[4]

This critical claim is supported not only by numerous arguments from the tradition of European educational thinking, but also by, for example, the current official curriculum of the Bavarian Gymnasium,[5] which contains the following:

> The Bavarian Gymnasium builds on a long and successful educational tradition. To this day it is a type of school which enjoys popularity because education at a Gymnasium is founded on an educational concept that transcends the mere transfer of knowledge and pursues the objective of personality development. Whoever successfully attends a Gymnasium will not only be thoroughly prepared for university or a vocation, he or she will also gain a cultural identity and experience certain values which give him/her self-confidence and which will enable him/her to develop positions and make judgement calls with self-assurance. In this sense, the Gymnasium forms the identity of young people so that they have cultural and ethical foundations which substantially contribute to a fulfilled life. The Gymnasium is still attached to the maxim of Wilhelm von Humboldt: 'The individual tries to grasp as much of the world as possible and to connect with it as intimately as he or she can'.

I will now discuss in more detail each of these three tendencies.

1) The focus on effective time management and time saving, and the acceleration of the learning process

This tendency can be detected on a macro as well as on a micro level. The most evident example on a macro level is the reduction of time spent in a Gymnasium from nine to eight years. Whatever one may think of the advantages and disadvantages of the G8[6] reform, it is certain that the motivation behind the reduction of school years was not educational, it was economic. Most importantly, the alleged competitive disadvantages of German Gymnasium graduates on the European and global labour market are thus to be compensated for. However, as far as I know, there is no empirical evidence that this is even necessary.

In addition, they were pursuing considerable financial savings.[7] Significantly, the impetus for this reduction did not come from the Department of Education but from the 16 regional ministers of finance. The leading trade associations were particularly strong supporters of the reform. In those circles, education is understood as human capital and therefore follows an economic 'time-is-money' logic. The winners are those who, with the least cost and in the least time, gain the most human capital and use it most effectively.[8]

The theoretical equivalent at the micro level in the classroom to this 'time-is-money' logic are the demands for more effective time management, an 'increase in pure learning time' (Hilbert Meyer),[9] 'time saving', and the effective use of difference in the classroom raised by the so-called 'new teaching culture'.[10] Herbert Gudjons makes no secret of where teachers and pupils can go to learn effective time management. The answer is the business world, which in his view has become a 'highly developed culture of work and time economy' (Gudjons, 2006: 174).

But what is worrying about the transfer of a quantitative understanding of time and the 'faster-is-better' principle, which are so important for today's economy, to the context of school? Why are there concerns that schools, which are driven by an economic understanding of time, can no longer form the personalities of their students in the Humboldtian sense? Käte Meyer-Drawe, for instance, fears that the 'high-speed learner becomes the turbo-condition prototype of the effective self-learner' (Meyer-Drawe, 2008: 125). Educational processes in the Humboldtian tradition essentially rely on inspiration, enough time, and the ability to wait. Furthermore, this tradition requires moments of deceleration and pauses from the march of chronological time so that curiosity, amazement, interest, personal involvement, calm reflection, and independent thinking can unfold. This is important so that the special time requirements and the particular nature of the subject matter as well as the challenge 'evoked by the material' (Meyer-Drawe) can be experienced and respected.[11]

In short: education takes time! Therefore, a valid theory of education must not be guided by a purely quantitative understanding of time. The qualitative dimension and the requisite impact of waiting and deceleration must be acknowledged. Otherwise, the pupil is reduced to a mere sack of stimulus-responses, educational programmes are turned into learning highways, the intrinsic value of knowledge is ignored, and schools become learning factories and brain-management institutions.

Such insights are to be found in the educational literature. Fiction also provides impressive examples of the pedagogic problems of school *Chronokratie* (sovereignty of time); for example, Hanno Buddenbrook's *Aufstehensgeschichte*[12] as well as Peter Høeg's *Der Plan von der Abschaffung des Dunkels*. In the latter, the struggle of the students against the linear timetable of school and the time and punishment plans of headteacher Biehl are portrayed. The story culminates when one of the students, Peter, climbs the clock-tower to set it back ten minutes – ten fictional minutes of chaos that for a short time turn the hell that is school into paradise.[13]

2) The focus on competence and output orientation

One of the most frequently used terms in the current debate over educational policy and schools is 'competence'. In addition to professional competence, the pupils are to be taught communicative competencies, and social, methodological, self, and media competencies. There is also talk of 'key competencies', 'foundation competencies', and, indeed, even 'life competencies'. In terms of content, these competencies are segmented into competence grids, competence areas, proficiency levels, domain-specific educational standards, and tests in the same style as that used in the PISA survey. They are evaluated in centralized examinations or central standardized tests as guidance, comparison, or parallel tests.[14] Furthermore, the teachers' tasks and roles are increasingly formulated in terms of competencies.[15]

Even though the term 'competence' has suffered from a major inflation of meaning, its positive perception in the educational field has not happened by chance. Despite any semantic inconsistencies, the term has kept a core meaning that contains three main points. First, the idea of output orientation. Second, the concept of predictability and governance. Third, the possibility of empirical evaluation and examination.[16] Through these specifications, the notion of education (as it was understood by Humboldt) will be reduced to predefined, manageable, and empirically measureable learning outcomes in much the same manner as the Anglo-Saxon notion of literacy. The competence and output-orientated notion of education has no room for, and does not value, sudden insights concerning scientific correlations arising from rigorous experimentation. The fascination with the consistency of a mathematical proof, the 'eureka' experience when, after lengthy reflection, one finally thinks of a striking figure of speech for a text, the joy of intellectual rapport and knowing oneself to be understood in conversation, as well as the goosebumps one gets (given one has an understanding of music and how to listen to it) when listening to a chorale from the St Matthew Passion – all of this is nothing in the world of competence and output orientation.

A functionalist, utilitarian, and performative understanding of teaching and learning, according to international student assessments, is essential.[17] The well-balanced formation of all the strengths of the individual and the improvement of his or her personality as valuable in themselves (Wilhelm von Humboldt) is no longer central. Instead, what is aspired to is the training of skills and the transfer of stored knowledge, which are believed to be conducive to the preservation and expansion of individual and common prosperity as well as the prosperity of German business in a globalized world.

In contrast to the above-mentioned claims for the curriculum, current educational aims are no longer primarily about individual pupils and forming their ability to judge objectively. Neither are they about preparing them for a responsible and meaningful lifestyle on the basis of broad and deep knowledge and contemplation. Primarily, the aims are about the most efficient transfer of testable knowledge and skills. Hence, they are about the improvement and increase of human capital. 'The unlearnable in every learning process' falls by the wayside.[18]

This means that the individual pupil is sold short. The intrinsic value of knowledge is brushed aside by this competence and output-orientated understanding of education. The educational content that has to become accessible to the students is no longer valued for its own sake. There is no more *Bildungsgehalt*,[19] as it is phrased in traditional pedagogy. Teaching syllabuses now are nothing more than training manuals and tools for the acquisition of formal competencies; in other words, competencies that are applicable in many content areas and that support lifelong learning. Primarily, the focus is on key competencies that in our modern 'knowledge-based' society are supposedly more important than getting thoroughly immersed in educationally relevant fields. Konrad Paul Liessmann characterized this trend for hollowed-out teaching and learning in favour of relatively content-neutral competence training as follows: 'One does not learn anymore in order to know things but for the sake of learning itself'. It is all about 'the kind of knowledge that can be produced, traded, bought, managed and disposed of as a commodity' (Liessmann, 2006: 27, 53). As a result of this 'removing of the heart of learning', the individual peculiarities, the uncontrollability, the intricate nature, and the mysteriousness of different subjects, as Horst Rumpf phrases it, are discarded.[20]

Apart from these basic pedagogical developments, the competence and output-orientated school creates tremendous side effects that I want to mention briefly:

First, as a result of obligatory standardized tests, the pressures to perform, in addition to the strain of having to repeat a class or being transferred to a lower school, are increasing.

Second, output orientation reinforces the danger of teaching-to-the-test and bulimic learning. Training and preparation for standardized tests are taking on an ever-larger role in teaching and learning. Increasingly, what is to be learned is no longer examined. Instead, only what is going to be in the exam is what is learned.

Third, this favours the problematic trend of ranking schools in league tables, since output orientation supposedly ensures the comparability of different schools. It also enables school administrators to increase competition between schools through ranking lists, as has been common in England since the 1980s.

Fourth, competence and output orientation lead to a strengthening of the so-called 'hard' subjects (mathematics, foreign languages, science, first language) and diminish and marginalize the 'weak' subjects (such as art, music, religion, ethics, social studies), as the output of those subjects is comparatively more difficult to evaluate.[21]

3) The focus on self-management and individualization

As illustrated in the example of the Neue-Max-Brauer school, one of the leading maxims of current school pedagogy and politics is the concept of self-regulated learning. 'Everyone is his own boss.' At first glance, this maxim seems to be the pinnacle of all progressive teaching claims, in which individual initiative, self-reliance, and independence in learning seem to be the fulfilment of the principles of autonomy, freedom, and maturity of the person. Are all previous objections (based on progressive educational ideas) to the use of education for non-educational purposes, and the narrow horizons placed on education, now obsolete? Appearances are deceiving, for the similarities to progressive education and educational enlightenment are rhetorical rather than substantial. Self-control is not synonymous with self-determination in the sense of autonomy and maturity, but merely acts as a modified control strategy in which the centre of control is shifted from the teacher to the student. The conventional external control (by the teacher) is replaced by a kind of contemporary internal control (by the student). Why?

Obviously, it is hoped that such a change in management leads to a smoother and more efficient accomplishment of the outcomes laid out in competence grids and standardized tests. In addition, a better kind of training in the key competencies that are believed to be essential for the mastering of the future is sought. Furthermore, this change is geared to the acquisition of transferable, soft skills that in our 'knowledge-based society' are considered to be the characteristics of the educated. These include employability, effective knowledge 'management', entrepreneurship, lifelong learning, self-management, flexibility, innovation, and self-evaluation competencies. In other words, everything that a thriving 'I as a PLC', 'I as a self-sufficient firm', supposedly needs these days in order to survive global competition.[22] In this concept of self-control, learners act as 'managers of themselves' and thus practically have to market and exploit themselves (Meyer-Drawe, 2008: 132). The freedom granted to them is reduced to a set of competencies to serve a specific, economic purpose and is no longer based on the Enlightenment's notion of maturity and the autonomous behaviour of people.

Following the analytical reflections of Michel Foucault, one could view this kind of freedom as a particularly ingenious and subtle form of domination and submission that is typical of the current transition from traditional forms of discipline to a society of control. This being the case, it amounts to a 'form of control with a libertarian veneer' in which the traditional techniques of maintaining discipline such as monitoring and punishment are substituted by a 'persistent quality tribunal'. This is made feasible via benchmarking, empowerment, assessment, ranking lists, and standardized tests.[23] Rousseau summed up the point well: 'There is no more perfect form of submission than the one that preserves the appearance of freedom'. ('*Il n'y a point d'assujetissement si parfait que celui qui garde l'apparence de la liberté*', in *Emile*.)

But where are the teachers in this concept of self-control? They are not redundant, but their role is changing from that of instructor to that of tutor, coach, and moderator and therefore from educator to development assistant and facilitator.[24] Their main task is no longer seen as the transformation of adolescents into mature and responsible people, teaching them in an appropriate and challenging manner. It is to provide them with the motivation to learn, and to accompany, advise, and support them (Gudjons, 2006: 17). What, for good reason, in the history of education was called the 'art of teaching and learning' has become 'classroom management competence'.

As a result of the allegedly technological understanding of teaching and learning, the central problems of the teaching profession are reduced to the simple alternative of: should control be exercised internally or externally? The issues in question are: the importance of the teacher's personality, the systematic coherence between leading and simply allowing to develop, and the question of whether the focus must be on the student or the content. The highly complex set of duties to be carried out by the teacher,[25] which has been debated on a sophisticated and systematic level for centuries, is thereby trivialized and marginalized.

In sum, on the basis of the tendencies I have demonstrated in school pedagogy and educational politics, it can be shown that German schools are diverging more and more from their own traditional educational standards. Just like other European countries, Germany is increasingly influenced by neo-liberal economic constraints and thought patterns. The main reason is that 'becoming educated' is primarily understood to mean 'becoming equipped with useful competencies for the purpose of maximizing one's "human resources"' (PISA-Konsortium, 2008: 26). Schools are primarily regarded as economic instruments in the global economic competition that work best according to market and economic principles. Wilhelm von Humboldt's maxim, which is quoted in the Bavarian curriculum (to grasp as much of the world as possible and to connect with it as intimately as one can), is no longer the touchstone for the educational quality of our schools, but the rank order achieved on the performance scale of a World Trade Organization called OECD.

Notes

[1] The episode can be found on the 1st and 2nd DVDs of the documentary 'Incubators of the Future' (2006) by Reinhard Kahl (Archiv der Zukunft/Beltz). A shortened version is available on YouTube.

[2] Website of the Neue-Max-Brauer school.

[3] This quotation can be found on the back of the booklet of the DVD 'Incubators of the Future' (see note 1).

[4] There is a long tradition of inherent pedagogic doubt about the educational attainment of schools. Especially in the 1970s these doubts were elaborated in the publications of Wolfgang Fischer, Jörg Ruhloff, and their students; for example, Wolfgang Fischer (1978) *Schule als parapädagogische Organisation*, Henn: Kastellaun. The term *Unbildung* (non-education) was brought back to pedagogy by Paul Liessmann in his 2006 work *Theorie der Unbildung*, Vienna: Zsolnay. In his well-known 2009 essay 'Bildung: Plädoyer wider die Verdummung', *Zeitschrift Forschung und Lehre* 9, 1–14, Andreas Dörpinghaus called attention to the danger of the dulling of the mind.

[5] A *Gymnasium* in Germany is the type of school for pupils pursuing the equivalent of A levels and potentially a university education.

[6] Eight years in a *Gymnasium*. Since the beginning of the new century, all federal states reduced the course of studies from nine to eight years.

[7] In Bavaria a thousand teacher positions can be 'rationalized', that is, dispensed with.

[8] As an example of this understanding of education, see the assessment of Alfred Herrhausen Gesellschaft (2002) *Wieviel Bildung brauchen wir? Humankapital in Deutschland und seine Erträge*, Frankfurt am Main: Deutsche Bank.

[9] 'Hoher Anteil echter Lernzeit' (increase of pure learning time) ranks second in Hilbert Meyer's 'Zehn Merkmale guten Unterrichts'. The question of 'real learning time' was the initial boost from the empirical studies of school effectiveness. In fact, the understanding of aptitude is characterized in an economic manner: you are gifted when you use your time most effectively and skilfully. If you need more time, you are less skilled. This 'time-is-money' logic becomes apparent when looking at the point

of 'wasted time'. In Germany, one lesson costs around €75. A teacher with the pay bracket A13 who is 5 minutes late for 3 of his 5 lessons wastes €25 per day (Hilbert Meyer (2004) *Was ist guter Unterricht?* Berlin: Cornelsen/Scriptor, 41ff.).

[10] Heinz Klippert (2010) *Heterogenität im Klassenzimmer: Wie Lehrkräfte effektiv und zeitsparend damit umgehen können*, Weinheim and Basel: Beltz.

[11] Particularly in: Andreas Dörpinghaus (2008) 'Schonräume der Langsamkeit'. *Zeitschrift für Erwachsenenbildung* I, 42–5; Andreas Dörpinghaus (2009) op. cit. (see note 4), 10f.; Horst Rumpf (2004) *Diesseits der Belehrungswut*, Weinheim and Munich: Juventa; Fritz Reheis (2007) *Bildung contra Turboschule: Ein Plädoyer*, Freiburg in Breisgau: Herder.

[12] cf. Irmgard und Helmwart Hierdeis (1993) '"Zeit, Verzehrerin der Dinge" (Ovid): Über Schulzeiten'. *Ethica*, 1 (4), 399–415.

[13] Peter Høeg (1995) *Der Plan von der Abschaffung des Dunkels*, Munich and Vienna: Hanser.

[14] Gertrud Hovestadt and Nicole Keßler (2005) give an overview of the various forms of competency-oriented evaluations in '16 Bundesländer: Eine Übersicht zu Bildungsstandards und Evaluationen'. *Friedrich Jahresheft*, 23, 8–10 (special issue on *Standards: Unterrichten zwischen Kompetenzen, zentralen Prüfungen und Vergleichsarbeiten*).

[15] The most important competencies are: professional competence, communication competence, and diagnosis competence, as well as personal, cultural, curricular, and evaluative competencies. In 2004 the conference of the ministers of education and cultural affairs settled on a table of 11 competence areas that is applicable to teacher training. Fritz Oser and Jürgen Oelkers issued a checklist comprising 88 competencies for the qualification of teachers. cf. F. Oser and J. Oelkers (2001) 'Standards: Kompetenzen von Lehrpersonen'. In Oser and Oelkers (eds), *Die Wirksamkeit der Lehrerbildungssysteme: Von der Allrounderbildung zur Ausbildung professioneller Standards*. Zürich: SKBF, 215–342.

[16] To read more about the pedagogic difficulties of the term 'competency', see Klaus Schaller (2009) 'Zauberformel "Kompetenz"'. *Vierteljahrsschrift für Wissenschaftliche Pädagogik*, 2, 389–412.

[17] Even in the first PISA survey in 2000 it says that PISA 'follows a functionally oriented literacy concept for which the use of competencies in authentic situations is the real touchstone' (17). 'It is not about the initialisation of different ways to look at the world' (20). Deutsches PISA Konsortium (ed.) (2001) *PISA 2000: Basiskompetenzen von Schülerinnen und Schülern im internationalen Vergleich*. Opladen: Leske and Budrich.

[18] Bernhard Waldenfels (2001) *Verfremdung der Moderne: Phänomenologische Grenzgänge*. Göttingen: Wallstein, 52. For further details, see Käte Meyer-Drawe (2008) *Diskurse des Lernens*. Munich: Wilhelm Fink.

[19] This is a reference to Wolfgang Klafki and his concept of the 'bildungstheoretische Didaktik'. Not all content is worth being taught.

[20] Horst Rumpf, op. cit. (see note 11).

[21] Particularly in Walter Müller (2007) 'Die KMK-Bildungsstandards: Ein Lehrstück für das Verhältnis von Politik und Pädagogik'. In W. Böhm and K. Hillenbrand (eds), *Engagiert aus dem Glauben*. Würzburg: Echter, 225–40.

[22] Agnieszka Dzierbicka and Alfred Schirlbauer (2006) edited a critical glossary of these terms, *Pädagogisches Glossar der Gegenwart: Von Autonomie bis Wissensmanagement*. Vienna: Löcker.

[23] Gilles Deleuze (1993) 'Postskriptum über die Kontrollgesellschaften'. In his *Unterhandlungen 1972–1990* (translated by V. Gustav Roßler), Frankfurt am Main: Suhrkamp, 255. For a pedagogical interpretation, see Ludwig A. Pongratz (2004) 'Freiwillige Selbstkontrolle: Schule zwischen Disziplinar- und Kontrollgesellschaft'. In N. Ricken and M. Rieger-Ladich (eds), *Michel Foucault: Pädagogische Lektüren*.

Wiesbaden: Verlag für Sozialwissenschaft, 243–59. Andrea Liesner (2004) 'Von kleinen Herren und großen Knechten'. In Ricken and Rieger-Ladich, op. cit., 285–300. And Carsten Bünger, Ralf Mayer, Astrid Messerschmidt, and Olga Zizelsberger (eds) (2009) *Bildung der Kontrollgesellschaft: Analyse und Kritik pädagogischer Vereinnahmungen* (*Festschrift* for Ludwig A. Pongratz). Paderborn: Schöningh.

[24] A more critical approach can be seen in Alfred Schirlbauer (2005) 'Vom Verschwinden des Lehrers und seiner Epiphanie', in his *Die Moralpredigt: Destruktive Beiträge zur Pädagogik und Bildungspolitik*. Vienna: Sonderzahl, 40–57; and in Walter Müller (2009) 'Schnee von gestern: Was ist das Neue an der "Neuen Unterrichtskultur"?'. *Vierteljahrsschrift für Wissenschaftliche Pädagogik*, 1, 26–38, especially 35ff.

[25] For example, see Theodor Ballauff (1985) *Lehrer sein einst und jetzt: Auf der Suche nach dem verlorenen Lehrer*. Essen: Neue Deutsche Schule.

References

Gudjons, H. (2006) *Neue Unterrichtskultur: Veränderte Lehrerrolle*. Bad Heilbrunn: Klinkhardt.

Liessmann, K.P. (2006) *Theorie der Unbildung*. Vienna: Zsolnay.

Meyer-Drawe, K. (2008) *Diskurse des Lernens*. Munich: Wilhelm Fink.

PISA Konsortium Deutschland (eds) (2008) *PISA '06: Die Kompetenzen der Jugendlichen im dritten Ländervergleich*. Münster: Waxmann.

Chapter 6

Whip me with carrots

The role of motivation in education and training

Frank Coffield

Is there any tonic in the world that bucks you up the way money does?

Michael Frayn (1999: 324)

It was a carrot and stick form of education, without the carrot.

Pete McCarthy (2001), on being educated by Christian Brothers in Liverpool

1) Introduction

During my 42-year career in education, I worked for 14 heads of department (I refuse to use the industrial term 'line manager'), and only two ever got the best out of me. Some were classic authoritarians who were sycophantic to their superiors, but oppressive to anyone lower than them in the hierarchy. Some were socially awkward egoists who found it impossible to praise anyone for doing a good job and tried to manage by issuing a stream of yellow sticky notes. One was a pompous control freak who, for instance, counted the number of chairs in the department and read the correspondence of his colleagues and the papers in their filing cabinets, which, he assured us, were university property. And one transferred the heavy responsibility of running examination boards to me and other junior, unpromoted colleagues, while he made serious money with his 14 external examinerships. Another even researched and wrote articles and books on motivation, but succeeded only in turning the majority of the department against him by constantly intensifying workloads without consultation.

One of the two people who motivated me (admittedly not the easiest of people to 'manage') divided up the work of the department equally between all members of staff, but only after he had taken upon himself twice the average amount. He also invited me to attend his lectures and then comment on them over lunch that he paid for – and he waited patiently for me to invite him to attend and comment on mine, all the while insisting on paying for lunch. The second motivating boss was a model of integrity with whom

I quickly developed a warm, trusting relationship and with whom I could discuss my problems with teaching, as he himself continued to teach despite running a multimillion-pound, research-intensive university.

Two out of 14 is a rather low figure, but I would suggest that it is pretty typical in education, if the replies from my higher-degree students over 30+ years are anything to go by. One of the things I learned when I became a manager myself is that management is the means whereby your strengths and weaknesses are endlessly discussed and exposed by your colleagues, who watch your every move and who dissect your every utterance for possible hidden meanings or clues to your future intentions. It is not for the faint-hearted.

The most difficult task I encountered as a middle manager of a large education department was finding a dignified way for those colleagues who were 'burnt-out' by many years of teaching to leave the profession. If they had dipped their hand in the till or had entered into a sexual relationship with one of our students, then my task would still have been unpleasant but clear. But how to deal with those whose teaching was repeatedly criticized by different cohorts of students for being dull and uninspiring, who did not improve even after intensive help, and who remained stubbornly unmoved by my cherished theories of change and professional learning? I used a visit from Her Majesty's Inspectors to break the deadlock. The leading inspector informed me that the department had a few 'dinosaurs' who should be encouraged to take retirement. I suggested that I wrote down their names on a piece of paper and handed it to the inspector, who nodded assent. Staff and students tend to know those who are struggling or treading water, and external regulation can be used to prevent any further damage to students or indeed to the staff in question, who are often desperately looking for an honourable exit.

I now turn to the job of motivating students, which has over the past few years become much more difficult and is very likely to become even more difficult for at least two reasons. First, from 2013–14, all young people in England will have to remain in education or training until they are 17, and then to 18 in 2015–16. This poses acute difficulties for the FE and Skills sector because, as Alison Wolf pointed out in her trenchant review, 'as a society *we are failing at least 350,000 of our 16–18 year olds, year on year*, because they are fed on a diet of low-level vocational qualifications, with little or no value in the labour market' (2011: 53, original emphasis). And this is before the participation age is raised. Woodin *et al.*, who studied the raising of the school leaving age to 16 in 1972, warn that this time 'local planning on a universal and coherent basis will not be possible given the eclectic and widening range of semi-autonomous stakeholders in education', by which they mean academies, trusts, and so-called 'free' schools (2013: 14). Moreover, young people may again respond with mass absenteeism, particularly if the 350,000 or so 18 year olds without Maths or English at GCSE C grade or above are compelled to take and retake exams in these subjects until they pass.

The second reason is that the psychological contract, whereby students are promised high-quality and high-paid jobs to provide them with access to the good life if only they work hard enough to gain the necessary qualifications, has been broken by 'an exponential increase in the global supply of high-skilled, low-wage workers' (Brown *et al.*, 2011: 13). So a simple-minded policy of driving up the skills of the workforce, of the kind advocated by all three main political parties in the UK, will not solve this problem, 'because the job market can no longer bear the weight of social aspiration, especially when there is an international bidding war for middle-class jobs' (ibid.: 146). I will return to this issue at the end of this chapter.

I do not intend to offer here an overview of all the theories of motivation, because I still remember being seriously demotivated by having to study them as a student of psychology. Instead, I shall be unashamedly eclectic in choosing only those ideas and practices that I and my students have personally found useful in our professional and private lives; these approaches have worked for us and so, I hope, they will for you. I divide what follows into two main sections: psychological and economic approaches to motivation. I will then critically examine some of the assumptions behind government policy in this area, say a little about the structure of the British labour market, and end with a few general comments. But first I want to make the point that we as tutors behave in much the same way as our students. For example, educators have become used to students who are so 'mark hungry' that they pay no attention to the carefully crafted comments on their assignments, because they are desperate to find out what grade they have been awarded. Similarly, staff who have had their lesson observed are so keen to find out the grade they have been given that the comments of the observers tend to be ignored.

2) Psychological approaches

2.1) Jerome Bruner

My favourite psychologist, Jerome Bruner, chose to highlight two groups of learners who are renowned for inquiring intensively into all sorts of problems – young children in kindergarten and higher-degree students. What, we need to know, dampens the curiosity of so many between the ages of 5 and 25 and what part does formal schooling play in turning them off learning? For Bruner, the task of moving students to higher levels of thinking involved freeing them 'from the immediate control of environmental rewards and punishments' (1974: 406). His studies showed that students learn information by heart and come to 'depend upon being able to give back what is expected rather than to make it into something that relates to the rest of their cognitive life' (ibid.). In other words, they do not make the knowledge their own. Indeed, bulimic learning explains how students do not hold onto the knowledge for long enough for it to be incorporated into their existing frames of understanding; the information is 'crammed' or 'mugged up' (the language itself indicates that something distasteful is taking place) in the days before the exam, the brain holds on to sufficient detail for exam purposes, and then the knowledge is quickly evacuated, leaving nothing behind but the bad smell of inauthenticity. Our students are learning how to 'do' exams, how to display knowledge for public evaluation, but not how to grow intellectually.

Bruner's advice is that, although we as educators may need to use extrinsic rewards (such as gold stars, grades, and prizes) to get learning started, especially among the unengaged, as soon as possible we should foster the intrinsic need that we all feel (primary school children and higher-degree students alike) to deal competently with our environment. In this way, motivation becomes intrinsic and inner-directed rather than manipulated by parents or tutors, and the gratification comes from coping successfully with whatever life throws at us. Besides, persistence in problem-solving and learning through discoveries that we make ourselves bring their own intrinsic rewards. Students are 'now in a position to experience success and failure not as reward and punishment', but as some of the best means of growing and maintaining competence so that they can go beyond the information given to generate new ideas (Bruner, 1974: 408).

I have myself used this competence motive to challenge students to work harder to understand the theories of, say, Basil Bernstein or Michel Foucault, not for the sake of a monetary reward, not for promotion, not for distinctions nor any other extrinsic reward, but for the sheer pleasure of being in command of ideas they had previously failed to understand. Jane Shilling writes of 'the pure exhilaration of learning something new' (2012: 222).

2.2) *Carol Dweck*

Over the past five years I have taken every opportunity to ask students from sixth-form and FE colleges whether they consider high or low intelligence to be something that one is just born with (see Box 6.1). Do they believe, for instance, that nothing can be done to change their fate? In the words the students use: do they see themselves as either 'smart' or 'thick' from birth onwards? I have been unpleasantly surprised by the very high percentage of students (over 30 per cent in some institutions) in even our most successful colleges who, at the ages of 16 and 18, are wedded to the notion that intelligence is fixed; and the effect of this implicit theory on their motivation to work hard is very likely to be seriously detrimental.

Box 6.1: Just imagine!

I developed the hypothetical vignette about failure below from the work of Carol Dweck, and have tried it out with various groups of academic and vocational students aged 16–18. The aim of the exercise is to tease out from their responses their typical pattern of behaviour when faced with failure. A large minority of students answered the first question by blaming their teachers: for example, 'It's her job to motivate me'. Most students offer only one strategy in answer to the second question and perhaps it would be helpful for classes to discuss the broad range of possible strategies, including asking their teacher for help. I offer the vignette as an activity for use with your students.

Just imagine!
At the start of the new term, you find out that you have a new teacher whom you instantly take a liking to for your favourite subject. You feel you're quite good at this subject so you study for only an average amount of time before the first test. Afterwards, you think you did OK, even though there were some questions you found hard and didn't answer as well as you could have. Then the class get the test papers back and you find out you have scored only 48%, which in this subject means grade D.

a. What reasons would you give for your poor performance?

b. What would you do about it?

Source: loosely adapted from Blackwell *et al.*, 2007

Carol Dweck and her colleagues at Stanford University have for over 30 years been carrying out experiments where, for instance, they have compared achievement in mathematics between students who believed that intelligence is fixed and those who have been convinced that it is malleable, fluid, and can be increased through effort (see Blackwell *et al.*, 2007). The latter group showed greater motivation to succeed as well as achieving higher scores in maths. Although samples have tended to be small (around 45 in both control and experimental groups), these findings are encouraging in that they show that students' attitudes to intelligence can be changed for the better and, as a result, they are prepared to work hard consistently and become more interested in learning in general. When faced with failure, the students with an incremental view of intelligence increase their efforts, explore how they could tackle problems differently, and learn from the challenges they face. Those who think intelligence is stable and unchangeable are anxious to be seen as smart, and if they fail, are more likely to avoid challenges in the future and even to stop trying altogether. Some very able female students who have been complimented year on year on their ability have been known to fall apart when they first encounter failure.

The positive advice that stems from Dweck's work is that educators should strive to change their students' thinking on three issues. First, students need to internalize the notion that they can learn to be more intelligent, that their abilities and skills will steadily improve through practice, and that the harder they work, the smarter they will become. Second, they must realize that they are the ones who need to make an effort and they cannot leave all of the work of getting them through their exams to their tutors. The *students* must do the learning; after all, their tutors already have a degree or long vocational experience or both, and so possess the requisite knowledge and/or skills. Third, they need to see that mistakes are part and parcel of learning; all of our classrooms and workshops should offer a safe and supportive climate where errors can be admitted and learned from.[1] I phrased my remarks to students as follows: 'If you are already good at something, you can become even better through practice. If you are not good at something, you can improve significantly through hard work.'

I like Piaget's insight that the mistakes children make (for example, saying 'digged a hole' for 'dug a hole') provide a window into their way of thinking. (The past participle in English is usually formed by adding -ed to the present tense; children do not formulate their hypotheses in such formal language, but they are nonetheless imposing order onto a notoriously irregular language.) What is true for students is also true for educators: if tutors are to innovate and take risks in their teaching, then they too need a 'no blame' culture, where they can acknowledge mistakes without being graded as inadequate.

Students who have convinced themselves that, for instance, they 'just can't do maths' because they are not 'brainy' enough can prove very set and inflexible in their thinking. One argument that I have deployed with reasonable levels of success is to point to athletes, tennis players, and body-builders who, through hard training and dedication to their sport, slowly improve their personal-best performances. Ignoring the problems of arguing from analogy, I appeal to students as follows: if hard work and commitment work for your body, why should they not work for your brain?

2.3) Dylan Wiliam

Pierre Daninos, the French author of the Major Marmaduke Thompson novels, once defined a colleague as someone who has absolutely no talent but, inexplicably, does the same job as you. Dylan Wiliam and I were colleagues at the Institute of Education and he is ... the exception to Daninos's rule. Dylan proposes a radical way of thinking about motivation that locates the 'problem' neither in the students ('They're just not interested in learning', 'They have low aspirations'), nor in the teacher ('Her lessons are deadly dull', 'She just can't seem to motivate them'), but in the match between challenge and capability:

> ... if we see motivation not as a cause but as an outcome, an emergent property of getting the match between challenge and capability right, then if the student isn't motivated, that's just a signal that the teacher and learner need to try something different.
>
> Wiliam (2011: 150)

I have produced in Box 6.2 an exploration of this approach, by describing the outcomes when challenge and capability are both high or low or when one is high and the other is low.

Box 6.2: Motivation not a cause, but an outcome

Challenge	**Capability**	**Outcome**
Low	High	Boredom
High	Low	Anxiety
Low	Low	Apathy
High	High	'In the flow'

Let me give an example of each to help bring these useful ideas alive. When the intellectual challenge is low and the student's capability is high (when, for example, able students are asked to copy into their notebooks definitions presented in PowerPoint slides), then the outcome will be widespread boredom. But if the challenge is high and the student's capability is low (when, say, a student has scraped through GCSE exams by memorizing large chunks of information off by heart and is then asked in AS classes to interpret conflicting evidence over the death of the two princes in the tower), then the outcome is likely to be anxiety. Now let us move to a classroom or workshop where both the challenge and capability are low (when, for instance, Level 1 students are offered 'busy work' in order to control rather than teach them, such as colouring in or cutting out photographs from women's magazines), then the outcome will be apathy. A problem with this model is that students of low capability have no desirable outcomes: they are made either anxious or apathetic. So the challenge set for them must be both motivating and within their reach, perhaps with help from their tutor. That is the beauty of the concept of 'scaffolding', which combines the teacher's informed guidance with the student's growing capacity for independence – the scaffolding is removed and the building stands on its own. Finally, if the challenge and capability are both high (where, for example, talented student actors and singers become totally absorbed in a performance of *The Phantom of the Opera*), then they can be described as 'in the flow'. I remember David Beckham scoring that glorious goal in 2001 for England against Greece that enabled England to qualify for the World Cup in 2002. He was 'in the flow'.

2.4) Jean Lave and Etienne Wenger

I want to introduce at this stage the ideas of these two American anthropologists who have formulated a fascinating new theory of learning, because they will provide an important corrective to the narrative so far. For them, the knowledge and skills learned by apprentices provide important intrinsic rewards, 'but a deeper sense of the value of participation to the community and the learner lies in *becoming* part of the community' (1991: 111, original emphasis). Newcomers to a trade or profession gain a sense of belonging and an increasing sense of identity as a chef, beautician, or painter and decorator.[2] In this way, participation in the activities of the group plays a powerful role in the apprentices' motivation and identity: they begin to talk, think, and act like experts. Lave and Wenger add, however, the following powerful rider:

> Problems of schooling are not, at their most fundamental level, pedagogical. Above all, they have to do with the ways in which the community of adults reproduces itself, with the places that newcomers can or cannot find in such communities, and with relations that can or cannot be established between these newcomers and the cultural and political life of the community.
>
> (1991: 100)

In my words, they shift the focus from internal states of motivation and from the transmission of knowledge or the acquisition of a skill to the social issues of access, information, resources, and opportunities to participate in what they call a 'community of practice'. By that phrase, they mean informal groups of people who share expertise and passion for a particular activity, such as running a charity shop, being a member of a golf or cycling club, or belonging to a pressure group such as Amnesty International. The problems that Lave and Wenger point to – unequal access, selection and control, and class-based structures of opportunity – provide a convenient bridge to the second approach to motivation: the economic.

3) Economic approaches

Ewart Keep answers the question 'What makes individuals want to learn?' by suggesting that incentives can be grouped into two types. Type 1 (internal) incentives are generated within the education and training 'system'. Type 2 (external) incentives are created within the labour market and in society. Let us examine both types more closely.

Examples of Type 1 incentives are curricula and teaching methods that are supposed to create and maintain the intrinsic pleasures that come from learning; similarly, forms of assessment, such as those described in Chapter 8, which encourage deep learning and understanding of the subject as well as a desire to progress and continue learning. Other examples are generous and widely available opportunities to progress, and cultures of learning within FE and sixth-form colleges that celebrate achievement.

At first glance, it may appear that Type 1 incentives are uniformly strong, but a moment's reflection suggests otherwise. For example, learning opportunities are not distributed equitably throughout the country or across class, gender, and ethnic divisions; and very few organizations within the Learning and Skills sector have so far been judged to be outstanding in TLA by Ofsted. Moreover, all of the examples I have given of Type 1 incentives are decreasingly in the control of colleges, as the government takes increasing power over what should be included in academic and vocational curricula and how it should be taught.

When we turn to examples of Type 2 incentives, the list includes: wages, job satisfaction, opportunities to travel, promotion and career progression, higher social status attached to some occupations, cultural expectations (for instance, a high value placed on education and training by some parents and many ethnic communities), licences to practise that regulate access to particular jobs, and the skills needed for lifelong learning and for participating in areas of civil society such as politics, voluntary societies, sporting clubs, and amateur dramatics.

Providers of education and training, however, are virtually powerless to control any of these Type 2 incentives. Moreover, there are a number of policy assumptions that affect the pattern and strength of these incentives and which have proved resilient to criticism from academics precisely because they are shared by the main political parties. I shall examine four of them.

Assumption 1: *'Incentives are uniformly strong and positive across pretty much the entire labour market and learner population'* (Keep, 2012: 31).

Keep reviews the empirical evidence, which shows that 'low-paid workers often see limited point in training, since it is outside their experience, their employer does not require higher skills and the opportunities to progress are circumscribed' (ibid.: 33). He concludes that strong, positive incentives are associated with higher-status, higher-paid work, and that those in low-paid employment have few, if any, incentives to learn.

Assumption 2: *Investment in learning always leads to higher earnings.*

Policy in education and training is driven by a touching but naive belief that there is automatic progression from participating in education and training to earning higher wages, greater productivity, and improved international competitiveness. The long, allegedly causal sequence, which apparently always works, is set out in Box 6.3. In the minds of politicians and policymakers, this is what they call 'a win-win-win scenario' for individuals, employers, and society.

Unfortunately, there can be, and often are, serious problems at every transition point in the sequence of eight stages shown in the box. At the first stage, for instance, students may enrol in apprenticeships or A level courses but there is no guarantee that they will pass; some fail or drop out for reasons that are beyond the ability of colleges or employers to influence, when, say, they, or their partner or a family member, fall seriously ill. Similarly, at the third, fourth, and fifth stages, qualifications act as a proxy for skill, and many workers have developed skills that are not made use of by their employer. In Keep's words, 'the link between skills, productivity and wages is massively more complex and subject to influence by a wider range of forces and structural arrangements than this simple formulation suggests' (ibid.: 32).

Box 6.3: From learning to earning and beating the world

Participation in Education and Training → Achievement → Qualifications → Skill → Higher Wages → Higher Productivity → Increased Competitiveness → Winning the Global Race NB: There is no automatic progression at each transition point, and students can, for instance, fall at the first hurdle – through no fault of their college, employer, or tutor.

Source: freely adapted from Keep (2012: 32)

Some of the interactive factors that need to be taken into account are: the employee's motivation and competencies, the structure of opportunities in local labour markets, the extent to which the labour market is regulated, and the use made of the employee's skills by employers.

Assumption 3: *Policy initiatives can swiftly transform education and training.*

There is a serious mismatch between the timetables of politicians, who understandably want hard evidence of improvements before they face the electorate in a general election in five years' time, and those of educators who know from hard experience that it can take ten years to turn a college around, never mind a whole system. As Walter Müller puts it in Chapter 5, 'Education takes time'. It is difficult to see how colleges or other providers of education and training could use either Type 1 or Type 2 incentives to create in the short term the 'step changes' or the 'radical and lasting transformations' that politicians demand. Changing the curriculum, teaching methods, and forms of assessment takes years to plan and many more years to enact successfully across thousands of institutions. Similarly, what can colleges do to change Type 2 incentives, particularly if they are serving a depressed area with limited employment opportunities and a predominance of poorly paid, unskilled, and insecure jobs? When I was studying youth unemployment in the North East of England in the mid-1980s, some young lads were interviewed for a casual job on a building site. They were asked only two questions: 'Do you have a pair of boots?' and 'Can you start tomorrow?' Their GCSEs were so irrelevant to their search for employment that they did not even bother to return to school to find out the grades they had achieved in these examinations.

Assumption 4: *Low-paid workers lack aspiration.*

People's aspirations are shaped, in the main, by their family background, educational history, and the structure of opportunities in their area. In many localities, the job opportunities are so poor that they lock families into long-term poverty. I am not discussing here unemployed people on benefits, but full- and part-time workers who earn their poverty. When the incentives of Type 1 and Type 2 are weak, people are forced, against their wishes and hopes, to adjust their aspirations downwards. Again, Keep reviews the evidence and concludes: 'the culture that policy wishes to change is rooted not necessarily in some form of self-defeatism on the part of the low paid, but rather within the structural features of the labour market, and the nature and distribution of the job opportunities that are actually open to them' (ibid.: 42). This makes a nonsense of the policy assumption that, if the government continues to increase the supply of better-qualified workers, it will be matched by an increase in the number of well-paid, high-quality jobs. Supply does not create its own demand.

Box 6.4: 2,500 apply for 80 jobs

Evening Chronicle

chroniclelive.co.uk

SATURDAY, FEBRUARY 2, 2013

TESCO receive a call every 49 seconds for vacancies

2,500 APPLY FOR 80 JOBS

MICHAEL BROWN

THOUSANDS of people have applied for 80 new jobs created at a new Tyneside supermarket.

More than 2,500 job hunters flooded an employment hotline for the new Tesco in Gateshead.

Company bosses – who have kept back a number of jobs for the long-term unemployed – said the amazing response showed the strong work ethic on Tyneside.

Mum-of-four Jacqueline Knight, pictured, was one of those trying to find work after months on the dole.

Full Story – Pages 2&3

Box 6.4 is an extract from the front page of *The Evening Chronicle* in Newcastle upon Tyne for Saturday, 2 February 2013. It tells the story of Tesco's plan to build a new supermarket in Gateshead, thus creating 80 new jobs: 'More than 2,500 job hunters flooded an employment hotline', so much so that the firm was receiving a call every 49 seconds. There is no problem with the work ethic in the North East of England.

4) The UK labour market

At various points in the preceding pages I have made reference to either the 'structure of opportunities' or the 'structural features of the labour market'. I want now to explain in more detail exactly what is meant by those phrases.

A levels used to provide (and still do for most) a golden staircase to higher education and to high-status, well-paid employment, but in this country we have still not produced a prestigious equivalent for those students who want to follow a vocational, rather than an academic, career. There are indeed a few highly sought-after apprenticeships, but most are of poor quality compared with their counterparts in Germany. The UK labour market is one of the least regulated among the developed nations, with politicians from all parties claiming that our labour market flexibility brings untold benefits but apparently no costs. The constant demand by employers for British workers to be more flexible has resulted in more than one million workers in the retail, catering, health, and education sectors on zero-hour contracts, where they work on standby and so cannot be certain of getting the minimum number of hours per week to ensure financial security for their families. It is shameful that so many universities and FE colleges make use of these 'flexible' contracts, which 'mean workers were unable to make financial or employment plans for the year or even the month ahead' (Butler, 2013: 13). Far from seeing such flexibility as a mark of a strong economy, Larry Elliott compared the powerlessness of workers on zero-hour contracts who have, for example, no rights to sick pay, to Marx's famous description of the 'reserve army of labour' (Elliott, 2013: 19).

Moreover, there is a robust body of evidence which shows that, while the labour market offers high returns in terms of wages to university degrees, it offers very low returns to vocational qualifications at levels 1 and 2. As I mentioned in the introduction to this chapter, Alison Wolf summed up this body of work as follows: '*many English low-level vocational qualifications currently have little to no apparent labour market value*' (2011: 32, original emphasis). Indeed, some of the returns to National Vocational Qualifications (NVQs) at Level 2 are actually negative; that is, those with this qualification earn less than those without it.

Add to this mix the fact that 'in 2006 there were around 7.35 million jobs that did not require any qualifications, but only around 2.47 million workers without qualifications' (Felstead *et al.*, 2007: 62). These figures suggest that, despite the relentless rhetoric of politicians about the imminent disappearance of unskilled jobs, such jobs are still plentiful. They also make the point that there are millions of workers in Britain with skills and qualifications but who cannot find jobs where these would be used. Lloyd *et al.* (2008) calculated that no less than 22 per cent of the British workforce and almost 33 per cent of female workers are in low-paid jobs. A report by the Resolution Foundation brings the story up to date by suggesting 'the emergence of a two-tier workforce in Britain, in which the lower tier is increasingly characterized by low-paid, low-skilled work which is often temporary, part-time or self-employed' (Whittaker, 2013). According to this report, 5.1 million of all employees (21 per cent) are low paid, and 3 million of these were women in 2013.

In the past 25 years, the youth labour market has collapsed, with around 35 per cent of 16–17 year olds now in employment, when it was almost 70 per cent of the same age group in the mid-1980s, when I was studying youth unemployment in the North East of England. Our 16 and 17 year olds summarized the choices open to them with the phrase: 'Shit jobs, govvie schemes, or the dole'. Their response to my question about the availability of job openings locally was: 'When one door closes, another shuts' (Coffield *et al.*, 1986).

I could continue in the same vein by discussing the downward cascade of graduate labour, which now takes over those jobs at an intermediate level that were previously the preserve of non-graduates;[3] or by referring to the constant 'churning' of low-paid workers who carry out the dirty jobs of society for as long as they can stand it – they then retreat into unemployment to recover, before being forced into another dirty job through financial necessity. In sum, the shape of the British economy is often depicted as an 'hour-glass', with the skilled occupations in the middle in serious decline. I hope sufficient has been said to justify the conclusion that the incentives to learn at the bottom end of the British labour market are so weak or non-existent that they create a major obstacle for colleges or private providers trying to motivate young people and adults. Hence the need for honest, up-to-date, and impartial information, advice, and guidance to be given to all young people.

5) Final comments

In this chapter, I have presented four psychological approaches to motivation and two types of incentives; I have also examined four assumptions that underpin much of government policy in this area and found them wanting; and I ended by giving the briefest of introductions to some of the baleful characteristics of the British labour market that are relevant to this debate. I want now to draw together the main strands of this chapter in a few general remarks.

First, there are a large number of interesting theories of motivation that I have not even mentioned – for example, Maslow's well-known hierarchy of needs (from hunger to self-actualization), Herzberg's two-factor theory (motivators such as challenging work and 'hygiene' factors, for instance, job security), and Alderfer's three groups of core needs (safety, personal relations, and growth). These have been omitted not because I think them uninteresting or unimportant, but rather because I did not want this chapter to become tiresome. Nor am I seeking to present a comprehensive review of all theories of motivation, but rather a brief, highly selective introduction to those ideas that have appealed most to me and my students.

Even so, I hope I have said enough to make the point that understanding the motivation of either students or tutors is a multifaceted, complex, and confusing task that calls for a fusion of insights from psychology, sociology, and economics. I have tried in this chapter to separate these out in a linear way, but senior staff in colleges, and educators in classrooms or workshops, are presented with a jumble of indistinct influences of varying strength; and they quickly have to come to a view about what influences are the most salient so that they can act in the best interests of their staff or students. This has been one of the leitmotivs running through this book: the messy, elusive, and unpredictable complexity and ambiguity of TLA; in contrast, successive governments have treated TLA as uncomplicated, effortless, and, above all, controllable. The unemployed 16 and 17 year olds I interviewed had a far sharper understanding of the harsh conditions at the bottom end of the labour market than I did; I hope that none of the tutors in the FE and Skills sector is similarly out of touch.

In adopting a more integrated approach to motivation by amalgamating both psychological and economic arguments, I have become indebted to the work of Ewart Keep, as this chapter has repeatedly testified. He is surely right in laying much of the blame for the problems we face squarely at the feet of the policies of successive administrations:

> government's fundamental misdiagnosis of the nature of the 'skills problem' – that it revolves around supply alone, rather than the complex interplay between skills supply, the demand for skills within the labour market and economy, and how skills are deployed within the product process.
>
> (2012: 25)

An emphasis solely on the supply side, such as we have seen for the past 30 years, has produced neither social mobility nor economic prosperity but some of the best-educated dole queues in the world.

These structural conditions are clearly not under the control of colleges or training providers. So it is perverse for Ofsted to suggest that in future it 'will shine a spotlight on the destination of learners' (Coffey, 2012: 17), as if colleges could reasonably be held responsible for the failings of local labour markets, which vary so markedly. We need to change the structure of opportunities rather than blame individual victims by claiming that their lack of aspirations is the root of the problem. If anything, it is the aspirations of government and business leaders that are too low.

Certainly, colleges need to discontinue the provision of low-level vocational qualifications that have little or no purchase in the marketplace and cease offering courses that are in their financial interest rather than in the best interests of students. Instead, they need to provide young people with honest, up-to-date, and accurate information, advice, and guidance. There is a desperate need for new, clear, and well-signposted progression routes out of poverty and dead-end jobs. That means putting some education back into FE by offering incentives to all those 16–19 year olds without a C grade at GCSE level in English and Maths ('the most generally useful and valuable vocational skills', according to Alison Wolf, 2011: 11), as well as providing high-status vocational courses for those young people neither in apprenticeships nor in quality employer-led programmes, and supporting the most needy by restoring generous grants such as Educational Maintenance Allowances. It also means persuading many more employers to offer high-quality apprenticeships, and creating not just more jobs but high-quality jobs. The education 'system' should no longer be expected to carry the can for the long-standing political failure to introduce an economic plan for high-skill, high-paid jobs, with businesses being rewarded for moving into higher-quality goods and services that would first use and then extend the skills of British workers. With such strategies in place, people of all ages would see the value of investing in vocational education and training: economic incentives could then be aligned with psychological approaches to provide the motivation that is currently lacking.

Notes

[1] Nietzsche commented interestingly as follows on the career of the Italian painter Raphael, who compared his early, rather mediocre efforts with the sublime works of the great masters Michelangelo and da Vinci in order to learn how to paint as well as them:

'Don't talk about giftedness, inborn talents! One can name all kinds of great men who were not very gifted. They *acquired* greatness, became geniuses (as we put it) through qualities about whose lack no man aware of them likes to speak: all of them had that diligent seriousness of a craftsman, learning first to construct the parts properly before daring to make a great whole.' Quoted by Alain de Botton (2001: 226, original emphasis).

[2] See Note 5 at the end of Chapter 2 for a very brief explanation of Lave and Wenger's theory of situated learning.

[3] '... the proportion of degree-qualified 24–29 year olds in the UK who are working in jobs that do not require this qualification is 26 per cent' (UKCES, 2011: 20).

References

Blackwell, L.S., Trzesniewski, K.H., and Dweck, C.S. (2007) 'Implicit theories of intelligence predict achievement across an adolescent tradition: A longitudinal study and an intervention'. *Child Development*, January/February, 78 (1), 246–63.

Brown, P., Lauder, H., and Ashton, D. (2011) *The Global Auction: The broken promises of education, jobs and incomes.* Oxford: Oxford University Press.

Bruner, J.S. (1974) *Beyond the Information Given.* London: Allen and Unwin.

Butler, S. (2013) 'Union criticises "murky world" of casual contracts in universities'. *The Guardian*, 5 September, 13.

Coffey, M. (2012) 'Promoting social mobility and securing economic growth – how the further education and skills sector can help bridge the gap and lead the way'. The first Ofsted Annual Lecture in Learning and Skills, 12 July, City and Islington College, Ofsted.

Coffield, F., Borrill, C., and Marshall, S. (1986) *Growing Up at the Margins: Young adults in the North East.* Milton Keynes: Open University Books.

de Botton, A. (2001) *The Consolations of Philosophy.* London: Penguin Books.

Dweck, C.S. (1999) *Self-Theories: Their role in motivation, personality and development.* Philadelphia, PA: Psychology Press.

Elliott, L. (2013) 'Why stop at zero hours? Why not revive child labour?'. *The Guardian*, 5 August, 19.

Felstead, A., Gallic, D., Green, F., and Zhou, Y. (2007) *Skills at Work: 1986 to 2006.* Oxford: Oxford University, Skope.

Frayn, M. (1999) *Headlong.* London: Faber and Faber.

Keep, E.J. (2012) 'Further education – the role of incentives'. In K. Hermannsson (ed.), *Further Education, the Scottish Labour Market and the Wider Economy.* Edinburgh: David Hume Institute, Occasional Paper No. 94, 29–51.

Lave, J. and Wenger, E. (1991) *Situated Learning: Legitimate peripheral participation.* Cambridge: Cambridge University Press.

Lloyd, C., Mason, G., and Mayhew, K. (eds) (2008) *Low Wage Work in the United Kingdom.* New York: Russell Sage Foundation.

McCarthy, P. (2001) *McCarthy's Bar: A journey of discovery in Ireland.* London: Spectre.

Shilling, J. (2012) *The Stranger in the Mirror.* London: Vintage Books.

UK Commission for Employment and Skills (UKCES) (2011) *The Youth Inquiry: Employers' perspectives on tackling youth unemployment.* Wath-upon-Dearre: UKCES.

Whittaker, M. (2013) *Low Pay Britain 2013*. London: Resolution Foundation.

Wiliam, D. (2011) *Embedded Formative Assessment*. Bloomington, IN: Solution Tree.

Wolf, A. (2011) *Review of Vocational Education*. London: DfE.

Woodin, T., McCulloch, G., and Cowan, S. (2013) 'Raising the participation age in historical perspective: Policy learning from the past?'. *British Educational Research Journal*, 1–19.

Chapter 7

Teaching and learning in context ...

with a little help from the web

Cristina Costa

> *If we teach today as we taught yesterday we rob our children of tomorrow.*
>
> Dewey (1916; in Dewey, 2008)

1) Introduction

This chapter focuses on the design of learning contexts in formal education. It deals with my experiences in trying to design learning activities that have the potential to create contexts for learning that are meaningful and authentic to students. In doing so, it offers a set of simple questions that aim to guide educators in the development of learning contexts in web-based environments. I advocate the use of the social web as a space for the participation and socialization of learning, and as a way of giving teaching a new dynamic by creating new forms of assessment.

2) Learning contexts: What are they?

Learning contexts can be broadly defined as environments that feature a set of characteristics to enable individuals to learn within and across social spaces. Learning contexts provide a more flexible structure in which individuals partake in different activities that will eventually inform their own learning. In this sense, learning contexts display similarities with learning in communities or guilds, which was a common practice prior to the rise of mass education in the nineteenth century (Dias de Figueiredo, 2005). Learning was contextualized in the activities individuals had to carry out or the issues they had to address as part of their daily tasks. Skilled workers learned through apprenticeships, with the workplace serving as the obvious context. In these cases, learning was situated in real settings (Lave and Wenger, 1991). Learning was authentic and therefore had direct meaning for the learner. The Industrial Revolution came to change that. As new types of job demanding a higher rate of literacy increased, there was a need to devise new forms of educating individuals: faster, more often, and with a specific set of skills. The educational system had to adapt. It developed a model that bore strong resemblances to the factory (Attwell, 2007). Mass education aimed to standardize teaching through strict curricula that stripped learning of real-world contexts.

This legacy is still, to some extent, felt today. It is not only visible in the learning spaces that most educational institutions offer to their learners and which often resemble the assembly lines in factories, but it is also noticeable in the curricula and assessment strategies through which teaching and learning are regulated. Learning contexts were thus ignored (Dias de Figueiredo and Afonso, 2006). As a result, learning became an activity with little relevance to the outside world. This is an issue that manifests itself more today than it did even 20 or 30 years ago, because the needs of business and commerce have changed and our educational system has not moved at the same pace. Hence, it no longer seems to provide an efficient answer to all of those industries and workplaces that rely strongly on digital technologies.

This leads to some fundamental questions:

- What is the obligation on education and educators to keep up with the times?
- How can we help learners, who carry a computer in their pockets (mobile phones) and have access to knowledge at their fingertips, relate to TLA?
- What is our duty as educators to prepare learners for this new digital world?

These are questions I constantly ask myself as an educator. This leads me to contemplate the current network society (Castells, 2000) as a source of inspiration for new forms of TLA. In the process of thinking of digital technologies for education, I have come to realize that the acquisition and reproduction of information is no longer the main required form of learning. Information can be accessible from multiple sources and at any time. Content is not learning. However, an appropriate context can facilitate learning.

The digital economy and society in which our learners are embedded needs people who are knowledgeable, but most importantly who have the ability to find and produce new knowledge – that is, who are 'knowledge-able' (Wesch, 2011). This is the age of problem-solvers, of people who can think creatively and work across different settings and with different groups of people. In the network society (Castells, 2000), individuals need to be ready to be flexible and to collaborate to solve emerging problems for which traditional education might not have prepared them. Learning in context not only explores learners' creative approaches to problem-solving, but it also provides them with the flexibility they need to put those approaches into practice.

Creating learning contexts means letting learners explore environments that exist beyond the classroom and giving them the freedom to experiment with different forms of learning (from self-study to joint projects). The design of learning contexts also means placing learners at the centre of their learning by making them actively involved. The emphasis on context over content (Dias de Figueiredo, 2012) means that content becomes a direct by-product of the learners' engagement with their own learning. The social web with all its interactive features helps create dynamic learning contexts, thus allowing learners to engage in much richer and wider settings than those the traditional classroom can provide.

3) Creating learning contexts: The role of the social and participatory web

The social and participatory web consists of web and communicating networks, applications, and environments in which individuals act as active participants and contributors of information and knowledge, personal views, and opinions. The social and participatory web has started to change the way individuals congregate and socialize. The richness of these connections can be seen in the artefacts created through the conversations and collaborative endeavours developed in those collective spaces, and the learning that is attained through those processes. From those contexts, content emerges as a product of peer participation. This represents a major shift in social and professional practices. In education, for instance, this offers a new set of possibilities for TLA.

The web is probably the most impressive technological phenomenon of the past 100 years and one that is effectively changing people's social and professional practices. It also shows how individuals learn and represent their learning. For instance, a close look at a video channel such as YouTube lets us know that both mature and young learners turn to this medium to teach and learn from others. YouTube has not only become the largest user-generated content video system (Cha *et al.*, 2007), but it is also the second biggest search engine on the web. According to YouTube's blog (n.d.), more than 60 hours of user-generated video are being uploaded to YouTube every minute, with more than 6 billion users accessing it every day. Individuals are taking to this new way of accessing and sharing information (Duffy, 2012).

It should therefore encourage us, as educators, to ponder how we can exploit these practices to make our classrooms more authentic. The same applies to the use of social networking sites and their potential as a support for connected forms of learning (Greenhow, 2011) around a given topic (Paolillo, 2008). There are also other approaches to collecting information and sharing one's learning, such as social bookmarking – a tool that allows us to list 'favourite websites' and share bookmarks of online resources with other web users (Churchill *et al.*, 2009) – and blogs (online journals with interactive features such as readers' comments) to name a few. These new tools and the learning opportunities they provide can bridge classroom learning with 'real-life' activities, thus making formal education a more meaningful activity for students whose social and communication practices are increasingly embedded in the so-called digital age.

At the beginning of the twenty-first century, Prensky initiated the much-popularized discussion on the types of web users with the metaphor of digital natives and digital immigrants (2001a and 2001b). It focused mainly on the age of the users and their computer competencies. The generational gap discussion has proved popular, supposedly because it is closely aligned with opinions that educators generally have of younger generations. This dichotomy is, however, too simplistic to explain how individuals are making use of the web. White and Cornu (2011) have since challenged this approach with a new metaphor, that of digital visitors and digital residents. They have tried to move the debate forward by devising a new topology that places an emphasis on motivation and engagement rather than on the age or ability of individuals. In this vein, they assert that digital residents 'see the Web primarily as a network of individuals or clusters of individuals who in turn generate content' (ibid.). To digital residents, 'the Web is a place to express opinions, a place in which relationships can be formed and extended' (ibid.). On the other side of the scale, there are the digital visitors to whom 'the Web is simply one of many tools they can use to achieve a certain goal' (ibid.). Hence, digital visitors are 'users, not members, of the Web and place little value in belonging online' (ibid.). The digital visitor/digital resident metaphor is more inclusive of the different ways individuals approach and use the social and participatory web. It looks at the frequency of use and explores the needs and motivations of individuals for using the web. Although this metaphor still offers a binary interpretation of a more complex reality (Harris *at al.*, 2013), it does provide us, as educators, with a basic understanding of how individuals are taking to the social and participatory web for learning and engagement with their peers. As a result, it is of paramount importance that education voluntarily takes into account the value of the online practices that individuals are starting to adopt outside, and explores the possibilities of the social and participatory web in providing meaningful opportunities and skills for (lifelong) learning. In promoting learning that is relevant to the current society, educators have a responsibility to promote contemporary forms of learning. Thus, it is also our role to promote digital forms of learning to learners who are less predisposed to engage with the social and participatory web.

Industry and services alike are also quickly recognizing the impact the social and participatory web can have on their practices. As a response to the emergent phenomenon that the participatory web represents in the workplace, there is a growing tendency for business and other sectors of society to start embedding it in their working strategy. This implies the introduction of new forms of internal communication and information management (Gray *et al.*, 2011), thus renewing working cultures. The twenty-first-century workplace is in constant transformation, and the participatory web is one of its main influencing factors. It affects the way individuals engage with, and are aware of, the needs of their target audiences. Turning to the web for customer service and customer opinion are now common practices, for example, if we are searching for a new product. We seek other customers' opinions before we purchase something, and we in turn are asked to review a product or service after we have tried it. Participating online is becoming entrenched in both our working and social habits. This leads me to ask:

- What is the significance of the social and participatory web for formal education?
- How can we appropriate the practices that are emerging in the outside world to make learning in classrooms an activity with relevance beyond the school walls?

In a nutshell, learning contexts rest on the fundamental principle of learning as a social process (Conole, 2010). The web as a space for participation can enable social interactions that are meaningful for learning in and out of formal education.

Given that education should reflect and serve the society in which it is situated, it is important that we, as educators, create learning contexts that are meaningful to the learner. This requires us to think of learning as an activity that puts a strong emphasis on the social, cultural, and economic contexts that frame the society for which the learner needs to be prepared. Currently, this means thinking of the digital technologies that abound in our social and professional spheres.

The above section has aimed to present the rationale for embedding technology in our teaching. The next section focuses on the design of learning contexts with the support of the social and participatory web. It provides a set of questions that aims to guide educators in the development of activities that contextualize learning by placing the learner centre stage; that is, the individual becomes the main actor and an active participant in his or her own learning.

4) Creating learning contexts: What to consider

This section offers a simple set of guiding principles in the form of questions that can be applied to the design of learning activities supported by the social and participatory web. I have employed and refined this set of guiding principles as part of my experiences with curriculum design using the social and participatory web. It provides a flexible structure that can be used across disciplines and by different areas of learning to cater for the creation of stimulating learning contexts. Moreover, the guiding principles are the result of an ongoing, reflexive action-research cycle and will therefore be accounted for here in a narrative form to explain more fully the practices of the practitioner-researcher, in this case, me.

4.1) The easy mistake: Lack of planning

It is very easy to misunderstand the role the social and participatory web can play in learning and how it should therefore be introduced as part of a given learning activity. As educators, we want our classes to be dynamic, meaningful, and also enjoyable, so that they can have an impact on the learning journeys of our learners. The integration of the social and participatory web can be, and often is, regarded as an element of curriculum innovation that has the potential to engage learners and boost their motivation. While this chapter does not aim to contradict research and practice that support such views, on the contrary, it is my goal to make it clear that using technology for the sake of using it has very little value as part of any learning and teaching experience. In fact, it can have serious negative consequences. It is the meaning, value, and purpose that the educator attributes to the use of the social and participatory web for learning, and which, in return, the learners adopt, that will make a real difference to how and what people absorb. I learned my lesson the hard way as I once set out to use technology in the classroom without a clear idea of what I was using it for. Blogs were one of the first web tools I used in my classes. Back in those days, in 2004, blogs were still seen as a novelty for TLA. As a new tool, blogs provided a fresh approach to writing, and as such it seemed like an exciting activity. With only that as a plan for integrating the social and participatory web in the curriculum, the project failed dramatically. It showed my inexperience, both as a teacher and as a web enthusiast, who had yet to understand the dynamics and philosophies underpinning the web for creating participation and deep learning. Nonetheless, this was a useful experience, which has become a landmark in my practice and it has helped me to develop and grow as a practitioner.

The project failed because it was too vague an idea – an unplanned attempt to diversify my teaching of English as a Foreign Language and thus introduce something new into my class. A blog was created and learners were asked to use it because it would be a good opportunity for them to practise their writing in a foreign language. And without further guidance to motivate their writing, not much happened. Although the idea might have been good – the intention certainly was – the outcome was a disaster, because there was no forward thinking about what the learners were supposed to achieve with this activity, nor were there, for that matter, clear guidelines regarding how they were supposed to engage with it or how their learning would be validated through assessment. This disappointing experience became one of the most meaningful lessons in my career so far, one that stimulated many questions about my practice and much-needed reflection. In the process of analysing this and future events, I decided to keep a record of my experiences in designing new learning activities and students' feedback on them. I also developed a set of simple questions that work as guiding principles for me when designing new learning activities involving the social and participatory web. I was not ready to give up on it as a tool for learning because I knew it worked for me. I was now on a journey to learn how I could make it work for others, especially my students.

4.2) The questions we need to ask ourselves to plan for context

The questions below derive from a long, reflective journey about my own career as an educator and curriculum designer. They have helped my practice as an educator in two ways: first, they give a clear, simple structure with which to work when designing learning contexts; second, they allow me to translate tacit knowledge into explicit knowledge, especially when designing curricula collaboratively.

These questions aim to stimulate reflection about the practice of teachers in refining educational activities to create learning contexts with relevance to the learner. The questions presented are supported with examples from my own portfolio of practice.

Curious as it may sound, technology should be the last element to consider when it comes to designing learning contexts with the support of the social and participatory web. Web tools should be regarded as elements to support the educational process; a medium through which learning can be fostered rather than a purpose in itself, as in the example of failure I described above. So it is crucial for educators to try to answer the questions listed below, before they decide on which technology to use.

4.2.1) Who are the learners with whom I will be working?

Knowing our audience is crucial to our understanding of what support there needs to be in place for learners to thrive and take ownership of their learning. This does not mean, however, that educators and curriculum designers should underestimate what learners can achieve, as will be illustrated in the examples below. On the contrary, it is important to acknowledge the strengths of the learners as well as recognizing the areas in which they will require further support. In identifying who the learners are, we should not limit their experience to our perceptions of what they might achieve, but rather allow them to test the limits of their own capabilities. Learning contexts serve that purpose. They aim to unleash the potential of learners beyond their own expectations as they come to play an active role in their own learning process. It is thus the educator's role to harness that potential by creating stimulating challenges. In trying to get a better understanding of the learners, educators should be able to prepare, support, and adjust their teaching approaches to foster engaging learning contexts.

4.2.2) What do I want the learners to learn and achieve?

Clearly defining what students will achieve at the end of a learning experience allows educators to set meaningful challenges that will ultimately become the learning contexts in which learners will hopefully become involved. Achievement is often associated with some kind of measurement. In formal education, that usually translates into assessment. It is important to make close, visible links between what is being learned and what learners are expected to achieve – that is, on what they will be assessed. The principle of linking learning activities with assessment is known in the literature as 'constructive alignment' (Biggs, 2003), and aims to provide learners with a coherent structure for their learning. This is a very important principle to follow when creating authentic learning contexts. Hence, the assessment should be embedded within the learning process as a continuous thread that guides and validates that learning throughout.

4.2.3) How do I want the learners to engage with their learning?

No less important for the development of learning contexts is the way learners will engage with their learning. As pointed out in previous sections, learning contexts are situated in social spaces and therefore involve social interaction (Conole, 2010). Deciding how learners will engage in their learning has a pivotal role in establishing meaningful contexts. Defining how learners will be actively involved in pursuing their own learning journey – be it by working in groups and/or in pairs, collaborating within or beyond the classroom, or connecting with extended networks and/or specialized communities – enables the educator to start preparing the ground for what can potentially become a fertile learning context. It is the role of educators to plant the seeds to stimulate the intellectual growth of the learner. Hence, it is of paramount importance that the learning context is set within a learning space where learners can exercise their creativity.

Once learners have been acknowledged as the main actors in the learning process, once learning outcomes and assessment have been defined, and once the activities that support the learning have been agreed upon, educators should consider what technology they can use to support the creation of a meaningful learning context. The question that remains is the following.

4.2.4) What technology can I use to create a stimulating learning environment?

The use of technology should show learners how to engage with their learning and with each other, as well as with their social environment. For technology to gain a meaningful place in the learner's experiences, it should not only support but also enhance those experiences.

Web technology is transforming the way we communicate, socialize, shop, work, and even learn (Attwell, 2007), and it adds a new dimension to TLA in that it promotes the learners as networked, informed, creative citizens who participate in multiple spaces. In this sense, technology can have a transformative role in the field of education, because it not only helps with the accessibility of new tools, but also changes approaches to TLA and the mindsets associated with it (Wetzel, 2001). Although technology may have opened up a new set of possibilities and opportunities for TLA, the human element often creates barriers to effective development, because changing practices and adopting new methodologies present a considerable challenge to one's working culture.

This major shift in educational thinking and practice that technology makes possible is grounded in social pedagogies aimed at the personalization of learning. Hence, it is difficult, if not impossible, to stipulate which technology to use. Rather than focusing on the technology, educators should focus on how they want to socialize learners into interactive forms of learning and teaching, and then select technologies that suit that purpose. Technology should be seen as a means to an end, not an end in itself.

5) Examples of learning contexts

The section that follows focuses on real teaching and learning practices on the web that led to the development of the four questions listed above. My decision to describe them here is an attempt to contextualize these guiding principles with concrete examples in order to make this approach more appealing to educators who might be willing to try this design format. The case studies were compiled with the support of diary notes that I have been in the habit of making throughout my practice.

5.1) First challenge: The motivation challenge

5.1.1) Who are the learners with whom I will be working?

The learners on this course were young adult students, mostly male, enrolled on an English as a Foreign Language (advanced level) course as part of their training in one of the branches of the Portuguese military forces. The students were competent in English, computer literate, but not highly motivated to learn in a traditional classroom setting. I introduced a challenge in the second week of classes as a response to the learners' lack of motivation.

5.1.2) What do I want the learners to learn and achieve?

The English language course aimed to help them achieve an advanced level of writing and communication in a foreign language. It also aimed to promote the learning of the specialized terminology used within the organization. Although the measurement of their learning was done through standardized tests, I felt it was important to provide learners with challenges that would increase their motivation to develop their proficiency.

5.1.3) How do I want the learners to engage with their learning?

Language learning has a strong social element associated with it. Thus, it was important to try to establish an environment where the learning of English could be stimulated. As part of the process, I wanted them to learn by working in small teams. I also wanted the entire class to collaborate as one big team. And it was important, too, that they could express themselves and reflect on their learning, so that their new learning could be publicly acknowledged both by their peers and by me, the teacher.

5.1.4) What technology can I use to create a more stimulating learning environment?

With that in mind, I posed this challenge to the class. It consisted of studying the life of the last living naval aviator in the navy, now a retired admiral. Their task was to work collaboratively on the development of a biography that would represent the working life of the chosen naval officer. The work was to be done in English and to be published on a website created for that purpose. The website, a tangible outcome of the students' learning and effort, aimed to pay respect and show admiration for the work and achievements of this naval officer. It served as a tool for engagement, as learners worked in small teams to gather information about the naval officer, learn the naval terminology associated with his career, and write the biography before coming together as a class to write a final version of his working life and achievements. The biography was uploaded onto the website that was created for this purpose. Students then decided to republish their work in a Wikipedia entry. The learners were also requested to write messages of appreciation to the person they had studied. As a form of practising their written and spoken English, they recorded short audio messages in a podcast website.

Another class in the school learned of the activity and asked to join in. Their contribution to the activity consisted of a photo-story that described the biography that the learners had written. All of the learners' activities were compiled in a website as part of the project and shared with the admiral himself whose career they had studied. A wider audience was also given access to the website and they contributed their appreciative comments. This served to validate the learners' work and they became rightly proud of their achievements.

5.2) Reflections about the motivation challenge

The motivation challenge was very successful in that it provided learners with a meaningful learning goal in which they could take ownership of their learning and use their creativity to achieve that goal. The real sense of achievement and learning came when their work was exhibited on a multimedia website that was validated by an external audience, which commented favourably on it. By shifting the learners' practices from content users to content producers, a meaningful, authentic learning context was created. It became a multidimensional social activity that was extended to peers in other classrooms and also provided links to the outside world as other people accessed and commented on their work.

5.3) Second challenge: The pronunciation challenge

5.3.1) Who are the learners with whom I will be working?

This challenge involved working with mature learners enrolled on an elementary-level English as a Foreign Language course. As is typical of this kind of learner, making mistakes in front of their peers is not thought to be an option. This made it hard to get them to speak.

5.3.2) What do I want the learners to learn and achieve?

The goal was to get these Portuguese-speaking learners to achieve elementary proficiency in English. It was important for them to learn how to pronounce words and speak in short sentences in order to practise speaking.

5.3.3) How do I want the learners to engage with their learning?

Language learning is by nature a social activity, and speaking is an act of communication. As a teacher, I wanted my learners to start communicating with each other in the foreign language. I wanted to encourage a culture of sharing so that they could learn and practise with one another other without being afraid of making mistakes or being laughed at.

5.3.4) What technology can I use to create a more stimulating learning environment?

This class started in January and finished just after St Valentine's Day. The challenge for this group of learners consisted in writing and recording Valentine's messages to their loved ones. The challenge tried to promote a relaxed environment that would enable learners to feel less inhibited and keener to practise their speaking. A podcast was the tool used to achieve that purpose. In the first phase, podcasts were used privately, just among the learners in the class as a form of practising the language and to help each other improve. Later, the Valentine messages were uploaded onto a public podcast site and shared with their loved ones through e-cards, which were also written in English. The podcasts were eventually shared more widely with a community of practice of language teachers, who surprised the learners by replying to their Valentine recordings.

5.4) Reflections on the pronunciation challenge

The pronunciation challenge became a crucial activity for the class, in that it set the learning context for all the other components of the course. The more learners engaged in the podcast activities, the less self-conscious they became. As a result, they were keener to participate in joint activities and share their learning – as well as their mistakes – with each other. It created a lively class dynamic and provided cohesion for the group as a whole. The use of the technology boosted their confidence: first, by having time to record, replay, and re-record their messages with each other's support; and second, by having their efforts validated and praised by those who served as their online audience. In this instance, the social and participatory web not only enabled participation through the creation of genuine content, but it also enabled contact with external people who 'legitimated' the product.

5.5) Third challenge: The Residence Abroad challenge

5.5.1) Who are the learners with whom I will be working?

The Residence Abroad challenge was based on a programme that supported university students during their placement or study year abroad. Students had never used technology for this type of learning before.

5.5.2) What do I want the learners to learn and achieve?

This time the goal was to engage students in deep learning while abroad by encouraging ongoing reflection about their experiences in their learning/working environments. I also planned that learners would create a digital footprint of their work in order to make visible the skills they were acquiring. The main goal of this project was to stimulate learners to learn from their experiences through reflection and to document the development of their skills in such a way that it could be used to promote their practice.

5.5.3) How do I want the learners to engage with their learning?

Going abroad to work or study can be a daunting yet rich experience that should be captured as part of students' learning. In previous years, students were assessed on their residency through a report they had to hand in at the end of their year abroad. This activity often produced a very low level of engagement with both their home institution and their reflection on practice. The purpose of the Residence Abroad challenge was to stimulate students to engage with their learning, provide evidence of their reflections, and keep in touch with their home institution. It was also a way of introducing an alternative form of distance pastoral support.

5.5.4) What technology can I use to create a more stimulating learning environment?

To meet this challenge, a networked learning environment was set up. Learners were asked to congregate in a social networking site in order to share their experiences with each other through thematic groups, and progressively work on their reflections – their assessment was based on these personal blogs. These online spaces aimed to stimulate the sharing of information and experiences and thus encourage the (re)presentation of learners' acquired skills through reflection, using different types of media, such as audio, video, and/or photography that learners could use to complement, or use as an alternative to, their written reflection.

5.6) Reflections on the Residence Abroad challenge

The Residence Abroad challenge aimed to stimulate change in how learners engage with their learning, provide evidence of their reflections, and help them keep in touch with their home institution. It was also a way of introducing tutors to novel forms of distance support.

The networked learning environment was created with the aim of providing a space where students and tutors could coexist and share learning by means of a new assessment strategy. A social networking site featuring personal blogs and thematic groups was put in place for this purpose. In Residence Abroad, shared blogs were used as a tool for assessment *for* and *as* learning in an interactive way. They served the purposes of:

- recording the ongoing reflection by learners of their practices and experiences
- creating a space for communication among peers and/or tutors
- developing a portfolio of practice showcasing the enhancement and acquisition of relevant skills
- creating a deeper understanding of their own learning.

The practice of blogging is known and valued in TLA as a tool for the sharing of one's practice through personal reflection. In the Residence Abroad challenge, reflection and the blogs are both used as a tool *for* and *of* assessment of learning, and as a mechanism that creates a record of practice in progress, capturing individuals' experiences and skills in real situations.

6) The impact of the web technology challenges on TLA

There is an assumption that students are proficient users of technology. Indeed, in most cases, they are very technically capable, but that does not necessarily mean they have the skills they need to curate their participation online (Bennett and Maton, 2010; Jenkins, 2009); that is, to select, organize, and contribute new information in online environments. There is also the assumption that, for the most part, teachers lag behind in the adoption of web technologies as part of their teaching. Although research shows that the take-up of learning technologies to support learning in institutional settings has been slower than predicted (JISC, 2009), making such generalizations can be a rather naive and false way of describing the digital phenomenon that currently pervades our society.

In the challenges presented above, I witnessed a mix of both realities. Some learners were really keen to engage in such activities and use technology, whereas others were less eager to change their practice where they felt less comfortable.

Such challenges aimed to introduce a more interactive approach to the way meaning is constructed, personal and collective knowledge is represented, and learning is assessed. In this sense, the integration of technology in TLA provides an opportunity to transform the practices of both learners and teachers. Web technologies can thus motivate alternative forms of creativity, autonomy, and the personalization of learning.

The feedback from the learners regarding the challenges mentioned above was generally positive, even if it meant taking them out of their comfort zones because the technology challenged their learning habits. Still, learners reported how such challenges 'boosted [their] motivation' and even provided a 'sense of validation', given that the technology allowed them to share and discuss their learning.

All in all, the challenges produced positive outcomes in terms of learner engagement. They also also stimulated a new culture of participation that is sometimes lacking in traditional classrooms.

7) Final remarks

In this chapter, I have tried to link theory to practice by providing real examples of how technologies can be used to support TLA in ways that make education more relevant to the society it aims to serve. Indeed, this approach can lead to learning environments that are conducive to autonomous and contextualized learning.

Designing a social learning paradigm challenges preconceptions of established teaching practices. It can present issues for both learners and teachers (Hirsh and Killion, 2009), as the former are asked to take control of their learning and the responsibility that comes with that, and the latter are required to give up a degree of control and engage in more of a pastoral role.

In summary, using learning technologies to enhance learning and to support teaching 'is one of the ways in which institutions can address their own strategic missions' (HEFCE, 2009: 1) regarding the digital and network society. The advantages of embedding digital technologies in education are many and include:

- encouraging the efficiency, enhancement, and transformation of existing processes (HEFCE, 2009: 2)
- enabling the engineering of learning contexts in that it pays 'attention to the activities and learning trajectory of each individual' (Roque *et al.*, 2006: 41)
- catering for the development of learning and teaching strategies focusing on the issues of flexibility, accessibility, and diversity (Mayes *et al.*, 2009)
- changing assessment and feedback strategies that can support the student experience in ways that are more relevant to the world of work (Nicol and Milligan, 2006).

However, attached to the new possibilities is a set of implications that needs to be addressed. These are directly related to the issues of equipping both learners and staff with adequate professional development, especially expanding the current vision of pedagogy (Mcloughlin and Lee, 2007). There is also a need to rethink the curriculum to incorporate diversity, digital literacies (Gilster, 1997; Goodfellow, 2011), and new ways of working (Tyner, 2010) that will propel not only the learner, but also TLA into the twenty-first century. As Mike Wesch (2011) reminds us:

> The new media environment can be disruptive to our current teaching methods and philosophies. As we increasingly move toward an environment of instant and infinite information, it becomes less important for students to know, memorize, or recall information and more important for them to be able to find, sort, analyse, share, discuss, critique, and create information and knowledge. They need to move from being simply knowledgeable to being knowledge-able.

While we, as educators, need to shift our practice from content providers in the classroom to knowledge facilitators in a world of digital connections, the social and participatory web can help in that process.

References

Attwell, G. (2007) *Personal Learning Environments – The Future of eLearning?* eLearning Papers 2.

Bennett, S. and Maton, K. (2010) 'Beyond the "digital natives" debate: Towards a more nuanced understanding of students' technology experiences'. *Journal of Computer Assisted Learning*, 26, 321–31.

Biggs, J. (2003) *Teaching for Quality Learning at University: What the student does.* 2nd edn, Open University Press.

Castells, M. (2000) *The Rise of the Network Society: Economy, society and culture v.1.* In *The Information Age: Economy, society and culture Vol. 1*, 2nd edn. Wiley-Blackwell.

Cha, M., Kwak, H., Rodriguez, P., Ahn, Y.-Y., Moon, S. (2007) 'I tube, you tube, everybody tubes: Analyzing the world's largest user generated content video system'. In *Proceedings of the 7th ACM SIGCOMM Conference on Internet Measurement,* IMC '07. ACM, New York, 1–14.

Churchill, D., Wong, W., Law, N., Salter, D., Tai, B. (2009) 'Social bookmarking–repository–networking: Possibilities for support of teaching and learning in higher education'. *Serials Review*, 35, 142–8.

Conole, G. (2010) 'Facilitating new forms of discourse for learning and teaching: Harnessing the power of Web 2.0 practices'. *Open Learning: The Journal of Open, Distance and e-Learning*, 25, 141–51.

Dewey, J. (2008) *Democracy and Education: An introduction to the philosophy of education.* Radford, Virginia: Wilder Publications.

Dias de Figueiredo, A. (2005) 'Learning contexts: A blueprint for research'. *Digital Education Review*, 11, 127–39.

— (2012). *Contextos de Aprendizagem.* Online. www.slideshare.net/adfigueiredoPT/contextos-de-aprendizagem (accessed 4 February 2014).

— and Afonso, A.P. (2006) 'Context and learning: A philosophical framework'. In *Managing Learning in Virtual Settings: The role of context.* Idea Group Inc (IGI).

Duffy, P. (2012) 'Engaging the Youtube Google-eyed generation: Strategies for using web 2.0 in teaching and learning'. In M. Ciussi and E.G. Freitas (eds), *Leading Issues in E-learning Research: For researchers, teachers and students.* Academic Conferences Limited.

Gilster, P. (1997) *Digital Literacy*, 1st edn. Wiley.

Goodfellow, R. (2011) 'Literacy, literacies and the digital in higher education'. *Teaching in Higher Education*, 16 (1), 131–44.

Gray, P.H., Parise, S., and Iyer, B. (2011) 'Innovation impacts of using social bookmarking systems'. *MIS Q*, 35, 629–44.

Greenhow, C. (2011) 'Online social networks and learning'. *On the Horizon*, 19, 4–12.

Harris, L., Costa, C., Harvey, F., and Earl, G. (2013) 'Curriculum innovation: Living and working on the web'. Paper presented at the International Conference on Enhancement and Innovation in Higher Education, Glasgow, United Kingdom, 11–13 June 2013.

HEFCE (2009) *Enhancing Learning and Teaching through the Use of Technology.* March, 1–4.

Hirsch, S. and Killion, J. (2009) 'When educators learn, students learn'. *Phi Delta Kappan*, 90, 464–9.

Jenkins, H. (2009) 'Confronting the challenges of participatory culture: Media education for the 21st century'. *Program*, 21, 72.

JISC (March 2009) 'Higher education in a Web 2.0 world'.

Lave, J. and Wenger, E. (1991) *Situated Learning: Legitimate peripheral participation.* Cambridge: Cambridge University Press.

Mayes, T. and Freitas, S. (2012) 'An overview of e-Learning: Review of e-Learning theories, frameworks and models'. In S. de Freitas and J. Jameson (eds), *The E-learning Reader.* Continuum, London; New York.

Mayes, T., Morrison, D., Mellar, H., Bullen, P., and Oliver, M. (2009) *Transforming Higher Education Through Technology Enhanced Learning.* York: Higher Education Academy. Online. www.heacademy.ac.uk/resources/detail/ourwork/learningandtech/transforming_he_through_technology_enhanced_learning (accessed 4 February 2014).

Mcloughlin, C. and Lee, M.J.W. (2007) 'Introduction : Social trends and challenges'. In 'Social software and participatory learning: Pedagogical choices with technology affordances in the Web 2.0 era'. Proceedings from ascilite 2007, Singapore, 664–75.

Nicol, D.J. and Milligan, C. (2006) 'Rethinking technology-supported assessment in terms of the seven principles of good feedback practice'. In C. Bryan and K. Clegg (eds), *Innovative Assessment in Higher Education.* London: Taylor and Francis Group.

Paolillo, J.C. (2008) 'Structure and network in the YouTube core'. In Hawaii International Conference on System Sciences, Proceedings of the 41st Annual. Presented at the Hawaii International Conference on System Sciences, Proceedings of the 41st Annual, 156.

Prensky, M. (2001a) 'Digital natives, digital immigrants', Part I. *On the Horizon*, 9 (5). Online. www.marcprensky.com/writing/Prensky%20-%20Digital%20Natives,%20Digital%20Immigrants%20-%20Part1.pdf (accessed 4 February 2014).

— (2001b) 'Do they really *think* differently?', Part II. *On the Horizon*, 9, (5). Online. www.marcprensky.com/writing/Prensky%20-%20Digital%20Natives,%20Digital%20Immigrants%20-%20Part2.pdf (accessed 4 February 2014).

Roque, L., Almeida, A.S., and Dias de Figueiredo, A. (2006) 'CISUC – context engineering: An IS development research agenda'. Online. www.cisuc.uc.pt/publication/show/771 (accessed 9 September 2013).

Tyner, K. (2010) *Media Literacy: New agendas in communication*. New York: Routledge.

Wesch, M. (2011) 'From knowledgeable to knowledge-able: Building new learning environments for new media environments'. UM Events, University of Michigan. Online. www.events.umich.edu/event/5894-1132837 (accessed 4 February 2014).

Wetzel, D.R. (2001) 'A model for pedagogical and curricula transformation for the integration of technology in middle school science'. In 'Building on the future'. Presented at the National Educational Computing Conference, Chicago, IL.

White, D S. and Cornu, A.L. (2011) 'Visitors and residents: A new typology for online engagement'. *First Monday*, 16 (9).

YouTube Blog (n.d.) 'Holy Nyans! 60 hours per minute and 4 billion views a day on YouTube'.

Chapter 8

Harnessing the potential power of feedback

Frank Coffield

> *Peter shows considerable creativity. It will, of course, be beaten out of him.*
>
> Report card sent to Peter Ustinov's parents by St Paul's School, London (in Ustinov, 1978)

1) Introduction

Feedback can be a powerful weapon, but, if it is wielded inappropriately, it can act more like a double-edged sword, causing as much harm as good. There is, however, a widespread and unquestioned assumption that just providing students with comments on their work is bound to improve it; in short, the prevalent notion that feedback is always effective. The story, however, that emerges from the long history of research into feedback (which stretches back over 100 years to the early 1900s) is far more complicated, interesting, and believable.

Before I give a brief version of that history, however, I would like to invite you, the reader, to predict the findings of the research, by asking you to carry out the activities in Box 8.1. Please spend a few minutes jotting down what you think makes feedback effective or ineffective, as well as what advice you would give a colleague about what to do (and what not to do) in relation to feedback. (If you like immediate feedback, please compare your responses with those in Boxes 8.3 and 8.4.)

Let me straightaway convey two of the most important messages that come from the research literature. First, in a seminal review of the effects of feedback on students' performance, Avraham Kluger and Angelo DeNisi found that 'over 38% of the effects were negative' (1996: 258). Not only that, but they found that many of the researchers had ignored their own inconsistent, variable, and contradictory results to such an extent that the notion that feedback is invariably positive came to assume the status of an established principle. The unacknowledged bias of these researchers in favour of feedback appears to have led them to discount the contradictory evidence that they themselves had produced; so they ignored the feedback they did not want to hear. Such a discreditable episode in the history of psychological research should alert the reader's critical faculties in order to become 'less immediately accepting of those who push too self-assuredly for [the] quick adoption' (Bennett, 2011: 20) of their pet ideas for intervention.

Box 8.1: Feedback

1.	What do you think makes feedback effective?
2.	What do you think makes it ineffective?
3.	What advice would you give a colleague about feedback? Please list five things. a. b. c. d. e.
4.	Please list five things to avoid. Please do not write 'broccoli'. a. b. c. d. e.

The second message concerns the original meaning of the word 'feedback', which comes not from psychology or education, but from engineering. Dylan Wiliam neatly uses the example of a thermostat that compares the actual temperature in a room with the desired temperature and then, by means of a feedback loop, either raises or lowers the heat: 'To an engineer, if the information fed back within this system does not have the capacity of changing the system, it is not feedback' (Wiliam, 2009: 9). Let me translate that idea into education: *if your feedback does not change either the thinking or behaviour of your students, it is not feedback*. Already we have moved some distance away from the simple notion that just providing comments is in itself sufficient, because if your students do not accept your comments, they will not act on them, rendering your efforts worthless.

In the rest of this chapter I shall indicate the size and strength of the evidence base, describe attempts to build an explanatory model or theory of feedback, outline effective and ineffective approaches, discuss the responses of students, review the experience of tutors, explain why feedback can so easily go wrong, offer some practical advice, and make some final remarks to pull my main arguments together.

2) The evidence base

I have been genuinely surprised by how extensive the research literature on this topic is and by the poor quality of so much of it. The researchers I have already quoted, Kluger and DeNisi, carried out a meta-analysis, whereby they pooled the results of a large number of investigations that measured the effectiveness of feedback. They collected over 3,000 reports, but only 131 (or 4 per cent) met their five basic criteria for quality research (for example, a control group, a measurement of performance, and a sample larger than 10, etc.). These 131 studies, however, were still based on no fewer than 12,652 participants and 23,663 observations. They then calculated the 'effect size' of feedback, by which is meant the size of the gain that can be attributed to any intervention. An effect size of 0.2 is considered trivial, one between 0.3 and 0.6 medium, and above 0.6 large. The average 'effect size' of feedback, found by Kluger and DeNisi, was 0.38, which suggests that it has a moderately positive effect on performance (1996: 273).

Eleven years later, in 2007, John Hattie and Helen Timperley studied 12 meta-analyses on feedback in classrooms, which included 196 studies and 6,972 effect sizes: 'The average effect size was 0.79 (twice the average effect)' of all types of intervention (Hattie and Timperley, 2007: 83). This comparatively high figure suggests that feedback can be one of the most powerful interventions, but the important rider is that some types of feedback are much more powerful than others, as we shall see later.

In 2012, John Hattie brought the story up to date by examining 24 meta-analyses, consisting of 1,310 studies and 2,086 effect sizes with an average effect size of 0.75, which, to repeat, is about twice the average effect of all the other interventions tried in classrooms. Although this average is certainly high, feedback in this study also had a broad range of effects, from the most effective (a mean of 2.87, where music was given as reinforcement) to the least effective (a mean of 0.12 for praise from teachers, a counter-intuitive finding that I will discuss in a moment). (See Hattie, 2012: 227–8.)

To sum up at this point then, what confidence can we place in these statistics?[1] One cannot fault the sheer number of studies, reviews, and meta-analyses that have been carried out; more significantly, methodological rigour has improved enormously since the first pioneering studies in the early 1900s. The main conclusion that can safely be drawn is that feedback can bring substantial, potential benefits, but also some serious (and at times surprising) limitations, of which more shortly. It has been tried with all age groups and across an impressive variety of learning tasks, although in schools and colleges the focus has tended to be on English, Maths, and Science. Higgins *et al.* estimated that employing feedback will 'require sustained professional development to improve practice ... [costing] in the region of £2,000–£5,000 per teacher per year' (2012: 12), depending on the number of days of cover that have to be paid for. A relatively inexpensive but effective intervention, then.

3) A model of feedback

A number of researchers have argued that a major part of the difficulty in explaining the large variability in the effects of feedback is caused by the lack of an overarching theory or model, and some have attempted to rectify this gap. The efforts made so far,[2] in my opinion, are preliminary but nonetheless appealing, and what follows is an amalgam of what I consider to be the most fruitful ideas produced by the key specialists in the area: Avraham Kluger and Angelo DeNisi (1996); Valerie Shute (2008); John Hattie (2009, 2012); Paul Black *et al.* (2003); and Paul Black and Dylan Wiliam (2009).

The barest outline of a model consists of three main parts, as shown in Box 8.2. This prototype of a theory of effective feedback suggests that tutors can make comments on any one of four areas of students' work (part A), in order to get students to internalize three questions (part B), so that they can reach the goal they want to reach (part C).

I shall now explain the four main areas that tutors can discuss in their feedback:

1. **TASK**: How well did the students understand the task that was set? Were their responses correct or incorrect? What should they learn next?
2. **PROCESS**: Did they know how to do the task? Did they use appropriate methods? Are there better, shorter, or more elegant methods they could have used?
3. **SELF-REGULATION**: Did they know how to monitor, direct, and evaluate their response to the task? Can they assess and manage their own learning? Can they set the next learning target for themselves? Are they independent, lifelong learners or moving to become so?
4. **PERSONAL**: Comment can vary from the positive, 'Well done! You're an excellent student', to the negative, 'You need to try much harder than this', usually written in red or green biro.

Box 8.2: A model of feedback

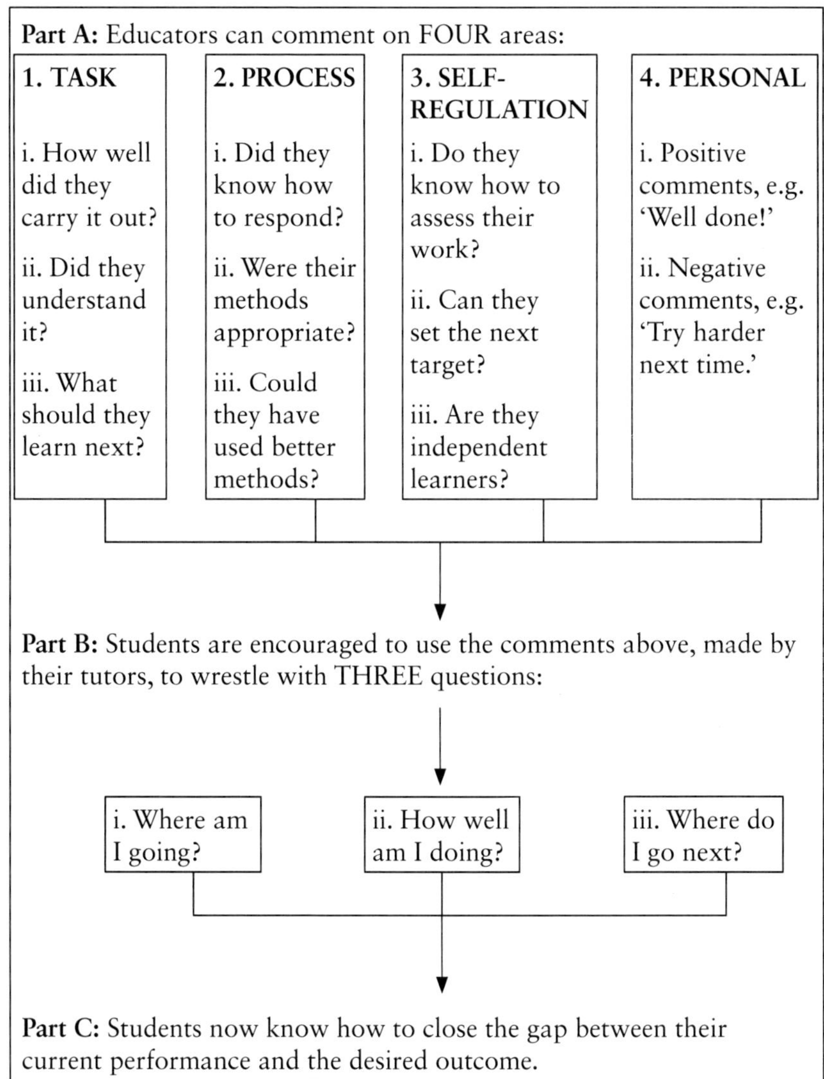

Source: loosely based on Hattie and Timperley (2007: 87)

The tutors' comments are aimed at getting student to ask themselves three questions:

i. Where am I going?

ii. How well am I doing?

iii. Where do I go next?

Now comes the pay-off. If stages A and B have been successful, then the students will know how to reduce any discrepancies or gaps between their current level of performance or understanding and the goal or standard they want to reach. In order to close any such gap, they will need to know: what a good performance in a particular assignment looks like; how to compare their performance with that good performance; and how to bring their current performance up to the desired standard.

4) Praise

> Nowadays we lavish praise on our children. Praise, self-confidence and academic performance, it is commonly believed, rise and fall together. But current research suggests otherwise.
>
> Grosz (2013: 18)

Stephen Grosz makes an important but unexpected point: the evidence strongly suggests that educators should confine their comments to the first three areas (task, process, and self-regulation) and refrain altogether from making personal comments; they are the least effective because they do not tell students how to improve their learning. I have found this topic to be highly contentious when discussing it with practising teachers (and even more so with members of my own family), namely, the advice from researchers to 'use praise sparingly, if at all' (Shute, 2008: 178). To prevent any misunderstanding, I want to stress that the researchers are *not* saying that students should be subjected to constant, nagging criticism and never congratulated for producing good work. Besides, tutors who are difficult to please, who home in unerringly on every trivial mistake, are most unlikely to inspire students to even greater effort.[3] Clearly, students, just like the rest of us, love praise, and hard-working students deserve it, not least because it helps to keep them motivated. The argument is rather, that if you write a general, empty comment such as 'This is a first-class piece of work', it does not let the student know what he or she should learn next.

Claudia Mueller and Carol Dweck have carried out extensive research on this topic and concluded that: 'Well-meant praise for intelligence, which is intended to boost children's enjoyment, persistence and performance during achievement, does not prepare them for coping with setbacks … as with criticism, it is better to separate "the deed from the doer" by applying praise to children's strategies and work habits rather than to' their intelligence or ability (1998: 50). Their findings, which were replicated with both sexes, different ethnic groups, and children from both rural and urban communities, help to shed light on the 'persistent and puzzling paradox … bright young girls who are academic stars in grade school often seen most vulnerable to later academic challenges' (ibid.). The problem appears to be that students whose success is attributed to their ability come to believe their intelligence is fixed, so they are thrown when confronted with failure, whereas those praised for hard work believe they can improve their intelligence through their own efforts and so do not fall apart because they can attribute a 'poor performance to a temporary state as opposed to a permanent trait' (ibid.).

So a more complete message to tutors would be: if over the academic year you have 300–400 assignments to mark, you need to make the best use of your main resource – your time – by confining your written feedback to how students can improve through hard work. You can always compliment the students orally on, say, their persistence in coping with challenging problems as you interact with them socially, when, for instance, you are handing back their assignments. Such praise will be part and parcel of the positive, encouraging learning atmosphere in which all students in your class feel good about themselves as hard-working, respected, and supported partners in learning. I want now to turn to a broader question: what are the characteristics of effective and ineffective feedback, according to the research?

5) Effective and ineffective feedback

Some general principles of good practice have been identified by David Nicol and Debra Macfarlane-Dick (2006) and I have freely adapted their synthesis of the research and presented it in Box 8.3.

In providing guidelines of things to avoid in Box 8.4, I have drawn mainly on the work of Valerie Shute (2008: 178–9) and John Hattie (2012: 115–37), but again I have added my own ideas and emphases as a result of running workshops with practising teachers and of assessing students' work over the past 40+ years. I have, for instance, noted the spreading practice of 'negotiated feedback', where a tutor agrees with a student which pieces of work will be rigorously assessed with detailed comments provided and those where a lighter touch is all that is needed.

Box 8.3: Effective feedback: Some suggestions

1. Show your student what a good performance is (for example, make sure that they understand the criteria for success).
2. Show them how to assess their own work; they need to acquire the assessment skills that you have.

3. Show them how to close the gap between their current and the desired performance. Students have to *change* their thinking and their behaviour in response to your guidance for your feedback to be effective.
4. Diagnose the strengths and weaknesses of their assignment, but always offer a prognosis as well – that is, what they need to learn now.
5. Discuss your feedback with the students (and encourage them to discuss it among themselves) to make sure they have understood it and agreed with it; and then give them the opportunity in class or at a workplace to act on it.
6. Your comments should increase their motivation to work hard, but confine them to the task, process, and self-regulation rather than making personal comments. Praise students for effort rather than for being able.
7. Set a specific target for the student's next piece of work. For instance, '*For your next target I want you to …*'. Limit yourself to three comments, to increase the chances of the students acting on them and to go easy on yourself.
8. Try to change the focus of students' attention from '*What grade did I get?*' to '*What do I need to learn now?*'

Box 8.4: Ineffective feedback: Some suggestions

1. Don't make invidious comparisons with the work of other students.
2. Don't just give grades. Provide the students with information about how they can improve, get them to incorporate your suggestions before resubmitting their work, and only then give them their grades.
3. Don't criticize learners personally. Draw their attention away from themselves to the task, the process, or how to get better at learning. Your feedback should make students pause, think, and act – not react emotionally to negative remarks.
4. Don't consume your precious time by praising students in writing for being able; instead praise them for working hard. Confine your written comments to how they can improve. (See the text for a more extended discussion of this point.)
5. Give them prompts, cues, and hints rather than the right answer straight away. We are trying to 'scaffold' their learning so that when the 'building' is complete, it can stand on its own, even when the scaffolding (your support) is removed.

6. Minimize your analysis of their errors. Concentrate instead on how they can put the matter right, but remember that their errors give you an insight into their current thinking. Are there any recurrent patterns in the type of errors your students are making? If so, they may have misunderstood what you taught them, or perhaps you have failed to teach them something vital.
7. Don't give your students dollops of rich feedback at the very same time as your colleagues are also doing so, or the students will be overwhelmed. The return of feedback needs to be planned and co-ordinated across subjects/departments and across terms; this is a role for managers rather than class tutors.
8. Don't see your feedback as primarily making statements about your students; it is more a reflection of your teaching.

6) The responses of students to feedback

Students choose how to respond to feedback; their reactions vary markedly, but they tend to employ four main strategies. Let us take a fairly typical case where students are told their work needs to improve and are then given detailed advice about how to go about it. They could first of all reject the feedback and, what is more, they could have good reasons for doing so. Suppose, for instance, a tutor set the following essay title: 'Describe John Hattie's main ideas about visible learning' and then she failed all those assignments that did not also evaluate his ideas. In this case, let us further assume that the students, having read my Chapter 4, have understood the critical distinction between description and evaluation, but carried out the task as required – and described Hattie's main ideas. They would, in my opinion, be right to complain that description had been reinterpreted to include evaluation after they had submitted their essays. Feelings of being unfairly treated can rankle for years and distrust of examiners can spread.

Second, students could come to the conclusion that the goal is beyond them and so they abandon it: 'I'll never understand the pluperfect subjunctive in French, never mind use it in conversation with that pretty waitress in the bistro'. Third, they could decide to settle for a 'B', or a Merit, because they consider the work necessary to obtain an 'A' or a Distinction not worth the extra effort involved: 'I'd rather spend the time on Facebook, walking the dog, watching *The X Factor*'. Fourth, they could, as the tutor hopes, accept the feedback, change their behaviour and/or thinking, and, as a result, work harder and more effectively: 'I'll do as my tutor advises and go back and read the original article rather than depending on secondary sources'. Kluger and DeNisi (1996) explain how difficult it is to predict what response any particular student will make because that depends on the quality of the cues given in the feedback, on the nature of the task the student has been asked to carry out, and on a variety of situational variables, including how late the student or the tutor was partying the night before.

Other researchers (such as Smith and Gorard, 2005; Price *et al.*, 2010; and Orsmond and Merry, 2010) have shown how dissatisfied students often are with the quality of the feedback they get. Students, for instance, have real difficulties in learning from vague and ambiguous comments such as 'Be more analytic/academic', or 'Clarify your aims and objectives'. What it means to be analytic needs to be explained to students in some detail when they come across the term for the first time. None of us was born with an inborn instinct for analysis: it is an intellectual process that improves with practice and training, as I explained in Chapter 4. Feedback needs to be specific, challenging, and focused on a particular target(s) for the student to aim at next. The skill lies in choosing a target that is neither so close that it does not stretch the student nor so far away as to be beyond reach. You are looking for the Goldilocks target – just right.

Certain characteristics of the students (for example, the level at which they are performing) are also likely to influence the type of feedback provided. Valerie Shute (2008) examined the evidence on this issue and concluded that low-achieving students need immediate, explicit, and directive feedback, especially when confronted with new tasks they find difficult. High-achieving students, on the other hand, seem to prefer delayed feedback that challenges them, with the proviso, however, that the steeper the challenge, the greater the need for feedback. These general conclusions strike me as just that – far too general. More importantly, they do not take sufficient account of the 'situated' nature of learning.[4] By this term, I mean that learning happens not so much in the brains of students, but as a result of newcomers coming to understand the social practices of a group of experts, and moving from the periphery of that group to the centre of their activities. So learning is situated in the sense that a particular group of novice biologists are being introduced to the way of thinking of biology by listening to and imitating the language and behaviour of an expert biologist – you, the teacher.

One other significant factor needs to be borne in mind before deciding on when to give feedback, namely, timing. Again, much research has been undertaken into the timing of feedback and the general finding appears to be that 'if the task is difficult, then immediate feedback is beneficial, but if the task is easy, then delayed feedback may be preferable' (Shute, 2008: 165).

To sum up at this point, tutors need to consider at least four dimensions when providing feedback – the capabilities of the students (for example, high or low achieving), the nature of the task (for example, easy/difficult, new/familiar), the principles, procedures, and understandings of the subject being studied (for example, the habits of mind of an historian), and any situational factors (for example, how well the tutor knows the students). In Valerie Shute's own words: 'there is no "best" type of formative feedback for all learners and learning outcomes' (2008: 182), and, I would add, for all subject areas.

This brings me to a teaching problem that dogged me throughout my career as a teacher: the large number of students even at higher-degree level who have to be reminded about incomplete, inaccurate, or inconsistent referencing. Tutors nowadays routinely supply detailed handouts that show students all the possible variations of entries in a bibliography, for instance, a chapter in a book, an article in a journal, or a reference to a website. Yet still some students submit work that, for example, contains full details of a publication in the text rather than in the bibliography. It took me some time to develop a tactic that encouraged students to reformulate the issue: I tried to persuade them that my insistence on them conforming to an internationally recognized referencing scheme should be interpreted by them as an invitation to acquire an essential professional skill, which they will need if they want their work to be taken seriously by the experts in whatever vocation they are keen to join. I did so after I overheard a student of mine say to his friend in a corridor, 'Oh, I've got a meeting now with that nit-picking Scottish pedant. He's got a thing about references.'[5]

A related problem often occurs when students are told to couch their arguments 'in their own words', a requirement that can represent a challenge to many native-born speakers of English. For students, however, who come from a collectivist culture (where teachers are rarely, if ever, challenged), and who are struggling to write clearly in English (never mind fluently), it makes little sense to be asked to present the key points of an article 'in their own words', when the article's author has already done so in succinct and attractive prose. All students need to be alerted to our rather strict views on plagiarism and originality; in addition, according to Hattie and Timperley, students from certain Asian cultures prefer 'indirect and implicit feedback, more group-focused feedback' and not personal comments (2007: 100). But again, are these generalizations not too sweeping? Do they apply, for instance, to all the millions of students in and from China and India?

7) Tutors' experiences of feedback

If students are frequently dissatisfied, then staff are 'frustrated about the way the process is working', according to Margaret Price and her colleagues (2010: 288). For a start there can be confusion between educators and students over the purposes of feedback, with many of the latter often more interested in a narrow range of purposes – having their errors corrected and receiving praise rather than being challenged to think more deeply. Moreover, Orsmond and Merry (2010) found that, although the tutors in their study claimed to be directing their feedback at encouraging future learning, in practice the majority of their biology tutors identified errors and offered praise – the well-established distinction between espousing one set of beliefs but practising another.

Margaret Price and her colleagues are, in my view, right to argue that feedback cannot be separated from the quality of the relationship between tutors and their students. Their advice is that tutors should, as a matter of course, discuss their feedback with students to ensure that their views on its purposes are aligned and to check that it has not only been understood but acted on. If, in addition, the students trust the tutor's professional judgement, then they are more likely to change their attitude to assessment. For students in England who have sat nationally assessed tests every year since they were seven years of age, it is no surprise that they have come to associate assessment with all that is punitive and painful in education; and yet we need them to reverse that judgement completely and come to realize that assessment is one of the main means of improving their learning.[6] They need to treat assessment as an integral part of the process of learning and not an unwelcome adjunct to it.

In discussions with tutors in the lifelong learning sector, I have also come to realize that the key variable in harnessing the potential power of feedback is the tutor's TIME. Here, for instance, is a list of the main tasks that I have suggested so far in this chapter. Tutors need time to:

- reflect on their students' assignments and write three challenging, specific, and clear comments on how each of their 200–300 students can improve
- carefully consider, before writing any comments, the capabilities of the students, the nature of the task, and any other important contextual factors
- engage their students in a dialogue about feedback, to check that they understand it and that they are agreed on its purposes

- be able to provide students with the time they need to act on the guidance offered and then make sure that the guidance has been acted on appropriately
- change students' attitude to assessment by giving them the assessment skills that tutors have, especially the insight that assessment, instead of being a bugbear, is one of the best means of improving their learning
- reflect on all that has gone on above before deciding what to teach next.

It is a tall order, and, in my opinion, asking far too much of staff who have 864 hours of teaching a year (or, on average, 24 contact hours per week over 36 weeks), especially if they are to add to their repertoire some of the suggestions contained in the other chapters of this book. If tutors are to devote more of their time to providing high-quality feedback, then managers will need to acknowledge and plan for this when deciding on contact hours. I will return to this topic in Chapter 9. When I reflect on the time-consuming demands of providing rich and effective feedback, I find it verging on the impossible to accept Dylan Wiliam's statement that 'the first fundamental principle of effective classroom feedback is that feedback should be more work for the recipient than the donor' (2011: 129). That would perhaps be true for an Oxbridge tutor with 10 or 12 students and three terms of only eight weeks per year, but wildly off the mark if you have 200 or 300 for 36 weeks; and even in the Oxbridge tutorial, students lack the stimulus of the views of other students.

8) What could possibly go wrong?

Let us take a pretty typical example of a teacher who teaches a new idea (entropy, say, or evolution) to her students and then sets them a test to see how much has been understood and by whom. She discovers that some students have misunderstood her lesson so she provides appropriate feedback. If we analyse in detail this standard teaching episode, we find that it can be broken down into a large number of constituent steps as shown in Box 8.5. The sequence is so long that errors or misunderstandings at any one point can sever the causal chain and render the feedback ineffective. For instance, let us examine steps 5 and 6. The teacher makes inferences from the evidence provided by the students in the test about what they know, what they do not know, and what they need to know next (step 5). She then decides what corrective and/or future action the students should take, provides appropriate feedback, and begins to consider what changes to make to her teaching (step 6). But, argues Randy Bennett, a teacher who has weak understanding of the subject area (for example, construction, catering, or chemistry) 'is less likely to know what questions to ask of students, what to look for in their performance, what inferences to make from that performance about student knowledge and what actions to take to adjust instruction' (Bennett, 2011: 15).

At each of the 12 steps in this causal chain, errors can creep in, so the surprise to me is not so much that feedback is sometimes ineffective, but that it is successful so often. The 12 steps in Box 8.5 are also a useful device for demonstrating yet again the sheer complexity and ambiguity of teaching and learning; it is very far from being a simple, technical matter of transmitting point X, never mind a full syllabus, from the mind of one teacher to the minds of 25 or 30 students.

Box 8.5: The steps behind one teaching loop

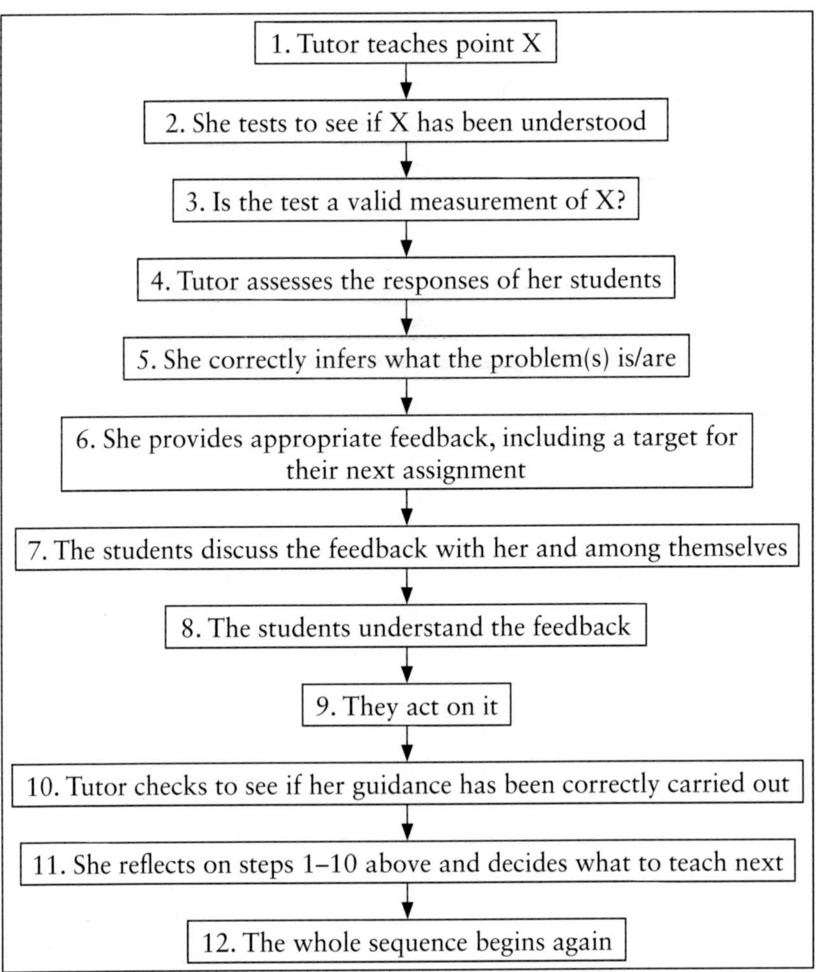

9) Final comments

Studying the theory and practice of feedback has reinforced for me the critical distinction between *performance* and *competence*. Any response from a student (whether it be an answer to a question in class, an exam script, or an assignment/portfolio) can be described as a performance on a particular day, produced under particular circumstances (for example, a reply off the top of the head, a pale reflection of ill-remembered handouts, or a seriously considered and insightful contribution). The art of assessment consists of making judgements from limited evidence, and in particular trying to infer what the relationship is between one particular 'situated' performance and the underlying competence or intellectual capability of the student. All sorts of social, cultural, and gender assumptions and stereotypes are, however, involved in making these inferences, as Valerie Walkerdine showed in her account of how girls' superior performance at maths was attributed by educators to rule-following and rote-learning, while the inferior performance of boys was paradoxically taken as a sign of their conceptual understanding: 'Throughout the age range, girls' good performance is downplayed while boys' often relatively poor attainment is taken as evidence of real understanding such that any counter-evidence (poor attainment, poor attention and so forth) is explained as peripheral' (1990: 66).

A few more concluding remarks. First, a leitmotiv running through the previous pages has been that the power of feedback is only a *potential*, and both its positive and negative features need to be understood to prevent this potentially powerful weapon becoming a boomerang. There is also the danger in formative assessment that the formation is towards the outcome that the teachers consider to be correct. John Webber in Chapter 3 has discussed teachers' questions, which can be open, closed, or pseudo-open. Feedback is no easy panacea to the complexities of TLA. Hattie and Timperley summarize it as follows: 'Feedback is not "*the answer*"; rather, it is but one powerful answer' (2007: 104). No one would sensibly operate a potentially dangerous tool such as a circular saw without some initial training or before reading the instructions or both; feedback is no different.

Second, I still remember with embarrassment reading over the Christmas vacation in 1965 the test papers of the first class I ever taught and having to conclude that not one of them, not even the brightest of the bright, had understood my 'brilliant' lessons. For months I had been making the elementary mistake, typical of young graduate teachers, of talking over the heads of very able, motivated, and delightful 12 year olds. The conclusion I was forced to draw was hard: there was no one to blame but myself.

Fifty years on, the pressures, the contexts, and the dangers are radically different: 'well-taught lessons by well-meaning teachers aimed at preparing students to successfully pass ... national standardized examinations lead to routinized procedures at the expense of understanding' (Jean Lave, 1997: 29). But I wish that back in the 1960s I had had the advantage of John Hattie's advice and had designed my teaching on the assumption that some/many/most students were not going to understand my lessons the first time around. In his own words, 'Teachers too often see assessment feedback as making statements about students and not about their teaching and hence the benefits of feedback from such testing are often diluted' (Hattie, 2012: 126).

Finally, I offer readers (again drawing on John Hattie's work) who are also parents a better question to ask their children at the end of the school day. Instead of enquiring 'How did it go today?' (which, in my experience as a father, tended to receive the I'm-too-bored-to-be-bothered reply of 'Fine, fine. What's for dinner?') I suggest you ask instead: 'How good was the feedback you got today?' or 'I wonder whether your teacher's comments ...'.

To return, one last time, to the heart of the matter, if you, the reader, retain and use the following question as a result of reading this chapter, then I shall have successfully conveyed my central message. When you are reflecting on your day's teaching, please ask yourself: 'Did my feedback change my students' thinking or behaviour?' If it did not, it was not feedback.[7]

Notes

[1] Hattie's approach has attracted some critical attention. Higgins and Simpson, for example, have reviewed his 2009 book on *Visible Learning* and urged 'mega-caution' about drawing conclusions from even well-conducted meta-analyses (2011: 200).

[2] There are a number of models to choose from, starting with Kluger and DeNisi's rather complicated Feedback Intervention Theory (FIT), which they produced in 1996. Nicol and Macfarlane-Dick also offered a model of self-regulated learning and feedback principles (2006), while Hattie and Timperley presented the 'model of feedback to enhance learning', which I have freely adapted and summarized in the text because it is, in my opinion, the most accessible (2007: 87). Black and Wiliam's model contains five principles of formative assessment, one of which is feedback (2009: 8) and which is discussed in a little more detail in Chapter 9.

[3] I still remember a history test that I took in 1949 at a primary school in Glasgow when I was seven years old. I got 9 marks out of 10, losing one mark because I gave the date for the execution of King Charles I as 1949 instead of 1649. I took my paper to my teacher, Miss Sweeney, and pointed out to her that I had made an unfortunate slip as she could not possibly believe that I thought King Charles had been beheaded earlier that year. So could the mark be restored? 'Francis,' she said, 'you made a mistake and you lost one mark for doing so. You should learn to check your work.' 'But, Miss,' I replied, 'I got three of the four numbers right. I should at least get three-quarters of a mark.' 'Sit down, Coffield,' she answered testily, 'You are beginning to get on my nerves.' More than sixty years later, the loss of that mark still rankles. So there were mark-hungry children long before the 1988 Education Act that ushered in

national assessment in England; and do not let anyone tell you that being assessed is a purely intellectual matter. Our emotions are deeply involved.

[4] See the end of Chapter 2, Note 5, for a brief account of Lave and Wenger's theory of situated learning.

[5] In a study of Scottish Higher National students making the transition from community college to university, Robert Ingram and Jim Gallacher (2013) found that one of the key skills these students lacked was how to reference their sources. The students also felt they had been spoon-fed, that assessment consisted too much of ticking boxes against criteria, and that they did not know what to do when asked to 'critically analyse' a passage of text. These problems of transition are very similar to those discussed by John Webber in Chapter 3, of students moving from GCSE to A level, and of first-year undergraduates with tutors trying to enhance their critical thinking and their skills of analysis and evaluation in order to move them slowly towards more independent study.

[6] In 2008–09 I carried out a small-scale, but intensive, research project with 24 students from academic, vocational, and foundation learning courses drawn from two large, general FE colleges, one in the north of England and one in London. I used a variety of research methods (interviews, questionnaires, learning logs, etc.) to explore their views on teaching and learning, and I quote one of my findings here: 'What I found most telling was that not one of these able and committed students made a connection between assessment and learning. Assessment was viewed as a necessary evil and the route to gaining qualifications, but it was not treated as constructive guidance about how to improve as a learner' (Coffield, 2009: 56). Changing their attitude to assessment through dialogue and argument strikes me as a powerful means of turning exam candidates into lifelong learners.

[7] We all need feedback, especially me. So if you have any comments, however critical, on this or on any of the other chapters in this book, please email them to me at f.coffield@ioe.ac.uk, with some guidance about what I should learn next.

References

Bennett, R.E. (2011) 'Formative assessment: a critical review'. *Assessment in Education: Principles, Policy and Practice*, 18 (1), 5–25.

Black, P., Harrison, C., Lee, C., Marshall, B., and Wiliam, D. (2003) *Assessment for Learning: Putting it into practice*. Maidenhead: Open University Press.

Black, P. and Wiliam, D. (2009) 'Developing the theory of formative assessment'. *Educational Assessment, Evaluation and Accountability*, 21, 5–31.

Coffield, F. (2009) *All You Ever Wanted to Know About Learning and Teaching but Were Too Cool to Ask*. London: Learning and Skills Network.

Grosz, S. (2013) *The Examined Life*. London: Chatto & Windus.

Hattie, J. (2009) *Visible Learning: A synthesis of over 800 meta-analyses relating to achievement*. London: Routledge.

— (2012) *Visible Learning for Teachers: Maximising impact on learning*. London: Routledge.

Hattie, J. and Timperley, H. (2007) 'The Power of feedback'. *Review of Educational Research*, 77 (1), 81–112.

Higgins, S., Kokotsaki, D., and Coe, R. (2012) *The Teaching and Learning Toolkit*. Education Endowment Foundation/The Sutton Trust.

Higgins, S. and Simpson, A. (2011) 'Visible learning: A synthesis of over 800 meta-analyses relating to achievement'. *British Journal of Educational Studies*, 59 (2), 197–201.

Ingram, R. and Gallacher, J. (2013) *Making the Transition from College to University: The experience of HN students.* Glasgow Caledonian University.

Kluger, A.N. and DeNisi, A. (1996) 'The effects of feedback interventions on performance: A historical review, a meta-analysis, and a preliminary feedback intervention theory'. *Psychological Bulletin*, 119 (2), 254–84.

Lave, J. (1997) 'The culture of acquisition and the practice of understanding'. In D. Kirshner and J.A. Whitson (eds), *Situated Cognition: Social, semiotic and psychological perspectives.* Mahwah, NJ: Lawrence Erlbaum.

Mueller, C.M. and Dweck, C.S. (1998) 'Praise for intelligence can undermine children's motivation and performance'. *Journal of Personality and Social Psychology*, 75 (1), 33–52.

Nicol, D.J. and Macfarlane-Dick, D. (2006) 'Formative assessment and self-regulated learning: A model and seven principles of good feedback practice'. *Studies in Higher Education*, 31 (2), 199–218.

Orsmond, P. and Merry, S. (2010) 'Feedback alignment: Effective and ineffective links between tutors' and students' understanding of coursework feedback'. *Assessment and Evaluation in Higher Education,* 36 (2), 125–36.

Price, M., Handley, K., Millar, J., and O'Donovan, B. (2010) 'Feedback: All that effort, but what is the effect?'. *Assessment and Evaluation in Higher Education*, 35 (3), 277–89.

Shute, V.J. (2008) 'Focus on formative feedback'. *Review of Educational Research*, 78 (1), 153–89.

Smith, E. and Gorard, S. (2005) '"They don't give us our marks": The role of formative feedback in student progress'. *Assessment in Education: Principles, Policy and Practice*, 12 (1), 21–38.

Ustinov, P. (1978) *Dear Me.* London: Penguin Books.

Walkerdine, V. (1990) *Schoolgirl Fictions.* London: Verso.

Wiliam, D. (2009) *Assessment for Learning: Why, what and how?* London: Institute of Education, Inaugural Lecture.

— (2011) *Embedded Formative Assessment.* Bloomington, IN: Solution Tree.

Chapter 9

Can we transform classrooms and colleges without transforming the role of the state?

Frank Coffield

My brother Denis once booked a seat on a train from Glasgow to Aberdeen and had only just settled into it when an announcement told him that all passengers were requested to move from platform 1 to join the train at platform 8. He arrived to find that those who had been standing on the first train now had seats while those with reservations had to stand. As the second train started up, the guard sought to explain: 'ScotRail apologizes to passengers for any inconvenience. It was caused by a management brainwave.'

1) Introduction

In this chapter I want to discuss the future of FE. Stephen Grosz recently argued that 'the future is not some place we're going to, but an idea in our mind now. It's something we're creating, that in turn creates us. The future is a fantasy that shapes our present' (Grosz, 2013: 157). I would add that any shaping of the future also needs to be based on an understanding of how the past is constantly recreated to justify a particular reading of the present. My hope is that the ideas presented in this book will offer an outline of a better future than the one we are hurtling towards.

This chapter is divided into three parts: transforming classrooms, transforming colleges, and transforming the role of the state, to which I add a few concluding remarks. I want to establish the minimal conditions for high-quality TLA for all. I have nothing to say about some major areas of work such as apprenticeships, work-based learning, and vocational learning, where I have no expertise and where there already exist substantial reports such as that by Bill Lucas *et al.*, who offer 'a theoretical underpinning for a vocational pedagogy' (2012: 9).

I begin with the question of what the FE sector is for. Over the past 20 years the language of learning and skills has eclipsed the language of education, and the measurement of inputs and outputs has replaced dialogue about the aims and objectives of FE (see Biesta, 2010). For me, the main purpose of FE is Further Education. The clue is in the name. FE does not stand for Further Employment or, that weasel term so beloved of the politicians, Future Employability, because that passes the responsibility for securing employment from governments to individuals. The main purpose of education is not the wages students will earn but the quality of the life they will lead. In providing second-chance education, vocational education, and lifelong learning for all, FE fulfils a vital role not only for individuals but also for society as a whole; and the wider benefits of education in terms of health, social cohesion, and active citizenship enable adults to sustain and transform their lives and those of their communities through what FE has to offer.

A sharper focus on Further *Education* will lead us to ask: are students leaving our colleges as educated people, prepared to take their place as skilled workers, discriminating consumers, *and* active citizens of a democracy? The Scottish government sets out clearly the aims for its *Curriculum for Excellence*, which are to create successful learners, confident individuals, responsible citizens, and effective contributors to society (see MacLellan and Soden, 2012). Have we provided them with the knowledge, skills, and values and with the democratic experience of political action that they will need to cope with the main threats to our collective well-being (see Coffield and Williamson, 2012; Biesta, 2006)? My answer to both questions is 'No'. FE students need general education as well as vocational training, and in Germany, France, and Scandinavia they receive it. That would prevent them from taking out an action against their FE college for contravening the Trades Description Act – 'You call yourself a Further Education college but you don't provide what it says on the tin'.

2) Transforming classrooms

Before we try to transform classrooms or 'learning spaces', we need to know what condition they are currently in. The constraints imposed on tutors in the sector are multiple, threatening, and intensifying. The most serious are:

- cuts in funding this year, next year, and the year after
- voluntary and compulsory redundancies as a result
- contact time is increasing, as are class sizes
- the pressures to 'ratchet up' test scores cascade down through every level in colleges

- the increasing use of part-time and agency staff to help cope with the constant changes in funding
- the wasteful competition for students between secondary schools, sixth-form colleges, academies, and 'free' schools has become even more intense
- Ofsted's 159 new criteria for inspection, which place a heavy, belated, but still welcome emphasis on TLA
- the grading of lessons on a four-point scale for all staff, although only around 1 or 2 per cent are considered inadequate
- the pace of change and the permanent revolution in structures, priorities, and qualifications.

Let us be clear about the source of all these stresses: the biggest obstacle to improving standards in education is, and has been since 1988, the policy of successive governments. The state in England controls what is taught, to whom, and how: it controls how learning is managed, funded, tested, and regulated. Despite all the political rhetoric about 'freedoms and flexibilities' (DBIS, 2011: 4), the daily reality of teaching in the sector consists of stress piled upon stress, as teachers strive to keep abreast of the ever-changing demands to 'drive up test scores'.

Yet, despite the continuing torrent of ill-considered and undemocratic government initiatives, it remains the case that 'learning – at least formal learning – does not take place in schools [and colleges]. It takes place in classrooms' (Thompson and Wiliam, 2007: 1). Ministerial initiatives become classroom realities only 'if they are embraced, understood and acted upon by classroom teachers' (Anderson and Krathwohl, 2001: xxii). It is the enduring commitment of the teaching staff to their students, with staff working over and above the call of duty, that keeps this show on the road.

Besides, there is only one Secretary of State, only one Chief Inspector, and Ofsted inspectors are not so numerous or ubiquitous that they are able to inspect every classroom every day, so when the classroom door is shut, educators still have considerable freedom to teach how they want to. They need to exercise that freedom more.

At the same time, there is a growing consensus, based on reasonably hard evidence, among the research community around the essential ingredients of effective TLA. I am NOT referring here to low-level tips for teachers to help them increase the test scores of as many of their students as possible; I refer instead to the evidence that I reviewed in Chapter 8 and which suggests that, for example, by providing students with formative feedback we can bring them to a deeper understanding and a love of the subjects they are studying. I refer to the work of Stephen Ball, Dylan Wiliam, Paul Black, Lorin Anderson, John Hattie, and Helen Timperley, among many others. I and my fellow contributors of chapters to this book have drawn on this substantial body of knowledge in order to offer a critical reading of present policy as well as a series of alternative approaches to TLA.

Just as importantly, we now know what NOT to do, and anyone who knows me will expect me to point out yet again that learning styles are unreliable and invalid and have virtually no impact on practice (Coffield *et al.*, 2004a and b; Coffield, 2012b and 2013). Recently, Philip Adey and Justin Dillon (2012) edited a collection of papers that debunk some of the more egregious but still prevalent and mischievous myths in education, such as fixed intelligence and emotional intelligence. For Dylan Wiliam the issue is more one of stopping tutors 'doing good things to give them time to do even better things' (forthcoming: 43).

FE should prioritize a major programme of investment in the initial and continuing professional learning of *all* the staff working in the sector, including the 51,000 tutors who are not on full-time contracts. The very high percentage of peripheral staff (over 40 per cent in some colleges) is one way SMTs have found to cope with the constant fluctuations in funding, but its impact on the quality of TLA and on the declining numbers of full-time, core members of staff needs to be acknowledged and the trend reversed.

Tutors, rather than managers, should be in charge of their own professional learning but it needs to be aligned with the needs of the students as well as those of the college. Their professional organization should not only be independent of government but capable of being critical of it; and so should Ofsted.

From the research I have carried out in FE and sixth-form colleges, I suggest that most classrooms can be positioned along a continuum according to the eagerness of teachers to embrace innovation and change. This typology would place at one end of that continuum the *enthusiasts*, who are prepared, for example, to be filmed while trying out new ideas and to have the results (both good and not so good) publicly evaluated by their colleagues. Then comes the main body of teachers whom I call the *healthy sceptics*, who sensibly try out one or two new ideas and carefully evaluate their effectiveness before adopting or rejecting them. Next are those I call the *unengaged*, who do not speak at meetings and who are hoping that all initiatives will come and go before they are challenged to reconsider their practice. Often their hopes are fulfilled. Finally, at the other end of the continuum come the *resisters*, whom I divide into two groups. There are those who have a principled objection to the proposed initiative because, for instance, they have launched an initiative of their own that they are putting to the test and they do not want their intervention contaminated by another. Finally, there is a small group of staff who appear to resist all new approaches and offer a variety of reasons/excuses for doing so: 'I'm doing that already', 'Is this the latest flavour of the month?', 'I haven't got time', 'I don't get anything out of that', or 'I'm just not bothered'.

All tutors in FE should receive initial training/education and then be consulted about how their professional learning should be developed: they are the best judges of what strengths they would like to build on and what weaknesses they need to address. Today, in England, gas fitters and the drivers of heavy goods vehicles require a licence to practise. The Lingfield report (DBIS, 2012) and the Secretary of State for Education have begun to argue that teachers do not need initial and continual professional education; in other words, they are telling us that gas boilers and heavy trucks are more valuable to society than our children.

Instead of educating tutors, the education 'system' is, at present, still running ever faster down the wrong road (Coffield, 2007). We, the professionals, need to stop running, admit publicly that we are heading in the wrong direction, face up squarely to the spreading malaises in the sector, and begin the fight for the adoption of a far better destination and better routes to it.

Let me summarize the damage that is being done to both students and staff by the three interconnecting policies of *performance management*, which turns staff into human resources to be managed, controlled, and changed; by *privatization*, which hands over responsibility for the education of this and future generations to firms driven by private profit; and by an *unregulated market*, which insists on inefficient, wasteful, and harmful competition.

First and foremost, there is damage to the very people who are supposed to be the beneficiaries of all our efforts, money, and time – namely, the students. I shall not repeat here the arguments made in Chapter 1 about the noxious effects of *bulimia* and *anorexia academica*, which, as I said in that chapter, I consider to be every bit as distressing as their medical counterparts.

British businesses are rightly concerned about the quality of the education our students are receiving; they are calling out for innovative, creative individuals who can think for themselves. Instead, *bulimia academica* is churning out people who can only think what others have thought, and *anorexia academica* disparages the central importance of knowledge.

Similarly, for too many staff, the atmosphere has become, and I use the word most often used by tutors in FE colleges, 'toxic'. In my words, they are working in a *sick* sector, which is part of a *sick* 'system', because the same malaises affect schools and universities. Stephen Ball has neatly summarized the baleful effects of government policies and managerialism on staff: increased stress, intensification of workloads, a decline in sociability, more paperwork and all the petty oppressions of bureaucracy, increased surveillance of teachers and the outcomes of teaching, and a 'developing gap between senior staff with a primary concern with balancing the budget, recruitment, public relations and impression management and teaching staff, with a primary concern with curriculum coverage, classroom control, students' needs and record keeping' (2008b: 52).

I want to explore a little further than I did in the first chapter this unhealthy gap in many, but by no means all, colleges that has grown up between SMTs and the teaching staff by presenting the case for both sides and leaving the reader to judge who has the better argument. Classroom and workshop tutors claim that SMTs proclaim TLA to be their number one priority, but they do not attend TLA events, they do not teach, in some cases they have not taught for many years, and yet they grade those who do teach, even in subjects remote from their own specialism – when, for instance, a manager with a degree in Modern Foreign Languages evaluates the teaching of an electrical engineer.

The major source of conflict between the two groups continues to be the grading of lesson observations. Teachers object to:

- being judged on half an hour's lesson out of a term's or a year's teaching
- being publicly humiliated if awarded a 3 or a 4
- all staff being subjected to termly grading when only 1 or 2 per cent are evaluated as inadequate
- teachers who 'work their socks off' for their students throughout the year being judged inadequate because they fall apart when observed by senior staff
- poor teachers, who serve up boring lessons all year long, being awarded a 2 or 3 because they are astute enough to produce one all-singing, all-dancing lesson for the SMT.

Matt O'Leary has conducted some empirical research into graded lesson observations in FE colleges, drawing data from 500 tutors (50 in each of ten colleges in urban, suburban, and rural areas). He concludes that this practice 'has emerged as one of the key tools to measure and control what tutors do in the classroom' and has 'reduced the assessment of TLA to the use of a simplified rating scale' (2012a: 117). More worryingly still, 'graded observation has resulted in a decline in the creativity and innovation of teachers' work in the classroom. There is a reluctance to want to take risks for fear of being given a low grade' (O'Leary, 2012b: 807).

Tutors sum up their objections by alleging that SMTs live in a parallel universe, comfortably ensconced in their corridors of power, where they manage via the data they collect three or more times a term from students and teaching staff. In one university, in a sector where the phenomenon of the gap between SMT and teaching staff is far from unknown, the 'executive corridor was known as Battlestar Galactica' (McNay, 2012: 2).

For their part, SMTs argue that they have begun to invest heavily in TLA. They also have the heavy responsibility of providing data for government, government agencies, funding bodies, for awarding bodies, and for Ofsted. One only has to look at the information Ofsted requires before an inspection to see how onerous this responsibility still is, despite repeated claims by different administrations to have cut back on red tape. (See Box 9.1 for details of Ofsted's current requirements; and in the next section I offer a more detailed account of the major roles SMTs have to fulfil.) In addition, SMTs point to the vocational experts in subjects as diverse as landscape gardening and painting and decorating who have to develop a corresponding expertise in the teaching of that subject, and some do not willingly embrace this requirement. Some still see themselves primarily as gardeners or painters and decorators, but they also need to become competent teachers of these subjects. The Institute for Learning (IfL) captures this notion well in its advocacy of 'dual professionalism': expertise in a vocational craft, together with deep knowledge of TLA in order to teach that craft well (see Crowley, 2014). SMTs also point to those teachers who are overly defensive of their practice, who resent anyone observing them teaching, who are critical of all new ideas, who can never find the time to try out new initiatives, and who are sometimes part of internal cultures who are disrespectful of their own curriculum managers, never mind those of the college as a whole.

Box 9.1: Information required by Ofsted for an inspection

The following list is a shortened version of the requirements laid out on pages 16, 18, 19, 21, and 22 of the *Handbook for the Inspection of Further Education and Skills* (Ofsted, September 2012). Some of the later entries ask for more detailed information on issues mentioned earlier.

1. Self-assessment report
2. Quality improvement plan
3. Data on learner recruitment, success rates, value-added, destinations, employment rates for past three years
4. Feedback from learners, parents, and employers

5. Report from previous inspection
6. Reports from Ofsted's subject surveys
7. Reports from Ofsted's monitoring visits
8. Any other information the provider wishes to offer
9. Information about the timetable and work-based activity
10. Number and type of subject areas
11. Current volumes and types of learners
12. Timetables of assessment
13. Staff names and responsibilities
14. Location and number of subcontractors
15. Names and email addresses of employers
16. Evidence of monitoring and evaluation
17. Evidence of improvement planning and progress
18. Performance management processes
19. Work of governors
20. Details of changes to normal routines
21. Checks and vetting of all staff
22. Records of complaints, racist, or bullying incidents
23. Strategic and operational business plans
24. Operating statements, subject area plans, staff development plans, action plans
25. Staff qualifications, experience, and development activity over past two years
26. Anonymized information on performance management of staff
27. Up-to-date list of Criminal Records Bureau checks
28. Reports from internal and external verifiers
29. A range of learners' work
30. Records of observations of TLA or information and advice sessions
31. Timetables of learners, showing locations and staff
32. Learner numbers and achievements
33. Minutes from key meetings
34. Evidence of effectiveness of learner support
35. Number of learners 14–16, 16–18, 19+; and in subject areas
36. Number of full-time learners at level 1 or below, level 2, level 3, and level 4
37. Number of intermediate, advanced, and higher-level apprentices
38. Number of part-time learners
39. Number of learners on employability skills programmes
40. Number of foundation learners
41. Number of learners in the previous contract year
42. List of learning programmes/courses at each level
43. Geographical spread of training premises and learners
44. Location and names of employers
45. Names and location of subcontractors and their postcodes

I cannot resist quoting Ofsted's claim in the Handbook: 'documentation is kept to a minimum' (2012: 19). Aren't we lucky that Ofsted shows such commendable self-restraint?

Whatever side of the argument you come down on, I hope it will be generally agreed that the chances of creating one learning community are substantially reduced by the presence in one institution of two colleges: the first consists of the SMT with their overriding and rational concern for protecting the organization from the latest government 'reforms'; the second college is made up of the teaching staff, whose main motivation is offering a first-class experience to their students. Some of those in the latter group complain that the SMT do not know their names, unless they start asking questions at staff meetings, a practice that ends up with them being labelled 'the troublemakers' or 'the awkward squad'. For what it is worth, I find the atmosphere in colleges that do not grade lesson observations to be palpably different and preferable to that in colleges that continue to grade.

One theme, one activity, and one shared concern – improving the quality of TLA – could help to bring the two internal colleges together and so close this dangerous gap. One conciliatory gesture would be to allow staff to *choose* how their teaching is to be evaluated. For instance, some tutors actually want their lessons to be graded, others would much prefer to share their successes and struggles with a respectful but challenging colleague, while yet others would like to improve their practice by having it assessed by other members of their teaching team. Whatever method is chosen, there have to be safeguards against complacent, mutual admiration.

What would also help, I continue to argue, is for SMTs to show leadership by returning to teaching, and I would like 'teaching' to be viewed broadly to include: senior staff observing and improving the teaching of new members of staff, carrying out 'learning walks' around departments, being in touch with the impact of social media on TLA, and participating fully in staff development days alongside classroom teachers. For their part, vocational tutors should embrace their dual professionalism – that is, expertise in a vocational subject as well as in the teaching of that subject. In these ways, the gap will start to close.[1]

3) Transforming colleges

Just as I positioned classroom teachers along a continuum from enthusiasts to resisters, so I suggest that colleges can be similarly arranged from successful businesses/skills factories at one extreme, to a small number of learning communities at the other, with the vast majority stretched out somewhere in between. It is, however, a formidable task to shift along this continuum a large, complex, social institution such as a general FE college, which will be operating: in a variety of workplaces and classrooms on multi-sites; with every age group from 14 to 90 year olds; with every subject from hairdressing to history; and with every level from pre-entry to degree. The continued existence of stable, confident FE colleges is, however, fundamental to the success of this government's educational, social, and economic policies.

In 2008 I wrote a booklet called *Just Suppose Teaching and Learning Became the First Priority…* (Coffield, 2008), mainly because I thought this essential topic had slipped down the list of priorities of SMTs. Understandably, when colleges were incorporated in the early 1990s, SMTs had to learn very fast to become successful business managers, while at the same time incorporation weakened the local identity of colleges and ended local democratic accountability. Many principals became chief executive officers and managed large groups of staff and students through the manipulation of copious amounts of data: data on recruitment, retention, student satisfaction, test scores, the tracking of students against targets, and on all other performance indicators. The responsibility for TLA was handed over to a middle manager, while the principalship concentrated on what were considered to be the more important functions – keeping a large, complex organization afloat, maximizing income from constantly shifting streams of government and private/commercial funding, and reconnoitring the horizon to spot trouble or financial opportunities coming over it.

That management style will no longer work because Ofsted has changed the rules of the game yet again. The recently revised Common Inspection Framework has made TLA the first priority, which will force colleges to change the very culture of their institutions.[2] But what does it mean in practice to create a culture of learning? In the first chapter I quoted the suggestion from Sir Michael Wilshaw, Chief Inspector, who has some idiosyncratic ideas about motivating staff. As he put it: 'If anyone says to you that staff morale is at an all-time low, you know you are doing something right' (Wilshaw, 2011).

The problem is not, however, an occasional ill-judged remark by the Chief Inspector, but the constant barrage of criticism directed at public education, which Stephen Ball neatly categorized as far back as 1990 as a 'discourse of derision'. In a more recent formulation, he argues that:

> blaming teachers has become over the last 30 years a political blood sport … Workplaces should be places where we flourish and grow and are encouraged and supported. They are social

> settings in which everyone deserves respect and has the right to feel valued. Just like students, teachers do not work well when they feel stressed. As *An Education Declaration to Rebuild America*[3] puts it: 'The working conditions of teachers are the learning conditions of students'.
>
> (Ball, 2013: 33)

I would also like to ask Sir Michael two questions: what theory of motivation suggests that it is a sensible strategy to denigrate, virtually on a weekly basis, the very people on whom you depend to enact your policies? And would Sir Michael be satisfied if the words 'student morale' were substituted for 'staff morale' in his infamous statement?

I would now like to outline what I consider to be some of the characteristics of a learning community.[4] First, learning is *the* central organizing principle of the college, which means that everyone from the youngest 14-year-old student to the principal demonstrates daily that they are still learning. If that were so, how did it come about that 'many staff attending the LSIS Aspiring principals and Senior Leadership Programme reported that neither the executive team nor the principal ever discussed with them their learning from the programme or how it might suggest improvements in individual or organizational practices' (Crowley, 2014: 139). One interpretation of that finding is that learning is something that students and teaching staff do, but not managers. On the other hand, I would like to know what structured support is available to help SMTs fulfil their multiple and multiplying responsibilities. The job has become virtually impossible, which helps to explain the reluctance of good candidates to come forward.

The second characteristic of a learning community that I would argue for is substantially more investment in the core activity of TLA, including an evidence-informed strategy to move students to higher levels of thinking and learning (as well as to A*/Distinction). Students in such a community become not complaining customers but partners in learning, who are gradually drawn into the democratic life of the institution, which not only surveys their views but involves them in dialogue about TLA, trains them to sit on appointment panels and jointly to plan and teach lessons (and carry out research) with the guidance and support of their tutors (Fielding and Moss, 2012). (See Box 9.2 for a brief account of Michael Fielding's six patterns of partnership between educators and students.) So the voices of students are heard loud and clear and are responded to appropriately. But so too are the voices of tutors.

Box 9.2: Patterns of partnership

Michael Fielding has produced a typology of six different patterns of partnership by means of which adults not only listen to, but also learn with students. I have also added a final level. In an ascending ladder of democratic participation, the seven patterns can be briefly characterized as:

1. **Students as a source of data**, e.g. staff use questionnaires to find out about students' satisfaction and well-being.
2. **Students as partners in dialogue**, e.g. staff involve students in discussions about TLA.
3. **Students as fellow researchers**, e.g. staff take the leading role in identifying plagiarism with active support from students.
4. **Students as creators of knowledge**, e.g. students take the leading role in studying bullying in college with active support from staff.
5. **Students as joint authors**, e.g. students and staff jointly plan the teaching of a section of the curriculum and jointly 'deliver' it.
6. **Students and staff live and learn democratically together**, e.g. students and staff share a commitment to, and a responsibility for, the common good.
7. **Students and staff as equal learning partners**, e.g. students and staff decide the key issues in the college, all with one vote.

Source: freely adapted from Fielding (2011)

There is now a solid and growing knowledge base on TLA that all tutors need to make their own, while acknowledging that 'research can only inform practice because it can never replace other knowledge which teachers bring to bear on practical problems; and that even the best research evidence is not available as fixed, universal relationships between methods and outcomes, but as local, context-sensitive patterns which have to be interpreted by practitioners within their particular working environments' (Edwards, 2000: 301).

We will know we have created learning communities when SMTs start discussing which theory (or theories) of learning they espouse and what influence it has on their teaching, as fluently as they chat about whether Arsene Wenger's days at Arsenal are drawing to a close. Libraries need to be stocked with the latest research on TLA and the staff given time to read, reflect, and discuss in their teaching groups how they will respond to it. A growing percentage of staff should be studying for higher degrees in TLA at their local university, which should be giving FE staff online access to its electronic library resources. Further proof will come when TLA also become the first, standing item on the agenda of SMTs, and governors are appointed who are experts in TLA to complement those who are experts in finance.

John Hattie challenges classroom teachers with the question: 'do the students believe that the climate of the class is fair, empathetic and trustworthy?' (2012: 165). I want to go further by asking a parallel question of SMTs: do your tutors believe that the climate of the college is conducive to their learning?

The third characteristic of a learning community is one where the climate encourages tutors to innovate, take risks, fail, and learn from their mistakes. It is one where tutors are able to argue for their practices by citing evidence of the effectiveness of their teaching, and where they have the freedom to debate different approaches openly and to see disagreements over practice as the basis for improving it. Principled dissent is therefore encouraged by SMTs, and democratic, collaborative learning becomes the road to renewal (see McNay, 2012).

Ken Robinson has identified nine principles that he argues are necessary to develop a 'systematic culture of creativity and innovation' (2011: 219). In Box 9.3 I have translated those principles into education, where, he argues the style of leadership needs to move away from command and control to collaboration and teamwork. His ideas are particularly relevant to all those in FE colleges and training establishments charged with leading the enhancement of TLA.

Box 9.3: Leading a learning community

Ken Robinson offers the following nine principles (to which I add a tenth) for promoting a cultural revolution in how our educational institutions should be led:

1. Release the creativity of every member of staff.
2. Give your staff the freedom to take risks, fail, and so improve. Value 'irreverence, the lively, the dynamic, the surprising, the playful' (2011: 228).
3. We can all learn to become better teachers. 'Professional development is at the heart of creating cultures' (2011: 231).
4. Form and support creative teams.
5. Creativity thrives on diversity. Don't hire, like David Cameron, people from the same background as yourself, who look and sound just like you.
6. Promote a culture of innovation.
7. Creativity loves collaboration, i.e. the interactions between colleagues improve the quality of TLA.

8. Provide staff with the time and physical spaces in which to think, discuss, and plan lessons.
9. Creating a learning community takes time. Don't expect to transform the culture of an institution within a year or two.
10. SMTs need not only to promote professional learning in all their staff, but also to participate in that learning.

Source: freely adapted from Robinson (2011)

I want to expand a little on two of the principles. The eighth talks of providing staff with creative spaces and yet I have been in a large FE college where the staffrooms were converted into teaching rooms, ostensibly because of a shortage of space, but the staff were convinced that the real reason was that the principal wanted to make it more difficult for them to meet and discuss her policies. For me, one of the marks of a learning community is demonstrated when the teaching staff are trusted to take work home rather than held to working 9 to 5, but in many organizations they are not. Flexible, family-friendly working arrangements are much appreciated by staff, but on the other hand it also means that they are on site less.

I have added the tenth principle in response to the research findings of Viviane Robinson and her colleagues, who studied the impact of different dimensions of leadership on student outcomes. They examined five leadership dimensions – ensuring order and support; providing resources for TLA; planning and evaluating TLA; establishing clear goals and high expectations; and promoting and participating in teacher learning. The final dimension (where the principal participates in staff development days as leader, learner, or both) proved to be twice as effective in terms of student outcomes than any of the other four. The reasons the researchers give for this important finding include the following: 'Leaders' involvement in teacher learning provides them with a deep understanding of the conditions required to enable staff to make and sustain the changes required for improved outcomes' (Robinson *et al*., 2008: 667). In my words, they are reminded just how difficult it is to teach well, 24 hours a week for 36 weeks of the year.

Quality in TLA becomes the desire of staff to be more than just employees, to get better for the sake of getting better rather than to get by or to satisfy the inspectorate (Sennett, 2008); it is not something imposed from on high, something controlled and assured by management. The budgets for CPD will have to be doubled and perhaps trebled if FE tutors are to update their technical/vocational expertise with local companies as well as learning to be better teachers, course designers, and assessors.

Learning for staff as well as for students requires a climate of trust rather than fear, so there needs to be a developmental rather than a judgemental model of CPD. I do not think a hybrid model (which grades lessons and then claims to be developmental by offering support) works, because those who are awarded a 3 or 4 simply 'switch off' or 'shut down' and cannot hear the advice being given, no matter how sensitively expressed. The grading of lessons will therefore have to cease, but to protect the paramount interests of students, the very small percentage of staff who repeatedly serve up inadequate lessons and who seem either unable or unwilling to learn from the plentiful support afforded, will be, with dignity and respect for their employment rights, removed from the profession.

The current Secretary of State for Education frequently uses comparisons with other educational systems to chide teachers in this country. What he has yet to concede is that those systems which repeatedly come top of the international league tables of student performance in English, Maths, or Science invest considerably more in their teachers. In Finland, for instance, teachers – all of whom must hold a master's degree in education – teach on average 15 hours per week; and in Singapore teachers are entitled to 120 hours of professional development per year, four times the entitlement in England (Pavett, 2013). Moreover, in Finland, there are no league tables of schools, colleges, or universities; there is no Ofsted, there are no state-prescribed curricula, and very few private schools. Michael Gove's aim to make the English education system 'world class' by allowing untrained teachers or ex-members of the armed forces into our classrooms is turning it into an international laughing stock.

Taken together, do all of the suggestions made in this and previous chapters amount to a strategy for TLA? First, I shall check our proposals against those made by Sir Michael Wilshaw, the Chief Inspector. He argues that successful leadership of TLA consists of three elements: 'passion and commitment for teaching in everything you say and do' (I prefer to keep the word 'passion' for my private rather than my professional life; and can you demonstrate commitment for teaching if you never do any?); 'committed to good quality professional development' (Yes, but who should be in charge of CPD? I think it should be the tutors.); 'monitor the quality of teaching effectively and ensure performance management is robust' (He is incapable of delivering a talk on education without the adjectives 'robust' and 'rigorous'. It is not a list that will inspire: it is not meant to, its aim is to frighten and control.) (2012: 3–4).

I would like to add two final suggestions. Of all the highly effective interventions that I have read about, seen in action, and evaluated in colleges, there are two that merit inclusion here: professional learning communities (PLCs) and Assessment for Learning (AfL). I shall briefly list the principles behind each and then comment on how I have found them working successfully in practice in the FE and Skills sector.

I would define PLCs as groups of 10 or 12 professionals meeting regularly to learn about TLA in order to improve the quality of students' learning (see Stoll and Louis, 2007). According to Dylan Wiliam (2011), there are five principles behind PLCs and they can be easily stated:

- **choice** – the key element in effective change is putting teachers in charge, provided that students' needs, management targets, and staff wishes are all in alignment
- **flexibility** – all interventions need to be adapted to local conditions
- **small steps** – change can only be integrated into existing routines slowly
- **accountability** – PLCs are not a soft option, as educators are held to account for the changes they choose to introduce
- **support** – from a coach or mentor or a group of colleagues.

Together these five principles constitute a model of change – a model whose effectiveness can be judged on three criteria, according to Ray Bolam and his colleagues: the *immediate* impact of the PLCs as successful groups; the *intermediate* impact on the learning, performance, and morale of the staff; and the *ultimate* impact on students' learning (2005: vi–vii). The danger is that either the governors or the SMT lose patience with the idea if the impact on students' learning is too long in coming.

In introducing these ideas into FE and sixth-form colleges, I have found the most useful question to ask is: 'What support do you need to make a success of this change?' Sometimes the answer is more funding or more IT support, but most often it is more time – the most precious resource of all. PLCs take time to bed down and for trust to grow among colleagues. I have witnessed a slow change towards a more collegial atmosphere among tutors who began to discuss TLA among themselves, but these encouraging signs were put at risk by a few governors demanding a return to the grading of lesson observations and an immediate improvement in test scores. Tutors reported that they no longer felt like solo performers but more like members of a supportive group; and AfL (discussed below) provided them with a common language with which to discuss TLA with colleagues from different departments, whose names they barely knew before the intervention.

I noted that PLCs were more difficult to develop within a large, general FE college than in a smaller sixth-form college because of their sheer size, the huge range of subjects taught, and the strong, and at times change-resistant, cultures of some vocational subjects within the former. Those PLCs that made the most progress appointed a leader for the group, had written agendas for each meeting, and drew up action plans for each tutor, who was expected to report back on progress at the next meeting. In both institutions, the clear majority of staff and students considered that feedback, of the kind described in Chapter 8, was the most effective of all the interventions tried. (For a more up-to-date account of research into putting PLCs into practice, see Wiliam, forthcoming.)

Let me present Assessment for Learning (AfL) in the same way: first the principles and then my experience of it in practice in FE. Somewhat to my surprise, I have discovered that the extensive research literature on TLA is not widely known in FE by either senior managers or by tutors, with the exception of those specializing in teacher education. For example, when I ask in FE colleges for a show of hands from all those who have heard of AfL and are using it in their practice, only a few arms are lifted. And yet AfL is well known in schools, although its implementation is often underdeveloped, and somewhat less so in universities – but in FE it is still something of a novelty. So FE is in the happy position of being a latecomer who could quickly learn from the 'superficial adaptations' (and other misinterpretations) of AfL in schools; in short, what Dylan Wiliam (2011) and others have learned from almost 20 years of research and implementation of AfL in schools could now be put at the disposal of FE tutors.

The essence of AfL can be quickly presented in five principles:

- students need to understand the criteria of success
- teachers need to collect evidence (via questions, assignments, tests, etc.) of learning by students
- tutors then provide students with formative feedback
- students learn from each other and are able to assess each other's work ('peer learning', as it is called, is seen as a strength to be cultivated, which helps to counteract the negative connotations of 'peer group pressure', about which see Smith and Swift, 2012)
- students are put in charge of their own learning (but remember the cautionary words of Walter Müller in Chapter 5).

Christine Harrison makes the valuable point that AfL aims not only to improve students' motivation, 'but also to ensure that they develop identities as capable learners' (2013: 74). In particular, for low-attaining students, 'AfL offers a way out of their downward spiral as it can refocus their attitude towards assessment as something that can help them learn rather than a process which highlights their incompetencies' (ibid.).

My practical experience of AfL has shown me that, as discussed in more detail in Chapter 8, providing high-quality feedback for 200–300 students is very time consuming; it needs to be planned across subjects and across terms to prevent, for instance, students receiving rich feedback from two or three tutors at the same time, feeling overwhelmed by their advice, and so failing to act on any of it. Tutors have also found that involving students in assessment (for example, by developing criteria by which their work will be evaluated) means giving up some power, but they have found the students' increased motivation has been ample compensation. To ensure that the students internalized the five principles of AfL, one college put them on posters, which they displayed in classrooms, and the principles appeared on the end-papers of the college diary given out free of charge to students. The principles were also explained in an open letter to new students (and their parents or guardians/carers) before they arrived at the college in September. Staff began operating with the five principles at the very start of the term.

AfL has also led me to pose two useful questions to teaching staff and students. First, 'What are the characteristics of a good learner?' Once the two groups had agreed on a list of characteristics, I got them to swap lists. These were by no means identical, and many students expressed surprise, for instance, at the staff including 'the willingness to ask challenging questions' as a mark of a good learner. Second, I asked tutors in their teaching teams a question that I took from the research of Paul Black and his colleagues: 'What does it mean to be good at English or maths?' (2010: 14). I invited the tutors in a wide range of subjects from music to motor vehicle maintenance to list the characteristics of a competent student in their subject at the three levels of GCSE, AS, and A2. All groups, irrespective of subject, found this task engrossing, not least because it exposed considerable variation within the groups on what constituted good work and the difficulty in plotting the growth of understanding, knowledge, and skills over the years 16 to 19.

To sum up, AfL is not another top-down initiative; rather, it is the tried-and-tested practice of successful classroom teachers organized into five principles that make immediate good sense to staff who have never heard of AfL. One of the advantages of AfL is that it encourages staff and students to treat teaching, learning, and assessment as one topic and not as three separate issues; indeed, when the five principles become integrated in students' work, a new culture of learning is in the making. After more than 20 years of research and writing about AfL, Dylan Wiliam reflected that 'Assessment for Learning is not about assessment, it's about better teaching' (*Times Educational Supplement*, 13 July 2012).

The learning communities I have been describing will not, however, be created if teaching staff have 24 contact hours per week; these need to be reduced to 20 hours and then to 16 to allow for planning, evaluation, feedback, collaboration, and research. This will mean significant new investment to include paying for sabbaticals for all staff. All of the characteristics of learning communities that I have just described exist now in some colleges in some embryonic form; they need, however, to flourish, spread, and permeate the 'system' as a whole.

4) Transforming the role of the state

The sector has been subjected by successive administrations to 25 years of continuous, radical reform, which, to be fair, has been compensated for by substantial increases in resources, especially under New Labour. I want to ask: why, then, are we not top of all the international league tables? Why are we not 'world class' already? How much longer is it going to take? How many more fundamental reconstructions will prove necessary?

I shall mention just two types of failures by successive governments that will have to do duty for a much broader range of incompetencies. First, the long list of initiatives, which were either abandoned or needed urgent revision within years of being launched, should be a source of shame to politicians and senior civil servants alike: the National Curriculum, National Vocational Qualifications, General National Vocational Qualifications, Curriculum 2000, Modern Apprenticeships, the University for Industry, the Open College, Training Credits, Learning Accounts, Training and Enterprise Councils, the Learning and Skills Council, Standard Attainment Tests, Diplomas, and now the English Baccalaureate. Before politicians embark on radical reform they should be obliged to state what steps they have taken to safeguard the interests of students during the transitional period (see Stanton, 2008). If the Department for Education were a college, Ofsted would have repeatedly judged it 'inadequate' and closed it down, and it would have been turned into an academy. This scandalous catalogue of failure means that England still does not have a high-quality vocational path that could offer a prestigious alternative to the academic route. This seriously disadvantages no less than 60 per cent of each generation of students, whose futures are not considered to be as important – or as politically sensitive – as the 40 per cent who are A level candidates; this amounts to 50 years of failure, since the problem was described in the Newsom Report of 1963, which was called *Half Our Future*.

Second, there have been no fewer than eight attempts by successive governments to create an efficient and effective developmental agency for the FE sector: the Staff College, the Further Education Unit, the Further Education Development Agency, the Learning and Skills Development Agency, the Quality Improvement Agency/Centre for Excellence in Learning, the Learning and Skills Improvement Service, the FE Guild, and the latest incarnation, the Education and Training Foundation. I have a suggestion to offer DBIS regarding the next reconstruction: let us complete an artistic circle and call it the Staff College.

Each of these acts of restructuring has been costly in terms of money (for example, redundancies) and even more expensive in human terms (for example, careers ended, able staff dumped into unemployment), so are we not entitled to ask all the political parties, when are you going to get it right? How many more shots do you need? Politicians would not have dared to behave so cavalierly with the equivalent bodies for HE. No wonder Ewart Keep (2006: 47) has called it 'playing with the biggest train set in the world'. And that is partly why matters do not improve: the opposition cannot wait for their turn to play with the train set. No minister and no senior civil servant has been held responsible for the blunders I have listed above, and yet they are constantly toughening the forms of accountability they impose on others.

But why, if one government initiative does not work, is the next very likely to fail as well? Administrations, no matter of what political persuasion, seem trapped by three false assumptions in addition to the four discussed in Chapter 6, and, as a result, they lurch from one failed initiative to another.

First, TLA is considered a simple, technical matter of transmitting facts from a teacher to students. Only someone who has never stood in front of a class could ask: what could possibly go wrong with such a straightforward process? Unfortunately, a few academics specializing in TLA appear to support that 'nonsense on stilts', as Jeremy Bentham would have put it, by using such phrases as 'The Teaching and Learning *Toolbox*', as if TLA were just a matter of choosing the right tool and the problem will be fixed in a jiffy (for example, Higgins *et al.*, 2012). We need to reassert the complexity, ambiguity, and deeply problematic nature of teaching, say, a group of 25 disaffected young people who have been reduced to thinking of themselves as incompetent learners after 11 years of formal schooling (Bourdieu, 1998). Governments have, in other words, an impoverished, simplistic model of learning that reveals a culpable, concerted ignorance of the relevant literature.

Second, education in England is not governed by a learning 'system'; there are no feedback loops whereby those who have to enact the plans of the Secretary of State can report back on what works and what does not. Governmental initiatives are imposed by diktat rather than improved through dialogue with professionals before enactment. The centre is not interested in listening to the views of practitioners; no teachers' representatives (whether in unions or professional associations) are consulted when policy is being formed.

The main driver in the FE sector is qualifications, but the tutors have little or no say over their content. 'What is in a qualification has to be taught, even if a college and local firms agree that it is not fit for purpose, otherwise money is lost. Conversely, what is taught is not funded unless it is in the qualification' (Stanton, 2013). In a similar vein, the rhetoric of the sector proclaims that 'students are at the heart of the FE and skills system' (Department for BIS, 2011: 3). Not so. The two Secretaries of State (in the DfE and BIS) are. A group of headteachers has, however, begun to insist that 'the teaching profession should be centrally involved in shaping future reform' (Millar, 2013: 32), a movement that deserves wholehearted support from the FE sector.

Third, government ministers have no adequate model of change. Change, as any educational practitioner or researcher knows, is a slow, painful, and incremental business because it is so hard, but politicians need miraculous, transformational change to take place before the next election because they need to demonstrate to the electorate that 'standards' (that is, test scores) have risen. There are, however, research-informed models of how to attempt the huge task of 'scaling up' success in some classrooms to success in colleges across the country (Coburn, 2003).

I want to sum up by suggesting that there is one underlying difficulty that helps to explain the educational state we are in. British politicians tend to preen themselves on our long-established democratic practices and values, made manifest in the Mother of Parliaments. But the truth, as Lord Hailsham pointed out in 1978, is that we live not in a democracy, but in an 'elective dictatorship', defined by me as: 'any government that has a majority, even a majority of one, in the House of Commons can pass whatever legislation it likes'. Governments like this coalition, which 'represents a minority of electors, and even a minority of those who actually voted' (Hailsham, 1978: 129), are given unlimited powers of legislation under our constitution. So educational policy swings to the left or to the right, depending on the political colour of the administration. Lord Hailsham, no member of the 'loony left', correctly predicted that our elective dictatorship 'will crush local autonomy. It will dictate the structure, form and content of education' (ibid.: 10). And so it has come to pass, both under New Labour and the Conservative-led coalition.

Sir Peter Newsam argued recently: 'How has Parliament allowed an individual politician to dictate what history is to be taught in the nation's schools? ... a statutorily enforceable national curriculum, controlled by an opinionated individual, has no place in a democratic society. It is the road to serfdom' (2013: 42). The current Secretary of State has assumed enormous centralizing powers that will affect not just the teaching of history, not just the primary and secondary curriculum, but the whole of the English education 'system', and all this damage is being done to promote the untested prejudices and the political career of the said Secretary of State.

The alternative, according to Lord Hailsham, is the theory of limited government, where the total quantity of legislation is reduced, it is more fully discussed, and all of the relevant parties are consulted in advance. More than 30 years have passed, Hailsham's advice has been ignored, the Houses of Parliament now pass more laws than can be properly scrutinized, and consultations over proposed legislation have long been an empty farce. As I argued in the introduction, we need nothing less than 'a new birth of democracy', to complement the 'new birth of freedom' that President Lincoln called for in 1863 (Goodwin, 2013: 586). This is not the place to explain in detail what that reaffirmation of democracy should consist of, but some of the main elements are obvious. We must reverse the galloping centralization of power in Whitehall, which will mean politicians giving up power by devolving it to the professions, regions, and local authorities. We need new, constitutional mechanisms to hold politicians, and especially the executive, to account in order to ensure, for instance, privacy and press freedom, as the unfolding scandal of the surveillance state underlines yet again how enfeebled our democracy has become. All of our educational institutions and the 'system' itself need to become far more democratic, with not only students but also staff being routinely consulted on the effectiveness of management and government policy. A 'system' as large and complex as education in England requires an intermediate tier of government, where local planning and local partnerships can ensure equity, value for money, and regulation via local, democratic accountability. 'We need to shift from the old model of vertical accountability to funding bodies, awarding bodies and inspectorates, to a framework based on horizontal accountability, directly to employer and community partners' (CAVTL, 2013: 28). But instead of any of these measures, the chains of elective dictatorship are being pulled ever more tightly, while democracy in education, as in the health service and all of the public services, is being dismantled before our very eyes.

5) Final comments

Let me try to answer the question I posed in the title of this chapter: can we transform classrooms and colleges without transforming the role of the state? I think some advances can still be made in classrooms by considered enactment and careful evaluation of the more effective interventions discussed in earlier chapters. We all have far more freedom than we imagine, but we must begin to exercise it. We are not living in a Stalinist or Fascist state; we need to start behaving *as if* we lived in a democracy.

On the other hand, over the past 25 years, government policies have become so numerous, invasive, ill-considered, and short-lived that the freedom of action previously enjoyed by educators and SMTs has become seriously curtailed. In particular, the key resource in this sector, namely the *time* of tutors and managers, is increasingly taken up with responding to the initiatives of ministers rather than to the needs of students. My own judgement is that the culture of fear, the constant raising of the barrier of minimal acceptable performance, and the 'high stakes' testing regime that pits college against college and colleague against colleague will prevent the widespread emergence of communities of learning. My prediction is that this sick sector will get even sicker, if a total change of direction is not made.

The FE sector rightly prides itself on being infinitely resourceful and responsive, but Geoff Stanton (2008) was surely right to question whether it is not at times *too* responsive. When do we collectively say that we also want to make some minimal demands upon government – to ask, for example, for our representatives to be routinely consulted when policy is being formed? For tutors to be consulted about radical changes to the curriculum before those changes are made mandatory? Please do not tell me that the Department for Education routinely consults on all new proposals. Yes, I know and I have seen the skip at the back of the Department where the replies are just as routinely discarded.

Democracy thrives on vigorous public debate and this book is our contribution to it. The education system in England has for some years been in crisis, and yet that great British institution, the BBC, has not one programme devoted to education, and every time I turn on the television or radio the education correspondent is someone different. I have argued in this book that the current 'system' has failed because generations of students are leaving our schools, colleges, and universities with a dangerously impoverished notion of education, profoundly ignorant about the major threats to our collective being and what they could do about them. Educational policy in England becomes ever more extreme, divisive, and inequitable; it is racing ever faster down the wrong road, reducing the professionalism of teachers to carrying out the detailed instructions of an opinionated politician, and the education of students to a narrow concentration on what can be measured and examined. The yearly application of more and more pressure for results is unsustainable. It is time to call a halt before any more damage is done.

What keeps me awake at night is not the hectoring demands of the market fundamentalists for more public assets to be turned into private profit, but the ghosts of those who built the sector we inherited, calling me to account: 'What,' I hear them ask, 'did you do, Frank, to defend this sector? What will you do to defend those tutors now threatened with unemployment? Will you fight publicly for those who need a second, and yes, a third chance to transform their lives through further education? What action will you take to build a democratic education system in this country?'

How, may I ask, will *you* answer these questions?

Notes

[1] These suggestions were made to me by a group of experienced practitioners and managers at a meeting organized by Lynne Sedgmore of the 157 Group to discuss an early draft of this chapter. I am very grateful to all those who took part in helping to improve this final version.

[2] Let me pass on the advice I once received from John Grey, Professor of Education at Cambridge at the time, which I hope is useful to those about to be inspected: in the presence of the inspectors, always speak well of your colleagues, no matter how much it may hurt.

[3] *An Education Declaration to Rebuild America* is an initiative by a group of leading educators, writers, and politicians who have come together to reclaim and reinvigorate public education in the USA. Online: www.educationopportunitynetwork.org/education_announcement/ (accessed 3 February 2013).

[4] This is not the first time I have tried to describe the main features of a learning community. In our book *From Exam Factories to Communities of Discovery: The democratic route* (2012), Bill Williamson and I set out 13 characteristics of such communities. Instead of just repeating that list here, I offer in this chapter what I have learned since that book was published and I refer readers to it (pages 49–54) for the earlier characterization.

References

Adey, P. and Dillon, J. (eds) (2012) *Bad Education: Debunking myths in education*. Maidenhead: Open University Press.

Anderson, L.W. and Krathwohl, D.R. (eds) (2001) *A Taxonomy for Learning, Teaching and Assessing: A revision of Bloom's Taxonomy of Educational Objectives*. New York: Longman, abridged edition.

Ball, S.J. (1990) *Politics and Policy Making in Education*. London: Routledge.

— (2008) *The Education Debate*. Bristol: Policy Press.

— (2013) *Education, Justice and Democracy: The struggle over ignorance and opportunity*. London: Centre for Labour and Social Studies.

Biesta, G.J.J. (2006) *Beyond Learning: Democratic education for a human future*. Boulder, Colorado: Paradigm.

— (2010) *Good Education in an Age of Measurement: Ethics, politics, democracy*. Boulder, Colorado: Paradigm.

Black P., Harrison, C., Hodge, J., Marshall, B., and Serrett, N. (2010) 'Validity in teachers' summative assessments'. *Assessment in Education*, 17 (2), 215–32.

Bolam, R., McMahon, A., Stoll, L., Thomas, S., and Wallace, M. (2005) *Creating and Sustaining Effective Professional Learning Communities*. London: Department for Education and Skills, Research Report 637.

Bourdieu, P. (1998) *Contre-Feux*. Paris: Liber, Raisons d'Agir.

Coburn, C.E. (2003) 'Rethinking scale: Moving beyond numbers to deep and lasting change'. *Educational Researcher*, 32 (6), 3–12.

Coffield, F. (2007) *Running Ever Faster Down the Wrong Road: An alternative future for education and skills*. London: Institute of Education, University of London.

— (2008) *Just Suppose Teaching and Learning Became the First Priority…* London: Learning and Skills Network.

— (2012b) 'Learning Styles: Unreliable, invalid and impractical and yet still widely used'. In P. Adey and J. Dillon (eds), *Bad Education: Debunking myths in education*. Maidenhead: Open University Press.

— (2013) 'Learning Styles: Time to move on'. Opinion piece, Leading Professional Development Level 2. Nottingham: National College for School Leadership.

Coffield, F., Moseley, D., Hall, E., and Ecclestone, K. (2004a) *Learning Styles and Pedagogy in Post-16 Learning: A systematic and critical review*. London: Learning and Skills Research Centre, LSDA.

— (2004b) *Should We Be Using Learning Styles? What research has to say to practice*. London: Learning and Skills Research Centre, LSDA.

Coffield, F. and Williamson, B. (2012) *From Exam Factories to Communities of Discovery: The democratic route*. London: Institute of Education, University of London.

Commission on Adult Vocational Teaching and Learning (CAVTL) (2013) *It's About Work … Excellent adult vocational teaching and learning*. Coventry: LSIS.

Crowley, S. (2014) 'Maintaining the challenge and the learning'. In S. Crowley (ed.), *Challenging Professional Learning*. London: Routledge, 133–44.

Department for Business, Innovation and Skills (DBIS) (2011) *New Challenges, New Chances*. London: DBIS.

— (2012) *Professionalism in Further Education*. Lingfield Final Report. Online. www.bis.gov.uk (accessed November 2012).

Edwards, T. (2000) '"All the Evidence Shows…": Reasonable expectations of educational research'. *Oxford Review of Education*, 26 (3 & 4), 299–311.

Fielding, M. (2011) 'Patterns of partnership: Student voice, intergenerational learning and democratic fellowship'. In N. Mockler and J. Sachs (eds), *Rethinking Educational Practice through Reflexive Research*. Springer, 61–75.

Fielding, M. and Moss, P. (2012) *Radical Education and the Common School: A democratic alternative*. Abingdon: Routledge.

Goodwin, D.K. (2013) *Team of Rivals: The political genius of Abraham Lincoln*. London: Penguin.

Grosz, S. (2013) *The Examined Life*. London: Chatto & Windus.

Hailsham, Lord (1978) *The Dilemma of Democracy: Diagnosis and prescription*. London: Collins.

Harrison, C. (2013) 'Testing times: Reforming classroom teaching through assessment'. In J. Clifton (ed.), *Excellence and Equity: Tackling educational disadvantage in England's secondary schools*. London: OPPR.

Hattie, J. (2012) *Visible Learning for Teachers: Maximising impact on learning*. London: Routledge.

Higgins, S., Kokotsaki, D., and Coe, R. (2012) *The Teaching and Learning Toolkit*. Education Endowment Foundation/The Sutton Trust.

Keep, E.J. (2006) 'State control of the English education and training system – playing with the biggest train set in the world'. *Journal of Vocational Education and Training*, 58 (1), 47–64.

Lucas, B., Spencer, E., and Claxton, G. (2012) *How to Teach Vocational Education: A theory of vocational pedagogy*. London: City and Guilds, Centre for Skills Development.

MacLellan, E. and Soden, R. (2012) 'Successful learners, confident individuals, responsible citizens and effective contributions to society: Exploring the nature of learning and its implications in curriculum for excellence'. *Scottish Educational Review*, 1, 29–37.

McNay, I. (2012) 'Leading strategic change in higher education – closing the implementation gap'. *Leadership and Governance in Higher Education*, 4, 46–69.

Millar, F. (2013) 'The headteachers' great rebellion'. *Education Guardian*, 5 February 2013, 32.

Newsam, P. (2013) Letter in *The Observer*, 24 February 2013, 42.

Ofsted (2012) *Handbook for the Inspection of Further Education and Skills*. Ofsted.

O'Leary, M. (2012a) 'Surveillance, performativity and normalised practice: The use and impact of graded lesson observations in further education colleges'. *Journal of Further and Higher Education*, 1, 1–21.

— (2012b) 'Exploring the role of lesson observation in the English education system: A review of methods, models and meanings'. *Professional Development in Education*, 38 (5), 791–810.

Pavett, D. (2013) 'What we are not told about Finnish education'. In T. Fisher (ed.), *Gove's School Revolution Scrutinised*. Socialist Educational Association.

Robinson, K. (2011) *Out of Our Minds: Learning to be creative*, 2nd edn. Chichester: Capstone.

Robinson, V., Lloyd, C., and Rowe, K. (2008) 'The impact of leadership on student outcomes: An analysis of the differential effects of leadership types'. *Educational Administration Quarterly*, 44 (5), 635–74.

Sennett, R. (2008) *The Craftsman*. London: Allen Lane/Penguin.

Smith, A. and Swift, D. (2012) 'Exploring the language of learning within FE'. *Journal of Further and Higher Education*, 1–19.

Stanton, G. (2008) *Learning Matters: Making the 14–19 reforms work for learners*. London: CfBT Education Trust.

— (2013) Personal communication.

Stoll, L. and Louis, K.S. (2007) *Professional Learning Communities: Divergence, depth and dilemmas*. Maidenhead: Open University Press.

Thompson, M. and Wiliam, D. (2007) 'Tight but loose: A conceptual framework for scaling up school reforms'. Paper presented to American Educational Research Association, Chicago, 9–13 April.

Wiliam, D. (2011) *Embedded Formative Assessment*. Bloomington, IN: Solution Tree.

— (forthcoming) *Sustaining Formative Assessment with Teacher Learning Communities*.

Wilshaw, M. (2011) quoted in *Times Educational Supplement*, 13 December.

— (2012) 'High expectations, no excuses'. Speech on 9 February, Ofsted.

Coda

The Secretary of State for Education I would like

Frank Coffield

Students are sometimes asked what sort of school or college they would like, and their positive suggestions tend to reveal what they think is missing, inadequate, or unacceptable in the education they are receiving. I thought to carry out the same exercise with regard to the Secretary of State for Education – not any particular Secretary of State, but the ideal characteristics of a highly successful minister in that post. Someone, for example, who regularly receives a standing ovation at teachers' conferences because the challenges she sets them stem from a deep and genuine respect for the teaching profession. (I shall alternate in each paragraph below the use of the pronouns 'she' and 'he' and use the acronym SoS to avoid repeating the full phrase, Secretary of State.)

First and foremost, my ideal SoS would act as a role model for the whole education system, in that he would publicly demonstrate in all he does that he does not just expect *other people* to change but that he himself has the capacity to learn – and not just a capacity but a willingness and even a love of learning. So he would make a point of learning from the recent history of education reform in order to avoid making the same mistakes as his predecessors, such as initiative overload and 'repetitive change syndrome'; he would also build on their successes, such as embracing institutions that are already strong. He would be the first to appreciate the limits of his own knowledge and skill base, and would know when and from whom he should seek help.

She would relish having her implicit and unexamined assumptions challenged, her pet theories about education tested (and at times found wanting) by research evidence, and her arguments for reform publicly scrutinized and thereby improved. She would respond positively to those sections of research reports that disconfirmed some of her most firmly held beliefs; and her most cherished innovations would be thoroughly evaluated in pilot projects long before implementation on a national scale.

His first consideration when introducing new legislation would be to consider carefully the chances of any adverse effects on students, who, for example, could be stuck with qualifications that are quickly found to be deficient and then abandoned; and within a few years no employer would remember that they ever existed.

Consultation would return to its original meaning and purpose – the first draft of plans would be published, views would be sought from all of the partners in education, and their suggestions, based on professional knowledge and long experience of teaching, would be incorporated into the final version. She would establish feedback loops so that, once the plans were being carried out in schools and colleges, teachers could report back systematically on their general effectiveness, their weaknesses as well as the improvements they are bringing about. Her major concern would be to find out whether the quality of students' learning (and not just an increase in test scores) had improved as a result of her innovations, not whether teachers were faithfully implementing the statutory guidance issued by her department. In so doing, she would be seeking to restore a key ingredient of success: trust in the professionalism of teachers and in their commitment to students.

His main aim would be to forge one education system from the existing set of separate sectors for primary, secondary, further, and higher education. These sectors would become more closely integrated to form coherent, easily recognizable, and navigable pathways for vocational as well as academic students. And his love of learning would become infectious and would spread to the thousands of civil servants at the Department for Education, who would be keen to find out how effective their policies turned out to be in practice; and they would be kept in post long enough for them to find out.

SoSs are, of course, in essence politicians, elected to carry out commitments set out in a manifesto and responsible for their actions to a Prime Minister, Parliament, a party, and constituents. They are very far from being free agents and are constrained by budgets, pressure groups, the power of the press, and the art of the possible. On the other hand, the office of SoS for Education has accrued more than 2,000 new powers through successive legislation since 1988, making it one of the most sought after in government by ambitious politicians.

She would appreciate the pressing need for a new settlement in education, devolving power to local authorities and to the professions to ensure local planning of all types of schools, an equitable distribution of resources, and a transformation in the status of teachers. She would see it as one of her main tasks to increase public confidence in the maintained sector of education, so that no minister, official, or inspector would be allowed to ridicule or denigrate teachers; they would all be too busy thinking of ways to improve teachers' professional learning to think of such distasteful politicking. As SoS she would stop the practice of junior ministers all insisting on a separate initiative being developed and attached to their name and career because she knows they would only be discarded as soon as they are moved on to another ministry.

In dealing with teachers, my ideal SoS would employ a psychological approach that has never been tried before – he would ask for their active support in enacting the reforms he proposed. That support would be forthcoming, because he had previously broken new ground by consulting the teachers' unions and professional organizations while policy was being formed. He would realize that teachers are not motivated by appeals to improve the competitiveness of British industry, so the wider purposes of education would be nationally and regularly debated before a new curriculum was devised or the current one revised. He would understand from his reading of the literature that punitive accountability led to compliance and game-playing rather than generic learning, and so he would introduce intelligent accountability, which will hold teachers and students to account without distorting educational objectives or practices (see O'Neill, 2013).

I would like to be as helpful as possible to my ideal SoS, so I will suggest activities for her first week in office. On Monday, she will install a large notice on the wall above her desk: **'The first requisite of a Secretary of State for Education is to Do the Minimum Harm'.** She will then announce that, in future, governments will withdraw from meddling in all professional matters such as curriculum and pedagogy. Tuesday's announcement will give details of the establishment of an independent unit (composed of representatives of teachers' unions and professional bodies, of employers, of parents, and of students), which sifts the evidence for and against any proposal for educational reform and advises the SoS appropriately about what action to take. On Wednesday, she will explain how all academies and so-called 'free' schools are to be returned to the family of locally maintained schools. Thursday sees her proclaiming the end of the market principle and of privatization being applied in education, so she abolishes school league tables and explains how from now on institutions will be judged according to how much they co-operate rather than compete with each other for the benefit of all pupils in the system. On Friday, Ofsted is done away with, as the evidence has continued to mount of it causing more harm than good; a rigorous system of local, collaborative peer-review is put in its place, and the millions saved as a result are diverted to a new billion-pound scheme to close the achievement gap between the most and the least academically successful students. On Saturday, she addresses a national conference of teachers, where her final act of the week is to make public her intention to withdraw charitable status from private schools, colleges, and universities.

In that speech he will explain that his first week's work had been organized to exemplify the practices and values of our democracy, and that in his second week he will turn to the great task of building together (rather than the pretentious phrase 'co-constructing') with teachers a democratic, innovative, and self-improving system in the service of all students.

There is no harm in wishing, is there? If you do not know what you want, and if you are not prepared to argue, struggle, and fight for what are reasonable, moderate, and long-overdue reforms, there is little, if any, chance of them being realized.

References

O'Neill, O. (2013) 'Intelligent accountability in education'. *Oxford Review of Education*, 39 (1), 4–16.

Index

Index